Clinical Psychology:
Issues of the Seventies

Clinical Psychology:

Issues of the Seventies

EDITED BY

ALBERT I. RABIN

MICHIGAN STATE UNIVERSITY PRESS

1974

★
★
★
★
★

Contents

PART 4 TRAINING FOR THE FUTURE

Foreword

THE YEAR 1973 MARKED THE 25TH ANNIVERSARY OF THE founding of the Psychological Clinic in the Department of Psychology at Michigan State University. The Clinic has been an essential component of the graduate program in clinical psychology. In fact, the graduate program in clinical psychology and the Clinic have grown in stature together.

Professor Albert I. Rabin was the first Director of the Psychological Clinic and served in that capacity from 1948 to 1961. At least as significant for clinical psychology, Professor Rabin provided leadership for the Michigan State University graduate program in clinical psychology as it developed into its increasingly robust status. Well in advance of the widespread use of the term in psychology, Professor Rabin was a *model* scientist-professional and continues to exemplify this difficult, complex standard in his career. The many individuals who have been associated with the graduate program in clinical psychology at Michigan State University and with Professor Rabin join in saying, "Well done and keep up the good work." His editorship of this work is one more example of his central place in clinical psychology.

On May 18 and 19, 1973, a large number of clinical psychologists who earned their doctoral degrees at Michigan State University returned to campus to exchange views and renew acquaintanceships. This volume contains many of the papers presented on that occasion.

C. L. WINDER
Professor, Department of Psychology
Dean, College of Social Science

Preface

AS A SCIENTIFIC DISCIPLINE AND AS A PROFESSION, CLINICAL psychology has been evolving since the end of the nineteenth century. However, not until the post-World War II years has the field flourished and reached its present-day proportions. Thousands of clinical psychologists, trained and educated in nearly one hundred universities, are currently active in various socially and scientifically meaningful endeavors. They are engaged in group and individual psychotherapy, in assessment and diagnosis of persons and families, in research, in teaching, and in many other related activities.

Unlike its sister professions, psychiatry and social work, clinical psychology had its origins in the university, in Academe. Unlike the other professions, it has not developed primarily as a field of practice. From its inception, and under the influence of the academic departments that somewhat reluctantly nurtured it, clinical psychology emerged as a field of scientific endeavor *and* as a field of professional practice. The most influential event in its history, the 1949 Boulder Conference, defined the clinical psychologist as both a scientist *and* a practitioner. The main rationale was that the field of psychology and the extent of our understanding of human functioning are too limited to support a class of strict professionals, that is, appliers and consumers of knowledge. The ideal that evolved for clinical psychology is training in research—the creation of new knowledge, and in practice—the application of available knowledge in the achievement of psychological well-being and social welfare.

The two decades that followed the Boulder Conference brought numerous changes in the field. Many of these changes are the results of the accumulated experience of practitioners and of new knowledge that has been accrued from clinical research. But perhaps most important have been the significant social changes in our society during the past two decades which, in addition to altering the pattern of professional activities have caused a redirection of our services to new targets, a reorganization of service settings, and a reordering of priorities in the practitioner's time expenditure. Psychotherapy has replaced assessment as the clinical psychologist's major enterprise. Group and family therapy, as well as community mental health, tend to replace individual psychotherapy. And professional preoccupation tends to push research and academic concerns into a corner. The clinical psychologist has had to adjust and change himself in a period of constant and accelerating change. He has had to assume new and emerging roles and to redefine himself and his profession.

This volume presents timely essays on clinical psychology in the seventies, written by a representative sample of young clinicians, whose primary activities range from university teaching and research to full-time clinical work in mental health installations and private practice of psychotherapy. These authors express a wide range of concerns about "clinical psychology in a state of flux."

Essentially, the book is divided into four main sections. The first, consisting of four papers, deals with broad issues—criticism of the field from a radical perspective, relationship between assessment and therapy, and the border zone of psychology and the law. The second part is more concerned with roles, models, and settings of the practicing clinician. Four papers on psychotherapeutic approaches and innovations comprise part three. Issues on training of future clinical psychologists are discussed in some detail in the five papers that constitute the fourth and final section.

Practitioners and teachers of clinical psychology, students and trainees, as well as intelligent lay people with serious interest in the mental health professions, will find this an interesting and instructive book. It represents *clinical psychology in transition*, described by a sizable group of knowledgeable teachers and practitioners of diverse viewpoints, from different parts of the country, who are products of recent and not so recent training programs.

These papers, among others, were presented at the 25th

Anniversary of the Psychological Clinic and the Clinical Training Programs at Michigan State University. The event, to which all Ph.D. graduates of the program were invited, took place on May 18 and 19, 1973. It was made possible through the cooperation and kindness of many friends, colleagues, and institutions (and with partial support by NIMH Training Grant MH–06663–14).

Professors Lucy R. Ferguson, Dozier W. Thornton, and Robert A. Zucker served with me on the organizing and program committee. Professor Thornton, in his capacity as chairperson of the clinical interest group and director of the program, was especially helpful in planning the conference and its activities. Professors Bertram Karon and the late Bill Kell joined us as chairpersons of the Anniversary symposia. The other members of the clinical faculty, as well as some of the nonclinical faculty, actively participated in making the event a success as well as Mr. Roger Halley. The critical, but kindly, review of many of the manuscripts by Professor John R. Hurley added considerably to whatever merit the present volume may have.

Special thanks are in order to Vice President Milton E. Muelder and Dean C. L. Winder for their encouragement and significant aid in making this publication a reality. Above all, thanks are due to all those former students who returned to the campus and shared with us their thoughts and experiences beyond the "ivory tower."

ALBERT I. RABIN

Contributors

JAMES F. ALEXANDER
Associate Professor of Psychology
University of Utah

ERMA DOSAMANTES ALPERSON
Associate Professor of Psychology
University of Northern Colorado

BENJAMIN BEIT-HALLAHMI
Senior Lecturer in Psychology
University of Haifa (Israel)

GERALD L. BOROFSKY
Senior Psychologist, Outpatient De-
partment
Erich Lindemann Mental Health Cen-
ter (Boston)
Instructor Department of Psychiatry
Harvard Medical School

HAROLD B. DAVIS
Associate Professor of Psychology
City College of the City University of
New York

ROBERT J. GREENE
Chief Psychologist
Midland-Gladwin Community Mental
Health Center
Assistant Professor of Psychology
Central Michigan University

LEONARD HANDLER
Professor of Psychology
University of Tennessee

DURAND F. JACOBS
Chief, Psychology Service
VA Hospital, Cleveland, Ohio
Adjunct Professor of Psychology
Kent State University

JOANNE H. LIFSHIN
Assistant Chief of Psychological Ser-
vices
Dept. of Psychiatry and Community
Mental Health Center
Brookdale Hospital Medical Center
(Brooklyn)

ROBERT G. MEYER
Associate Professor and Clinic Director
Department of Psychology
University of Louisville

KEVIN M. MITCHELL
Associate Professor of Psychology
University of Georgia

HERBERT M. POTASH
Professor of Psychology
Fairleigh Dickerson University

JOHN M. REISMAN
Professor of Psychology and Director of
Clinic
Memphis State University

RAYMOND S. SANDERS
Assistant Professor and Clinical Psy-
chologist Student Health Center
Oregon State University

MARK H. THELEN
Professor of Psychology
University of Missouri

JUDITH A. VAN EVRA
Consulting Psychologist
Waterloo, Ontario

Part I

General Issues

Clinical Psychology, Values, and Society:

A Radical Perspective

BENJAMIN BEIT-HALLAHMI

DISCUSSIONS OF VALUES, AS OPPOSED TO DISCUSSIONS OF technology and ethics, are relatively rare among psychologists, and constitute only a limited component of graduate training. One major reason is that many clinical psychologists consider their technology to be value-free. Personally, I find this view rather amusing. I can recall several case conferences, when a statement by one participant is reacted to by another with a victorious, critical "But this is a value judgment!" My reaction is "But I thought everything we were doing here was based on value judgments." This last statement is likely to enhance my reputation as a cynic who has little respect for the sacred cows of the profession and the delicate feelings of his colleagues. It is interesting to note that those who emphasize the role of values in professional work are often labeled "cynics," those who remind us of glaring inequalities and exploitation are labeled "materialists," while those who deny the importance of values and morality and justify exploitation and inequality are, of course, idealists and purists. What becomes clear is that, for most psychologists, there is no need to talk about values, since these are taken for granted and are agreed upon by a majority of their professional colleagues. Discussion is more likely to arise in cases of conflict, and not on what we all agree about.

What we take for granted may be ego-syntonic, personally and professionally, may be consistent with our self-image, and is probably consistent with our self-interest and the need for survival in this society.

Yet, what we take for granted most clearly affects our biases; but, since so many of our values are taken for granted and have become a part of our technology, we do not talk about them. Technology is mostly what professional education is about. Several reasons may explain the emphasis on technology in graduate education in clinical psychology. Possibly technology teachers are guided by their feelings of urgency, believing that the technology they teach is vital and desperately needed for the betterment of human existence. Possibly they are guided by simple dogmatism and inertia, or by their personal needs for certainty and clarity in an uncertain world. The desire to make clinical psychology look professional and mature is undoubtedly a major motivation. If we do not have a technology to offer the world, then perhaps we are not as professional or scientific as we claim to be. Preoccupation with technology is the best way to avoid discussion of values and principles, thus avoiding potential conflicts. Assuming that we agree on principles, then we can only disagree on technique.

The emphasis on technology and on means, rather than ends, is the homage we pay to the system of rationality and efficiency which surrounds us, a system that tries to reduce every question into a technological question. Roszak asks: "Is it intellect our scientists and strategists and operational analysts lack? These men who preside with an impersonal eye over a system of mass murder . . . is it their capacity to reason that is flawed?"[1], and he continues quoting Captain Ahab's chilling confession, "All my means are sane: my motives and objects mad." The failure of mass murder technology in Vietnam, and the victory of the human spirit over cold-blooded imperialism, showed us the limitations of rationalist technology and its eventual defeat.

A major cause of our reluctance to discuss values is that psychologists are "social scientists," committed by training to the idea that our scientific activities are "value-free."[2] Yet, social science is never value-free. We start every inquiry by deciding on questions to be asked or solutions to be attempted. Since much of social science, and clinical psychology in particular, is devoted to studying "social problems" or "personal problems," we have to encounter the question of values when we choose and define these problems. Our biases are reflected in what we take for granted, as when we assume general agreement on the nature or the definition of a problem. The positivistic approach makes a claim for a new beginning in the study of man. It denies the value-based humanistic traditions of the past as unscientific and irrelevant and claims that our new start makes us superior to those thinkers who did not use "scientific" methods.

The extent to which psychological training results in the ability to divorce values from technology and science is illustrated in an incident reported by a nonpsychologist, playwright Arthur Miller.[3] Speaking to an APA meeting, Miller discussed the importance of values in science. As an example, he mentioned an experiment conducted by the German Nazis, in which the drowning process was studied by direct measurements of changes in the bodies of people who were dropped into swimming pools. Undoubtedly, this was an advance in scientific knowledge, since the only source of information before that had been autopsies. The reaction of Miller's audience was to tell him that there was nothing unscientific about the German experiment. We can all see that the psychologists were right, and Miller was wrong. Naturally, Miller never had any courses in methodology or philosophy or science. The experiment was perfectly scientific, and the only problems with it were moral.

Another source of the reluctance to discuss values is the "medical model" of "mental health" and "mental illness," which is still influential in clinical psychology. If what we are involved in consists of diagnosing "disease entities" and giving "treatment," then there is little room for value decisions beyond the basic decision to cure illness and relieve human suffering. This is naturally a value decision, but it is assumed to be universally supported. The orthodox psychoanalytic view similarly sees our only value as the promotion of health in a scientific way. Thus, Hartmann[4] declares that the only aim of the psychoanalytic method is to undo repressions and all other defenses against seeing unpleasant truth, and that it has nothing to do with ideologies, indoctrinations, religious dogmas, or teaching a way of life or a system of values. The psychoanalytic position, with its emphasis on basic needs and their gratification, may lead to another kind of escape from the value question. This is what I have labeled the relativistic-superior position. Here, the psychologist is an armchair observer of the human situation, pipe in hand and omniscient smile on his face. He tells us that there is no need to get involved in value questions, since what we see around us is all a part of the great mandala, specific manifestations of universal human needs and impulses. He may tell us that both Adolf Hitler and Richard Nixon have acted out unconscious oedipal fantasies, and the only person Nixon really wants to kill is his father, who is already dead anyway. According to this view, poverty and inequality are universal and inevitable and all social systems are the same; so no one needs to get excited over values and politics.

Contrary to the psychoanalytic position that emphasizes the human comedy of errors, perversions, and disguised manifestations of basic impulses, the existential position may lead to what we can call the human tragedy view. This "tragic view of life," as described by C. Wright Mills, ". . . is a way of saying to oneself: We're all in it together, the butcher and the general and the ditchdigger and the Secretary of the Treasury and the cook and the President of the United States. So let's all feel sad about one another. . . . But we are *not* all in this together—so far as such decisions as are made and can be made are concerned. 'We' are *not* all in this together—so far as bearing the consequences of these decisions is concerned."[5] Both a human comedy approach and a human tragedy approach lead to escaping from our own value responsibilities and from the question of taking sides.

What we normally deal with when we talk about values in psychology are "professional ethics."[6] As defined by most psychologists, professional ethics deal with the rules of our game vis-à-vis society. They reflect both an honest concern with the rights of others and a wish to preserve our professional monopoly and privileged status, but these rules of professional conduct stay within the realm of technical questions and our reputation as good citizens. Professional ethics concentrate on the moral implications of our relationship with the client, but do not deal with the moral implications and the political, consequences of this relationship as they extend to other areas of the client's life.

What professional education in clinical psychology concentrates on, almost to the exclusion of everything else, is the question of how to change human behavior. The metatechnological questions, which may be just as important, are the Who and the Why of changing human behavior. Who do we want to change and Why do we want to change them? These questions are rarely discussed, since the answers are assumed to be obvious or universally agreed upon. The Why question has, or should have, clear implications for the How question. Our answers to the Who and the Why reflect our notions of the good person and the good society. In our actions as clinical psychologists, we express our implicit theories of human nature and society. Normally, we discuss our theories of human nature and refrain from talking about our theories of society. It is hard for us to conceive of the teacher in a personality theory course discussing the political theories of Freud, Maslow, or McClelland. It is assumed that we can leave the task of dealing with the nature of society to others, and the decision to do that relegates the political implications of psychology to the professional unconscious, where it is destined to lie repressed unless uncovered through some radical treatment or some severe trauma.

Analyzing implicit value statements in our professional work will lead us to focusing on the political implications of our daily activities. The relationship of professional psychology to the rest of society, and especially its political implications, are evidently open to several interpretations. One view simply asserts that psychologists always serve those in power, whether they are aware of it or not. Another view regards psychology as a major force working for cultural change or cultural rebellion. Later on, we will have a chance to check both views against reality and to find that the truth does *not* lie somewhere in between.

One starting point for a discussion of the societal role of psychology as a discipline and as a profession is that of the sociology of knowledge.[7] This viewpoint assumes that systems of knowledge and the analysis of reality are always socially determined. The way we organize our knowledge of reality reflects our social environment. American psychology today reflects the realities of American society today; and the values of American psychology reflect the values of American society. Any psychological system is only as good as the society that produced it. This, in turn, leads us to an historical question: why is it that psychology is an academic discipline and psychology as a profession appeared and were developed in this particular society at this particular point in history? Was there something in this society that created the need and the readiness for it? Psychology is only one among the "helping professions" that have been growing in all Western industrial societies since the beginning of this century. The dominant psychological force in all these societies is that of alienation; the dominant social fact is the development of absolute and complete social control. To understand the development of psychology, we have to consider both alienation and social control.

ALIENATION AND THE HELPING PROFESSIONS

The term alienation, as it is used here, has nothing to do with dissatisfaction and estrangement from the central values of society, as it is used when writers refer to "alienated students." Rather, I refer here to alienation as a normative and normal experience, which is the lot of most workers in this society, and is accompanied by justified feelings of meaninglessness and powerlessness. Alienation, as described by Marx[8] and Marcuse,[9] has two major aspects: self-estrangement and powerlessness. Most people work because otherwise they would starve. This is the basic fact of alienated labor. For most people, if it were not for the threat of poverty, work is something to be avoided. And it is to be avoided for several good reasons: because in most cases it is meaningless, dehumanizing, and wasteful. Alienating work is that which a person does because it is a means to something else. In most cases, that something else is money, which in turn is a means to having something else again. So work becomes further and further estranged from the self, and a lifetime of working for money is a lifetime of increasing estrangement from the self and others. This type of career is undoubtedly the fate of most people in advanced industrial countries. This kind of existence, where motivation is always extrinsic and never intrinsic, in turn leads to feelings of powerlessness and meaninglessness. Alienated labor is a central fact of life in capitalist society. Despite all the efforts of our colleagues in industrial psychology, most workers still hate their jobs. What industrial psychologists, and some clinical psychologists, are doing is trying to make the workers forget that they are alienated, without changing anything.

As a result of alienation and constant manipulation, the major problem in terms of the individual's life experience is realizing authenticity. When we are always manipulated to want what we should want and to need what we are supposed to need, how can we trust our own experience? Do we engage in sex because we want to and desire to, or is it because we have been manipulated to believe that it proves our own self-worth and desirability? Even the most basic desires are no longer authentic. We cannot trust ourselves because we cannot trust everybody else.

The development of clinical psychology and other "helping professions" can be understood in the context of growing specialization and alienation. Since love is no longer exchanged freely as it once was, the "helping professional," who is the

love specialist, takes care of the needs for love and companion-
ship. This solution, which itself is alienated, does not lessen
alienation. Psychology can be seen as a result of alienation, a
reaction to alienation, and another form of alienation. The
work of the psychologist is in itself mostly nonalienated, since
he is able to satisfy personal needs. It may surprise many psychologists to know that they are using more libido in their
work more directly than most other workers in the society.[10]
Since we work to keep other alienated workers in their places,
our own work has to involve some personal satisfactions.

Psychological activity can become alienated if it follows the
rules set by those who emphasize "professionalism"[11] and
want psychologists to be just as respectable as dentists. One
example of how psychology becomes alienating and alienated
is the conducting of research with funds from government
sources. Many psychologists claim that taking money from the
federal government does not imply support or legitimation.
Some even spend Pentagon money on "peace research" and
are naive enough to believe that they are indeed fighting the
war machine with its own money. Here is a process of mutual
exploitation, with each side believing that it is using the other.
In reality, by conducting research for those in power, we are
working for those in power and are promoting their view of
political realities. When psychologists do research on television
violence and political "violence" and assassinations, they accept the ruling class definition of what constitutes legitimate
action and what constitutes illegitimate violence. Psychologists
thus support the view that violence is what we see in TV
westerns, or what assassins do to politicians, but not what
politicians do to people. When a single man kills a president,
this is assassination; when a president kills millions, this is politics.

CLINICAL PSYCHOLOGY AND SOCIAL CONTROL

Szasz's analysis[12] of the psychiatric profession seems pertinent to what most clinical psychologists do. Psychiatric ac-

tivity, according to Szasz, is a form of social control. The psychiatric professional activity is a combination of three roles: (1) theoretical scientist—one who is expert on game-playing behavior; (2) social engineer—one who sorts out players and assigns them to games they can play; and (3) social manipulator —one who influences people to induce them to play, or cease to play, certain games. In the psychiatrist's main role as a social engineer, he sorts people into pigeonholes of "identities" in which they belong; and in his role as a social manipulator, or therapist, he makes sure that they stay there. The extent to which most therapists foster social conformity and social control, rather than self-actualization, is clear in a nationwide survey of therapists by Goldman and Mendelsohn.[13] One of the major ways in which psychology functions as an instrument of social control is through providing explanations for inequality and human suffering, which are reflected in what we preach and what we practice. The problem is not the gap between the two, but rather both the preaching and the practice, since a lot of our practice consists of preaching.

One important distinction suggested by Mills[14] is that between personal troubles and social issues. Personal troubles are those which occur within the character of the individual and within the range of his immediate relations with others. Social issues transcend individual relationship and have to do with the institutions of society as a whole. The distinction between the personal trouble and the social issue is often overlooked or denied as irrelevant. Individual unemployment, for example, is a personal problem, severely affecting the life of one person. But this problem cannot be solved without changing the economy that produces unemployment. The psychological bias is clearly to direct attention to personal troubles, and even generalize them to social issues. As Szasz[15] suggested, the major impact of the psychological model of human suffering, as it is used today, is to de-ethicize and de-politicize ethical and political problems. Thus, questions of value are turned into questions of technology.

The dilemma is summarized in a quotation from the play

The Cocktail Party, by T. S. Eliot. Going to a psychiatrist, the
heroine starts her interview with:

> I should really like to think there's something wrong with me
> —Because, if there isn't, then there's something wrong. . . .
> With the world itself.

Our clients, when they come to us, ask the same question: is
there something wrong with them, or is there something
wrong with the world around them. And with few exceptions,
psychologists tell them that there is something wrong with
them and nothing wrong with the world. We usually ignore
the possibility of structural social problems, which in turn
cause some of the discomfort in our clients. The importance of
interpersonal and social conflicts tends to be obscured by our
preoccupation with internal conflicts.[16]

In individual work and in theorizing about groups, we come
up with explanations for emotional states, especially those that
are likely to create conflict. We do have ideas about the sources
of interpersonal conflict and personal unhappiness. We normally refer to anger and sadness as "hostility" and "depression," and a crucial part of our social role is to explain their
sources. We are called upon to explain the sources of oppression, and the way it is felt by the individual. The major question
is whether the sources of oppression are external or internal.
The traditional psychodynamic view saw the disturbed person
as oppressed by his symptoms, inhibitions, and other inappropriate behaviors. This view of oppression as mainly internal is
still accepted by most psychologists today. Those who explain
their problems and oppression as caused by external sources
are rejected by us as externalizing, defending themselves
against the more demanding internal frame of reference.

A major problem in so-called "community mental health"
centers is the conversion of clients from the external to the
internal frame of reference. The unsophisticated lower-class
client often thinks that his problems may be related to his
poverty and oppression. We teach him to ignore the material

world and concentrate on his feelings. Psychologists practicing in community mental health centers are selling the ideology of internalization to the lower classes. The message is: "Look into yourself. See why it is that you always end up as the victim. There must be something in you." If we are successful, we induce in our clients a desire to deal better with the internal representations of previous relationships, and we move them away from their present circumstances. The realities of oppression and inequality become justified and mystified in the process of immersion in individual perspectives.

Similarly, we emphasize the sources of aggression as being internal. This is a newer version of the innate evil theory: some people are born more aggressive or become more aggressive because of early experiences. Little attention is paid to the environment in which they are being aggressive. We concentrate on the universal in human behavior and feelings, and our emphasis is again internal, rather than external. We pay attention to universal crises, conflicts, and urges. We pay less attention to common destiny or social situation. By concentrating on the universal and the internal, we may claim to be liberating the individual from the constraints of his society, moving him from the relative to the universal, helping him to transcend society and realize his essence as a human being. Our focus, when dealing with an individual, is on factors that are internal, historical, and unique. We pay attention to past experience rather than present situation. We often tell people that the events determining their present situation happened when they were children, inside their family of origin, and our analysis usually stops at the boundaries of the family.

A major function of psychologists today is to rationalize inequality or, in more elegant language, to explain the differential allocation of rewards in society. Psychologists are called upon to make individual judgments as to who shall not be rewarded, and they are also involved in more general explanations as to who shall inherit the earth, and why. The way psychologists rationalize inequality is by saying that people at the bottom of the social ladder are: lower on I.Q. tests, show less ego strength, have weaker superegos and are unable to delay gratification.[17] If only psychology had been sufficiently developed in the 1840s in the U.S., we would have read a psychological analysis of slavery, describing slaves as "unable to delay gratification, low on frustration tolerance, having psychopathic tendencies, scoring lower on intelligence tests, and in general being unmotivated, impulsive, and violent." An interesting conclusion would have been that slavery is a psychological syndrome, transmitted from generation to generation. Support for this conclusion would have come from the observation that children born to slaves tend to become slaves. If this description seems absurd, one should look at how psychologists discuss the problem of poverty today. Then this absurd pattern will become familiar.[18] The extent of person-blaming as a strategy in psychological research of social problems, and the various forms this technique takes, are brilliantly described by Caplan and Nelson,[19] who provide several illustrations.

The psychological view of human suffering is discovered to be, upon a closer look, a repetition of the old conservative-religious morality: man is by nature sinful and corruptible. Most of an individual's suffering is blamed on himself in a variety of ways. The modern psychological way of doing it is by describing a variety of personality deficiencies: lack of motivation, inability to delay gratification, low frustration tolerance, "psychopathic personality," and so on. When we look at psychology as a mechanism of social control, an interesting analogy comes to mind. If we combine the emphasis on individual responsibility, internal causation, and individual solution to problems, it all sounds a little like a call for soul searching and individual salvation, and indeed it may be. The similarity between the functions of religion and psychology was also noted by London,[20] who described the enterprise of psychotherapy as "the salvation of secular man" and psychotherapists as "secular priests." When we look at the content of what both psychology and religion offer the individual, the similarity is rather striking: both move away from the social and material world, to deal with the invisible world of feelings and fantasies. Both offer salvation at the individual and internal level, not in any social, political, or economic way. Both psychology and religion tell us that the road to happiness is through individual change and not a change in the world around the individual.

IS PSYCHOLOGY A FORCE FOR SOCIAL CHANGE?

Is psychology indeed the opium of the people, as I have implied? Most psychologists see themselves as part of a movement toward positive social change, and will be terribly offended if we suggest to them that they are part of a social control mechanism. Many psychologists have an image of themselves and their profession as counterdependent, rebellious, and critical of society. Many clinical psychologists see themselves as the vanguard of a new humanistic revolution. Recent development in the technology of psychotherapy, and especially new group approaches, are hailed as signifying a new age and a "human potential movement." Some claims of this movement rest on the assumption that the whole atmosphere of social groups and organizations can change, and the age of Aquarius will dawn upon us as a result of greater individual awareness and liberation. A popular book detailing "awareness exercises" is appropriately entitled *What to Do Till the Messiah Comes*. The title implies an expectation of a major change in this world, and in this society. But until this eschatological event comes, the reader is offered a series of experiences to tide him over. These are all temporary measures, but this is what we must do while we are waiting for real change. We can change our private environment, but the Messiah is expected to do the rest. This anecdote raises some serious questions: (1) Can psychology change society in any way? (2) Do we have the potential or power to bring about change? (3) What is the real effect of the things we do until the Messiah comes? Is it possible that all these temporary measures may be delaying change?

One claim heard most often from psychologists who are involved in changing individuals goes like this: "We help people get their heads together, so that they can change the world around them." As Halleck[21] suggests, helping people get their heads together often results in the elimination of their desire to change the world. People who are thoroughly pleased with their lives do not make good revolutionaries. Both Halleck and Halmos[22] show how psychological interpretations and emphasis on individual motivation neutralize potential political energy.

One answer to the question of the gap between what psychologists are doing and what they think they are doing has to do with the social origins of people who become clinical psychologists. Marginality is central in the experience of clinical psychologists, both individually and as a group. As a group, psychologists are notoriously deviant. They differ from majority views in both attitudes and life styles. They are openly critical of social norms and social roles. How can we integrate this view of psychologists with their role as social engineers and social controllers?

A paradox is indeed here—the paradox of those who are marginal and deviant and who are put in a position of being controllers and resocializers. We might say that the minimally deviant psychologists are resocializing the extremely deviant, those who are defined as "mentally disturbed," "mentally ill," or "criminal." Society's way of recruiting social controllers is based on both individual dynamics and societal needs. Often the social regulator is close to those he has to regulate, both in dynamics and origin. We frequently comment on how policemen are similar to those they arrest, in both dynamics and social origin. The difference between the cop and the robber is that the cop becomes aware of his impulses early enough to control them by becoming a controller. Similarly, choosing the career of a social engineer may have something to do with recognizing one's own impulses and defending against them. In terms of individual dynamics, we may speculate that this career choice is related to an incomplete identification with the parents in early childhood. This identification is completed by assuming the parental role in work with deviants, and by identifying at the same time with the client, who is rebuilding his own identification. In terms of individual mobility, choosing the career of a psychologist means for most individuals who make this choice moving upward and assimilating into the majority, since most clinical psychologists came from socially marginal groups.[23]

After an examination of the social control function of psychology, we may reach the conclusion that it is involved not with real social change, but with maintaining the illusion of change. Clinical psychologists talk today about the choice of life styles and about helping people choose their own life styles. The problem with the prophets of "life style" and "the greening of America" is that they refuse to look at the basic problems and inequalities in society. It may be appropriate to say about clinical psychologists what B. F. Skinner said about Albert Schweitzer; "He wanted to help mankind—one at a time".

RECENT DEVELOPMENTS AND THEIR IMPLICATIONS

Recent developments in professional practice can be examined from the perspective of their relationship to the traditional approach presented above. These developments will be viewed either as challenges to or derivatives of traditional approaches. Most changes in practice originate from the internal frustrations and failures of the profession itself, and present themselves as innovations in technology. Some changes, mainly those which arose in response to external pressures, may involve a different value perspective.

Perhaps the major development over the last ten years in terms of clinical practice has been the rise, maybe the triumph, of behavior modification. In terms of the values and the political views described so far, behavior modification is paradoxical, since it is both the embodiment and the natural consequence of the conservative trend in psychology, and the only psychological school that is openly and consciously value-laden. We should commend our colleagues who are practicing behavior modification for their honesty in stating their value preferences. Most of them are quite open about the fact that they work to inforce social norms and prevent deviance. Contrary to other therapists, they are ready to tell us exactly what kinds of changes they want to bring about in their clients, and why. Their starting point is always what is socially desirable and socially acceptable. One of the promoters of behavioral approaches to deviance, J. V. McConnell, suggests the following: "We must begin by drafting new laws that will be as consonant as possible with all the human behavior data that scientists have gathered. We should try to regulate human conduct by offering rewards for good behavior whenever possible instead of threatening punishment for breaches of the law. We should reshape our society so that we all would be trained from birth to want to do what society wants us to do."[24]

The behavioral approach recognizes the importance of the environment in shaping the individual; but, when dealing with human suffering and dissatisfaction, it attempts to reshape the individual rather than the environment. In this respect, behavior modification is in total agreement with most other clinical approaches. Philosophically, it is the logical result of the "end of ideology" and the "end of values" movement in clinical psychology, the reduction of all moral questions to technical ones. "End of ideology" theories, in both psychology and politics, are promoted by conservative forces. The assumption behind them is that of a broad consensus, which unites most members of society, and most members of the profession, so only "technical" problems remain to be solved.[25] Behavior modification is the logical result of our emphasis on "functioning" and on our "big machine" model of society. We start with the belief that the big machine is all right; we just have to keep it oiled and running. Individuals, who can best be conceptualized as little machines, should adjust to the big machine, and they too should be kept oiled and running. Psychologists help people adjust to the reality of the big machine.

On the other side of the spectrum in terms of scientific claims and rigor are developments in the area of group work, which have also gained prominence over the last decade. Sensitivity training, encounter groups, group marathons, and all other varieties of temporary and intense interpersonal contact in groups can be regarded as a reaction to the alienation and shallowness in normal human relations in society.[26] Viewing such group situations as opportunities for the exchange of love and intimacy makes clear why they have become so popular. In terms of ideology and political implications, encounter groups cannot be regarded as radical, since they still concentrate on individual changes and immediate relationships. Other changes in practice present more of a challenge to the narrow ecological view of the causation of human suffering, since they go beyond the individual and attempt wider system intervention. The newer developments of family therapy and network therapy show that the preoccupation with individual causation can be constructively overcome. These newer approaches also give due recognition to what is going on within the family at present, not just what was going on within the family twenty or thirty years ago. Dealing with systems may lead psychologists to looking at wider and more encompassing ones. It is impossible to ignore the continuity between the family and society as a whole, and so psychologists are already looking at whole communities and they may find themselves looking at whole societies.

More serious challenges to the traditional model of the individual come from those who attack the basic definition of deviance. The drive toward politicalization of private problems offers us concrete examples of an alternative way of viewing our clients. One clear example of the redefinition of deviance is the tendency of homosexuals and others to view themselves as a minority group, rather than as a group of individual deviants. Their problem then is regarded as social and political, and not as individual or therapeutic. Our emphasis on what human beings have in common internally is countered by the new emphasis on what they have in common externally, such as race and sex. We are used to dealing with individual and universal insecurities involved in the process of growing up in human society. The new approaches emphasize the insecurities involved in growing up as a member of a social group. The difference between growing up powerful and growing up powerless, the difference between growing up upper-class and growing up working-class, growing up white and growing up black, all lead to differences in psychological experiences and self-concepts.

The experience of every woman is affected by her social position. Belonging to an oppressed group is one of the major determinants of individual experience. Politicizing women's problems is significant, since women make up the majority of our clients. The feminist viewpoint implies that there are external forces and necessities that shape women's behavior into forms that are then regarded as deviant or pathological. The external social forces are those that determine what appears to be prevalent forms of psychopathology. The hysterical woman is a product of a society that teaches women to be hysterical; the depressed housewife has some pretty good reasons to be so; and identity conflicts in college women are a result of reality pressures. When we look at minority groups, the radical viewpoint emphasizes reality factors in the causation of personal difficulties, and underscores the relativity of clinical concepts.

The lessons of "community mental health" and studies in psychiatric "epidemiology" are quite clear. They show that the poor and minority groups are high risk populations in terms of mental health, which means that members of these groups are more likely to become inmates in mental hospitals or prisons. One of the daring suggestions of the recent "Nader's raiders" report on community mental health was that employment opportunities and better housing could do more for the mental health of the poor than community mental health centers. This suggestion was properly ignored by mental health professionals, since it obviously indicates defensive externalization.

Many of us have become sensitized to the problems of

women and are less likely to take a totally individualistic position when looking at the problems of individual women. Many are recognizing more and more the effects of the social situation on members of minority groups, and are willing to examine critically the social consequences of our measurements and definitions. We can then generalize and suggest that there are general social conditions affecting most members of this society, and not merely minority groups. Growing up and living in a society which regards people and treats people as commodities affects every individual, every individual's self-concept, confidence, and abilities. In working with individual clients and in our attempts to generalize from work with individuals, we have to recognize social and political realities. Both the psychologist and the client are subjects of enormous social pressures. Often clients come to us when they have to make real-life decisions, and all too often we tend to ignore the impact of political and economic realities to which they respond. What we are all interested in, or that is what we say, is the maximal actualization of human potential. The question before us is whether such an actualization is possible without a major transformation of society. Most psychologists today are committed to a viewpoint that sees self-actualization as totally dependent on the individual. Most psychologists are totally satisfied with a role definition that demands that we leave society intact, while changing only the individual. Those of us who are committed to a different choice of values are in the unenviable position of reminding the majority of its repressed responsibilities.

References

1. Theodore Roszak, *The Making of a Counter Culture* (Garden City, N.Y.: Doubleday, 1969), p. 78.
2. Cf. A. Gouldner, "Anti-Minotaur: The Myth of a Value-Free Sociology," *Social Problems,* 1962, 10:199–213.
3. Arthur Miller, "The Writer as Independent Spirit: 1. The Role of P.E.N.," *Saturday Review,* June 4, 1966, pp. 16–17.
4. Heinz Hartmann, *Psychoanalysis and Moral Values* (New York: International Universities Press, 1960).
5. C. Wright Mills, "A Reply to Critics," in *C. Wright Mills and the Power Elite,* edited by G. W. Domhoff and H. B. Ballard (Boston: Beacon Press, 1968), p. 243.
6. American Psychological Association, *Ethical Standards of Psychologists* (Washington, D.C.: APA, 1963).
7. B. G. Rosenthal, *The Images of Man* (New York: Basic Books, 1971).
8. Karl Marx, "Economic and Political Manuscripts," in E. Fromm, *Marx's Concept of Man* (New York: Ungar, 1961).
9. Herbert Marcuse: *One Dimensional Man* (Boston: Beacon Press, 1964) and *Eros and Civilization* (Boston: Beacon Press, 1966).
10. Cf. Marcuse, *Eros and Civilization.*
11. N. A. Milgram, "The Clinical Psychologist—A Man for All Seasons?" *The Clinical Psychologist,* 1972, 25:2–15.
12. T. S. Szasz, *The Myth of Mental Illness* (New York: Harper & Row, 1961).
13. R. K. Goldman and G. A. Mendelsohn, "Psychotherapeutic Change and Social Adjustment: A Report of a National Survey of Psychotherapists," *Journal of Abnormal Psychology,* 1969, 74:164–72.
14. G. W. Mills, *The Sociological Imagination* (New York: Oxford University Press, 1959).
15. T. S. Szasz, *Ideology and Insanity* (Garden City: N.Y.: Doubleday, 1970).
16. Cf. Szasz, *The Myth of Mental Illness.*
17. A. Hollingshead and F. C. Redlich, *Social Class and Mental Illness* (New York: Wiley, 1958); M. R. Levy, "Issues in the Personality Assessment of Lower-Class Patients," *Journal of Projective Techniques and Personality Assessment,* 1970, 34:6–9; M. R. Mehlman and J. E. Fleming, "Social Stratification and Some Personality Variables," *Journal of General Psychology,* 1963, 69:3–10; F. Riessman, J. Cohen, and A. Pearl (eds.), *Mental Health of the Poor* (New York: The Free Press, 1964).
18. A. Billingsley, "Black Families and White Social Sciences," *Journal of Social Issues,* 1970, 26:127–42; E. Herzog, "Social Stereotypes and Social Research," *Journal of Social Issues,* 1970, 26:109–25; W. Ryan, *Blaming the Victim* (New York: Pantheon, 1971).
19. N. Caplan and S. D. Nelson, "On Being Useful—The Nature and Consequences of Psychological Research on Social Problems," *American Psy-*

chologist, 1973, 28:199–211.
20. P. London, *The Modes and Morals of Psychotherapy* (New York: Holt, Rinehart, and Winston, 1964).
21. S. L. Halleck, *The Politics of Therapy* (New York: Harper & Row, 1971).
22. Ibid.; P. Halmos, *The Faith of the Counsellors* (New York: Schocken, 1970).
23. W. E. Henry, J. H. Sims, and S. L. Spray, *The Fifth Profession* (San Francisco: Jossey-Bass, 1971).
24. J. V. McConnell, "Criminals Can Be Brainwashed—Now," *Psychology Today,* April 1970, p. 74.
25. Cf. Halmos, *The Faith of the Counsellors.*
26. U. G. Foa and G. W. Donnerworth, "Love Poverty in Modern Culture and Sensitivity Training," *Sociological Inquiry,* 1971, 41:149–59.

Issues in the Diagnosis and Classification of Personality Functioning

GERALD L. BOROFSKY

AT TIMES, WE PSYCHOLOGISTS TEND TO BE A CONTENTIOUS lot. Often our professional attitudes and theoretical orientations are used as much for the generation of internecine debates as for the generation of new understanding. However, one of the few things that most psychologists seem to agree upon is that the current system of diagnosis and personality classification.[1] Although this system has some clinical utility, its heuristic value seems to be highly limited.

This paper represents a preliminary effort to review some of the conceptual and theoretical issues involved in personality classification. It is hoped that this approach has both heuristic and clinical value.

PART I. IS CLASSIFICATION USEFUL?

The tendency to classify experience appears to be an innate function of the human brain. Classification enables us to make order out of the various, (and seemingly chaotic, elements of human experience. It allows us to be more efficient in our psychological functioning. It is one of the principles underlying our ability to learn, and it is inherent in the language we use.[2] Without this capacity to classify, we would be unable to learn. It is through the classification of our experience that we form concepts, by generalizing from one psychological event to other related events. Because classification enables us to bring order out of seeming chaos, it is one of the basic requirements for the development of science.

But, Is Personality Classification Necessary?

Many writers have been highly critical of attempts to systematically classify and diagnose personality.[3] Albee's thoughtful and concerned opposition to psychodiagnosis raises the following major objections to current systems of classification: (1) most systems of diagnosis tend to focus on pathology and weakness rather than on adaptive functioning and ego strengths; (2) most systems view psychopathology as being discontinuous with adaptive psychological functioning; accordingly, they classify disturbed individuals into one of several discrete types, rather than viewing emotional disturbance as an exaggeration or disruption of normal adaptive functioning; (3) most classification systems tend to ignore the individual personality and the possibility of individuality and uniqueness in the search for adaptation; they tend to focus on a nomothetic approach to deviancy and adaptation; (4) diagnostic systems use typologies rather than traits; and (5) diagnostic classifications are used to make value judgments in legal or moral matters. The first four objections noted above seem to be highly reasonable ones that can easily be integrated into a system of personality classification.

The last point, however, is a speciously reasoned basis for opposing a system of personality classification. It is clear that individuals can be given a socially unacceptable label because of their emotional disturbance. It is also true that such labels can have disastrous social consequences for individuals including deprivation of their civil rights. Although such misuses are repugnant to us, they can hardly be used as arguments for doing away with personality classification. They are signposts that caution us to guard against the misuse of our science.

Analogous situations demonstrate this point. Atomic energy holds the potential for misuse as a weapon of war or for use as a revolutionary source of energy. Some have suggested that such knowledge be suppressed because of its potential for misuse. History has clearly shown that the suppression of knowledge only leads to greater evils. The challenge has always been to create constructive and socially beneficial uses for potentially dangerous and destructive knowledge.

In the psychological development of the individual there is a similar situation. During the course of development, id demands are subordinated in the service of growth and adaptation. Socially acceptable expressions of the drives—i.e., sublimations—must be developed if the person is to enjoy continued psychological growth. If these drives are simply repressed and no adequate structure is developed to adaptively channel these drives, then the person is generally conceded to be emotionally disturbed. The development of an adequate psychic structure which allows expression of the drives in the service of adaptation is considered to be a sign of emotional strength.

We are confronted with a similar situation in our efforts to develop a science of psychology. In that science deals with a body of facts which are *systematically* arranged, it is necessary for us to *systematically* classify our knowledge about psychological functioning. It was noted earlier that all humans innately seem to classify their experience. Doing this in a *systematic* manner earns us the title of psychologist.

To guard against the misuse of knowledge, we cannot do away with knowledge. The challenge of using new knowledge for the advancement of humanity is a challenge that is probably as old as civilization. The use of knowledge for constructive, rather than destructive, ends will undoubtedly continue to be a major challenge.

Some General Conceptual Issues Involved in Classifying Personality

Some general issues relating to the structure and content of a system of personality classification include: (1) discrete typologies vs. continua in psychological functioning; (2) classification based on maladaptive functioning vs. classification based on adaptive functioning; (3) behavioral vs. intrapsychic factors; (4) clinical utility vs. heuristic value; and (5) clinical data vs. psychological test data.

1. *Discrete Typologies vs. Continua in Psychological Functioning.* It should be noted in passing that the current APA system of diagnosis and personality classification is essentially a typology of psychopathological functioning. Like any typology, it groups individuals into discrete categories based on the presence or absence of certain criteria. Allport[4] has summarized the main objections to a typological approach to the study of personality. He notes that regardless of the specific types involved, typologies "always fall short of depicting the *whole* individual." And elsewhere he notes that typologies "say nothing more than that certain people resemble other people *in some respect.*" He also observes that no single person can be found who embodies the pure or ideal type. That is, any one individual may possess certain characteristics of a given type, but at the same time lack others. Similarly, most individuals possess personality characteristics that would simultaneously place them into several different types. The situation is even more confusing with regard to the APA diagnostic system, since the types themselves are not independent of each other. Considerable overlap exists between the various diagnostic types.

Another major problem with typologies is that they leave one with the impression that the structures and dynamics of personality functioning are somehow discontinuous. Even though it is widely accepted that psychological functioning is continuous and not discrete, we still find ourselves with a diagnostic system that prevents us from directly conceptualizing the underlying psychological processes that constitute personality. Although we repeatedly speak of psychological processes as ranging along a continuum, we nonetheless persist in using a diagnostic system which, at best, only *implies* such an underlying continuity of functioning. Rather than speaking of the presence or absence of a certain variable, one should speak of the degree and intensity to which a given variable characterizes the psychological functioning of an individual.

The concept of a continuum allows us to take a given psychological variable and to scale the quality and quantity of its contribution to the psychological functioning of a given individual. This is in contrast to an instrument such as the MMPI, which scales the relative contribution of psychological factors that are *typological* in nature. It does not scale the underlying psychological structures and processes that operate dynamically.

As with the APA diagnostic system, the MMPI only *infers* the presence of underlying continuity in psychological functioning. To better understand the nature of psychological functioning, it is necessary to use instruments that allow us to study the underlying *continuous* processes directly and explicitly.

2. *Classification Based on Maladaptive Functioning vs. Classification Based on Adaptive Functioning.* Systems of diagnosis and personality classification have generally tended to focus heavily upon the pathological aspects of personality functioning. Much of our awareness of psychological functioning has been drawn from clinical experience with disturbed individuals. The argument has always been raised that the study of psychopathology does not allow us to draw conclusions about progressive or growth-oriented psychological functioning. However, Freud[5] repeatedly argued that there were no fundamental differences between normal and neurotic—only qualitative and quantitative differences. He insisted that the study of pathological functioning would provide valuable contributions to the understanding of growth-oriented functioning. Psychoanalysis has provided us with a highly refined outline of how individuals cope maladaptively with conflict. For whatever the reasons, however, the classification and under-

standing of growth-oriented functioning has not reached a similar level of sophistication. As a result, the more refined systems of classification are those dealing with psychopathology.

However, a general classification of personality should not merely include pathological aspects of functioning; it should also classify progressive and growth-oriented functioning. If we accept the concept of a continuum and the notion that psychological functioning is continuous, then we must assume that a continuum exists between progressive and regressive psychological functioning. Freud had this in mind when he stated:

> Every normal person, in fact, is only normal on the average. His ego approximates to that of the psychotic in some part or other and to a greater or lesser extent; and the degree of its remoteness from one end of the series and of its proximity to the other will furnish us with a provisional measure of what we have so indefinitely termed an "alteration of the ego."[6]

Thus, any system of personality classification, if it is to have maximal heuristic value, must view all psychological functioning as being continuous. It should not separate maladaptive from adaptive functioning. The underlying variables being examined must be able to explain both adaptive and maladaptive functioning as simply reflecting a difference in degree and intensity.

It would be worthwhile briefly to clarify the concept of adaptation at this point. Psychoanalysis uses this term to describe the process by which the ego reaches an integration of a complex set of conflicts that interact with one another. In speaking of adaptation, I have intended to use a broader meaning of the word. I mean to use the word in the Darwinian sense, in which adaptation is a natural state toward which the individual strives in order to enhance his survival value over the long run. This typically involves increasing the flexibility of potential responses to changing demands both internal and external. This contrasts to the psychoanalytic usage, which is concerned with the more short-run goal of equilibrium. Adaptive functioning, as I mean to use the term, may result in a large-scale upset of equilibrium over the short run.

3. *Behavioral vs. Intrapsychic Variables.* Many approaches to classifying personality make exclusive use of external behavior. This is extremely problematic if the classification system is to have maximal heuristic value. According to the concept of *overdetermination*,[7] a given behavioral phenomenon may be caused by more than one intrapsychic factor. Waelder in his *principle of multiple function*[8] asserts that a given piece of behavior serves several functions. That is, behavior is typically the most economical synthesis of a whole series of intrapsychic states. These concepts suggest that the relationship between intrapsychic functioning and overt behavior is far from simple.

To base a classification system on the presence or absence of certain discrete behaviors or symptoms seems to be a highly dubious undertaking. First of all, these discrete behaviors are typically treated as being discontinuous. In view of what has been said earlier, it would seem unwise to use discontinuous variables as the basis for classifying personality. Secondly, since behavior can have multiple determinants, it is hard to know what different combinations of intrapsychic factors can produce the same piece of behavior. Thirdly, since behavior has the purpose of satisfying multiple internal functions, it would seem more profitable to examine the underlying functions involved.

Anna Freud has summarized the problems involved in classifying personality by simply describing the manifest behavior that has been observed.

> As in the field of adult analysis, the descriptive nature of many of the current diagnostic categories runs counter to the essence of psychoanalytic thinking, since it emphasizes the identity of or difference between manifest symptomatology while neglecting those of the underlying pathogenic factors. It is true that in this manner a classification of disturbances is achieved which seems orderly and comprehensive to the superficial glance. But such a schema does nothing to advance deeper understanding

or to promote differential diagnosis in a metapsychological sense. On the contrary, whenever the analyst accepts diagnostic thinking on this level, he is inevitably led into confusion in assessment and subsequently to erroneous therapeutic inferences.[9]

To place primary reliance upon intrapsychic factors is admittedly a difficult and challenging task. This is particularly so for the inexperienced person. Experienced clinicians, particularly those trained in psychoanalysis, tend routinely to make use of a metapsychological approach to diagnosis.

On the other hand, psychologists, with their unique training in psychological testing and personality assessment, are in a good position to carefully study and classify the functioning of intrapsychic factors. Psychological tests, particularly the WAIS (WISC), and projective techniques (especially the Rorschach) provide us with more than sufficient raw data to make an assessment of personality functioning based on intrapsychic factors.

Thus, in developing a system of personality classification, it would seem wisest to rely primarily on the functioning of intrapsychic factors. This would provide for the greatest heuristic value.

4. *Clinical Utility vs. Heuristic Value.* For all its limitations, the APA diagnostic categories do provide some amount of clinical usefulness. We are able to distinguish between cases that require hospitalization and those that can be treated on an outpatient basis. We are able to distinguish between individuals who require intensive treatment, possibly including the use of various types of medications, and those who only require weekly psychotherapy. Other classification systems have been developed that allow us to predict an individual's success or failure in psychotherapy. Such systems, and there are many of them, are concerned with classifying individuals for specific clinical purposes. Typically, such approaches have limited heuristic value. In addition, they are based upon discontinuous phenomena and tend to resort to typologies. While

they may have considerable clinical utility, they have little or no value in increasing our overall understanding of how human beings function psychologically. They are designed to attack specific issues and are typically lacking any formal theoretical foundation.

Since our primary goal is to generate new understanding about psychological functioning, it is important to classify personality in a manner that has the maximal heuristic value. A system of classification should perform two functions: (1) organize existing knowledge and (2) promote the generation of new knowledge.

5. *Clinical Data vs. Psychological Test Data.* The dimensions or variables included in a system of personality classification should be *both* clinically observable and measurable by psychological tests. It makes little sense to have a system that is based solely on clinical observables and cannot be measured on psychological tests. It is just as futile to develop a system that uses variables that are measurable on psychological tests but cannot be clinically verified.

Summary of General Issues Involved in Personality Classification

In summary, an adequate system of personality classification and diagnosis should: (1) view all psychological functioning as ranging along a continuum rather than classifying it into discrete and discontinuous types, (2) utilize the same variables, mechanisms, and logic for explaining both adaptive and maladaptive psychological functioning, (3) be based mainly on intrapsychic factors, (4) be such that heuristic considerations take precedence over short-range clinical utility, and (5) use variables that are observable and measurable both clinically and from psychological test data.

PART II. GENERAL THEORETICAL CONSIDERATIONS

In selecting specific variables for inclusion in a system of classification, it seems necessary first to outline some basic as-

sumptions about the nature of human psychological functioning. These assumptions will set the directions in which we
search for specific variables.

It is assumed that:

1. All humans have an innate drive toward increased psychological development and an increased realization of their innate developmental potential. Whether this is called a developmental instinct,[10] a drive toward self-actualization,[11] or
Eros,[12] it is assumed that all humans have an innate drive
toward continued development and realization of their potential.

2. All humans have an innate drive toward increased adaptation and mastery of both their internal and external environments. Adaptation in the Darwinian sense[13] enables the individual to enhance his survival potential, through the
development of increased flexibility of response to changing
demands from internal and external sources. Psychologists
have called this innate tendency by such terms as competence,[14] an instinct for mastery,[15] striving for superiority,[16] or
transcendence of the environment.[17] Whatever the name, this
drive reflects the innate tendency of humans to proceed toward mastery of their environments.

3. Conflict is a normal and omnipresent aspect of human
functioning. Lampl-DeGroot notes that conflict is,

> an inherent part of the life process. . . . The process of develop-
> ment is centered around and *stimulated* by inner and outer
> conflicts. The decision whether a "normal" solution of a conflict
> is achieved or whether a symptom or some other pathological
> outcome finally emerges, depends upon the intactness of an
> ego-capacity, the integrative or harmonizing ability.[18]

Similarly, Dabrowski[19] insists that experience with conflict is
an essential precondition for psychological development. It is
not the presence of conflict that is considered pathological. On
the contrary, the seeming absence of conflict is probably a sure
indicator of psychopathology. Pathological functioning occurs
if the ego is unable to integrate conflict in the service of growth

and adaptation. Zetzel[20] has suggested that the capacity for emotional growth hinges on the ability to recognize, tolerate, and master conflict. In fact, it has been proposed that humans innately and automatically induce stress and conflict in order to cope with it and subsequently master it.[21] This process, which has been called the *conflict cycle,*[22] leads to enhanced psychological growth and adaptation through producing, coping with, and resolving conflict.

4. Psychological development and adaptation involve both regression *and* progression. According to the Theory of Positive Disintegration,[23] regression or "disintegration" is a necessary precondition for any type of psychological growth. Borofsky[24] proposed that the superior level of psychological functioning observed in creative individuals was due to their heightened ability to use regression in the service of growth. Similarly, Lampl-DeGroot[25] has noted that "healthy" character traits allow for a certain amount of oscillation—i.e., progression and regression—around a central point that represents the "character-constancy" or personality of the individual. That is, normal personality functioning involves a dynamic ongoing process that is characterized by regression as well as progression.

5. The nature of an individual's psychological functioning is dependent upon his level of psychological development. At more primitive levels of development, the functioning of the psychic structure is less articulated, less differentiated, and generally less developed than at more advanced stages of development. At each level of development, the nature and functioning of the psychic structure is somewhat different. This view is embodied in the concept of *developmental lines.*[26]

These assumptions regarding the nature of human psychological functioning lead us to certain conclusions as to what factors should be included in a system of personality classification. First, a system of classification should not focus on the presence or absence of conflict and regression, since these are natural parts of human psychological functioning. *The more important issue is the manner in which the psychic structure functions in its attempts to integrate and use conflict and regression in the service of increased development and adaptation.* Second, the system should attend to the individual's potential for development as well as his vulnerability to arrests in psychological development. And, third, the system should pay attention to the importance of the concept of developmental lines and to whether the functioning of an individual is phase-adequate, precocious, retarded, or regressed in terms of a given model of psychological development.[27]

Of necessity, the selection of specific variables to include in a system of classification and diagnosis is largely determined by the theoretical orientation from which the system evolves. The specific theory must be comprehensive enough to contain a wide range of theoretical constructs, which in turn can account for the widest possible range of psychological functioning. At the same time, the theory must regard these psychological processes as operating along a continuum. It was noted previously that a system of classification must be based mainly upon intrapsychic factors if it is to be maximally heuristic. With this in mind, it seems most reasonable to use psychoanalytic theory as the basis for developing a system of classification and diagnosis. If there were other equally comprehensive theories of psychological functioning, presumably they could serve equally well as the basis upon which to develop a system of personality classification.

Psychoanalytic Theory and Personality Classification

The Structure of Psychoanalytic Theory. In his attempt to present systematically the structure of psychoanalytic theory, Rapaport[28] noted that there were *ten* basic propositions, or "points of view," embedded in what is called general psychoanalytic theory. He concluded that ultimately these ten orientations could be condensed into five—the dynamic, economic, structural, genetic, and adaptive points of view.

The *dynamic* point of view states that "the ultimate determinants of all behavior are the drives." The *economic* viewpoint states that "all behavior disposes of and is regulated by psychological energy." According to the *structural* point of view, "all behavior has structural determiners." The *genetic* view states that "all behavior is part of a genetic series, and through its antecedents, part of the temporal sequences which brought about the present form of the personality." The *adaptive* point of view proposes that "all behavior is determined by reality."

No single viewpoint is sufficiently comprehensive to adequately organize the various constructs that are collectively called psychoanalytic theory. It is clear that these approaches are not independent of one another. It is also true that some approaches have significantly greater heuristic value than others. Likewise, some orientations are much more comprehensive than others. The challenge has been to integrate these various approaches into a unified model of psychological functioning.

The Structural Theory in Psychoanalysis. Based upon Freud's formulations[29] of a tripartite model of the mind, as well as recent advances in ego psychology, Arlow and Brenner[30] attempted to clarify and resolve the numerous inconsistencies that Rapaport[31] had shown to exist within psychoanalytic theory. In doing so, they provided an integrated model of psychological functioning that includes all five of the orientations discussed in the previous section.

This model places primary emphasis upon the dynamic interactions of id, ego, and superego and their role in the determination of how one functions psychologically. In doing so, however, it does not ignore the dynamic, economic, genetic, and adaptive viewpoints. The basic role of the drives (dynamic view) is embodied in the concept of the id. The vicissitudes of drives and their derivatives, however, are determined by the functioning of the psychic structure as a whole. The functioning of the ego and superego are central to the manner in which drives and their derivatives effect psychological functioning. Similarly, it is the functioning of the psychic structure, as a whole, that determines how psychological energy regulates behavior (economic view). The role of reality and its influence upon psychological functioning is primarily determined by the adequacy of ego functioning (adaptive view). Likewise, the structural theory emphasizes the developmental vicissitudes of the psychic structure (genetic view). According to Arlow and Brenner, it

> emphasizes the gradual maturation and development of ego functions and their gradual integration into a functional unity, the ego. It also emphasizes the genesis and gradual development of the superego.[32]

Thus, the structural theory is able to integrate all five points of view by placing the dynamic interactions of the psychic structure in a developmental context. Accordingly, it seems to provide the conceptual basis for a comprehensive and integrated model of psychological functioning. As such, it provides the basis for the formulation of a system of diagnosis and personality classification.

The Structural Theory and Personality Classification. In the structural theory, the mental functions dealing with the management of conflict and regression, as well as management of the drive toward continued development and adaptation are all considered to be ego functions. Furthermore, it is the adequacy of the ego's ability to synthesize and integrate that determines an individual's developmental potential and vulnerability to developmental arrest. Analysis of ego functioning also allows for a determination as to whether the functioning of the psychic structure is phase-adequate, precocious, retarded, or regressed. With these factors in mind, it is clear that a system of personality classification should give primary attention to the nature of an individual's ego functioning.

To study and classify ego functions, one must first compile a list of the numerous mental functions subsumed under the rubric of ego functions. This is a difficult task, but some representative lists are presented below in order to convey the wide-range of functions that fall under this classification.

Arlow and Brenner[33] include the following variables in their list of ego functions: (1) consciousness, (2) sense perception, (3) the perception and expression of affect, (4) thought, (5) control of motor action, (6) memory, (7) language, (8) defense mechanisms and defensive activity in general, (9) control, regulation, and binding of instinctual energy, (10) the integrative and harmonizing function, (11) reality testing, and (12) the capacity to inhibit or suspend the operation of any of these functions and to regress to a primitive level of functioning.

As part of an extremely comprehensive system of personality assessment, Bellak[34] lists the following twelve functions as being subsumed under the concept of ego functions: (1) reality testing, (2) judgment, (3) sense of reality, (4) regulation and control of drives, (5) object relations, (6) thought processes, (7) adaptive regression in the service of the ego, (8) defensive functions, (9) stimulus barrier, (10) autonomous functioning, (11) synthetic functions, and (12) mastery-competence.

A given system of classification should probably include all these variables. Each should be analyzed as to how adaptively or maladaptively that particular function is operating.

In similar fashion, a system of classification should assess superego and id functioning. The main issue here is the degree to which the ego has been able to differentiate and reintegrate primitive superego forerunners and drive representations.

The list of potential variables that can be included in a system of personality classification is enormously long and quite beyond the scope of the present paper. Work is in progress to develop such a list and to reduce the number of variables to a workable size.

Quantification and Measurement of Variables

A system of personality classification must be able to quantify and measure the specific variables contained in the system. The method of measurement and quantification must take into account both the *quality* of how that variable functions, and the *quantity* or *intensity* with which the variable manifests itself in a given individual.

More traditional approaches to assessment have tended solely to emphasize the quantitative assessment of a given variable. For example, the *Problem Appraisal Scales*[35] use a five-point scale to score whether a given variable (e.g., delusions) is not present, slightly present, mildly present, moderately present, or markedly present. Similarly Beck[36] has used the Q-technique to rate whether a given variable (e.g., inadequate reality testing) is highly characteristic or highly uncharacteristic of an individual's functioning.

The limitation of these traditional approaches lies in the fact that the psychological processes involved are not conceptualized as being continuous. Typically, the extreme end of the continuum is selected as the variable, and then a rating is only made of the intensity with which this variable manifests itself.

Keeping in mind the requirement that variables in a system of classification should be continuous, it would seem that the technique of scaling lends itself admirably to the measurement of a given variable. Ideally, each variable should be formulated so that it can be represented along a *bipolar* dimension— ranging from highly maladaptive or pathological at one end, to highly adaptive or growth-promoting at the other end. For example, in discussing the variable "reality testing," which is an ego function, Bellak describes the pathological or maladaptive extreme of the scale as follows:

> Person is primarily deluded and hallucinated; extremely disoriented with respect to time, place, and person; no awareness that his perceptions are in any way inaccurate.[37]

Reality testing at the highly adaptive end of the scale is described as being:

> Optimal. Sharp and flexible (as opposed to hyper-vigilant) reality testing; even in stressful or emotionally burdensome circumstances. Person is well-oriented, and perception resists social contagion, such as suggestion and group effect. Distinction between percept and idea holds up even under many drug states and other physiological alterations. Inner reality testing and psychological mindedness are optimal.[38]

Any given individual's reality testing is placed at some point along this scale. Bellak uses a thirteen-point scale in his system of classification. Such an approach not only stresses the continuous nature of psychological variables, but also allows for a *qualitative* assessment of how a given individual is functioning on that specific variable.

The technique of scaling can also be used for a *quantitative* assessment of a given variable. A quantitative assessment measures the strength or intensity of the variable. Once a qualitative score is assigned for a given variable, we can then rate the intensity with which this qualitative score manifests itself in the functioning of a given individual. The result is a *quantitative* assessment of that specific variable. For example, Silverman and Bellak[39] use a six-point scale to make a quantitative assessment. Their categories measure the frequency with which a given *quality* of a specific variable manifests itself in the functioning of a given individual. The extremes of the scale range from occurring "all or almost all the time" to occurring "not at all."

The above approach to measuring psychological variables can be conceptualized in the form of a two-dimensional matrix. Qualitative assessment of the variable is scaled along one axis, while the quantitative assessment of that variable is scaled along the other axis. The data for a large number of variables can also be presented schematically in the form of a profile, with the individual variables either color-coded or presented along a third dimension. This approach to measurement maintains the discreteness of each specific variable so that it can be studied in isolation from other variables in the classification system. At the same time, it allows for the possibility of grouping several variables together (e.g., by factor analysis) if this is desired for specific research purposes. However, the basic system of classification should not combine individual variables into clusters, since this would simply result in the formation of a new system of psychological types.

Existing Systems of Diagnosis and Classification Which Meet Some of the Criteria Presented

Of the various classification systems reviewed in the process of writing this paper, the system developed by Bellak[40] is the most comprehensive. He has formulated his specific variables in a continuous manner and has scaled them so as to obtain a qualitative assessment of each variable. Apparently, the provision for quantitative assessment, which was included in an earlier version of the system,[41] was deleted from the most recent 1969 edition. While one could argue that more variables and perhaps different variables should be included, the system is clearly the most comprehensive, in spite of the problems noted above.[42]

The metapsychological diagnostic profile developed by Anna Freud[43] is also a relatively complete system of diagnosis. However, this system is mainly a descriptive one and does not readily lend itself to quantification. The specific variables, while not formulated in a continuous manner, are comprehensive and, like Bellak's system, are directly derived from the structural theory of psychoanalysis.

Beck[44] has formulated a partial system of personality classification, which developed from his studies of psychological functioning in schizophrenia. The specific variables were derived both from clinical observation and psychoanalytic theory. The list of variables is perhaps the most comprehensive (120), but they are not formulated in a continuous manner. Thus, his system allows for a quantitative assessment of the variables, but not a qualitative one. In addition, since the system was designed to study psychological functioning in schizophrenia, it does not attend to the areas of adaptive and growth-oriented functioning.

Holt,[45] in his efforts to develop a manual for scoring primary process manifestations in the Rorschach has also developed a system of personality classification, which has a high degree of usefulness. Again, this system provides a comprehensive list of specific variables related to psychological functioning. It provides for a rough measure of both qualitative and quantitative assessment. It is incomplete as a system of personality classification but, then, this is not its intent. However, it certainly is an excellent example of the directions that a system of personality classification should follow.

Kroeber[46] compared what he called defensive ego functioning, which is basically maladaptive, with coping ego functioning, which is basically adaptive. In doing so, he formulated each of these ego mechanisms in a continuous fashion, thus making it possible to assess their function both qualitatively and quantitatively. Since this approach only deals with the ego mechanisms of defense and coping, it is quite incomplete as a system of personality classification. Nonetheless, as with the Holt system, it is an excellent example of the direction that a system of personality classification should follow.

In his classification of character pathology, Kernberg[47] provides a comprehensive list of variables derived from psychoanalytic theory. He provides a rough qualitative assessment of these variables, but not in a manner that is directly quantifiable. The variables are partially formulated in a continuous manner, but do not attend to the areas of adaptive and growth-oriented functioning.

Despite what might be the individual shortcomings of these classification systems, they are all excellent examples of what should be included in a system of personality classification. In addition to the points discussed, all these systems are based mainly on intrapsychic factors, have major heuristic value, and are designed in such a manner that the specific variables are observable and measurable both clinically and from psychological test data. Also, all these approaches allow for an assessment of how the psychic structure functions in its attempts to integrate and use conflict and regression in the service of increased development and adaptation. They also allow for an assessment of both an individual's developmental potential and his vulnerability to arrests in psychological development. All these approaches also allow for an assessment of the functioning of the psychic structure along developmental lines.

PART III. IMPLICATIONS FOR THE TEACHING
OF DIAGNOSIS AND PERSONALITY ASSESSMENT

Some of the major implications for the teaching of assessment and diagnosis are:

1. The variables underlying the psychological functioning of an individual should be taught explicitly and specifically, rather than indirectly inferring their operation as is done in the current APA typology. It is not possible to assess, for example, an individual's developmental potential, the quality of his adaptive functioning, or the relationship of progression to regression if one uses the APA set of diagnostic categories. However, by directly assessing the functioning of specific psychological variables (e.g., reality testing, degree of differentiation in object representations), which are continuous in nature, it is possible to evaluate the quality and quantity of these specific aspects of an individual's functioning.

Similarly, the use of a diagnostic type provides little or no information about what specific variables are functioning maladaptively in a given patient. In order to proceed with psychotherapy, it is necessary to know what specific aspects of the psychic structure are not functioning in an adaptive manner. One cannot treat the label schizophrenia by psychotherapy. However, the therapist *can* treat a disruption in reality testing, concretization of the concept, dedifferentiation, and so forth. Traditionally, these specific ego defects are inferred from the label schizophrenia. However, by teaching how to assess specific variables directly, the psychologist is in a position to maximize his effectiveness as a therapist and as a diagnostician.

2. Traditional methods of assessment tend to delineate areas of conflict in the functioning of the psychic structure. Typically, the focus is upon the *content* of these conflicts. The approach taken here is that the presence of conflict is of secondary importance, and that the specific content of these conflicts is of tertiary importance. The major task in assessment is to make an adequate evaluation of the quality of the psychic

structure's attempts to cope with conflict. Since conflict is universally present, the important issue is the adequacy of the individual's attempts to cope with and resolve it. The specific coping mechanisms used by a person should be assessed as to their adequacy.

3. Similarly, the specific libidinal fixations in a given individual are far less important than how the structure attempts to cope with them. To speak of oral, anal, or phallic fixations is not directly heuristic. By assessing how the structure copes with fixations, we can directly comment on the adequacy of one's psychological functioning. In similar fashion, the presence of drives and their derivatives is of secondary importance for assessment. The degree to which the ego has differentiated and integrated these drives, however, is of critical importance. To speak of the presence of conflict over aggression is not particularly useful. However, it is much more heuristic to speak of the degree to which aggression is integrated into the functioning of the structure in the service of growth and adaptation.

Such an approach is basically a developmental one. However, rather than focusing on the content or intensity of the drives and fixations, the diagnostician should focus on the degree of development (differentiation and integration) that is reflected in the functioning of the structure, through the assessment of specific variables.

4. Traditional methods of assessment have tended to note the presence of regression or regressive tendencies, without assessing whether these are pathological or in the service of growth. It is important to assess the quality of regression and its role in the overall functioning of the structure. As was noted earlier, regression and conflict act as the stimuli for increased psychological growth. Thus, these phenomena cannot simply be observed and recorded as signs of pathology. They must be viewed in the overall context of how the psychic structure is functioning.

5. The previous comments serve to underscore the need for assessing how the quality and quantity of *specific* variables

interact as part of the overall functioning of the psychic structure. To make such assessments from psychological tests, it is necessary to place primary emphasis upon the *structural* or *formal* characteristics of the test protocols.

It has been somewhat of a shock to discover that many psychologists, even those with doctorate degrees, have never learned to adequately use the formal aspects of a Rorschach protocol. An even greater number fail to score protocols in any kind of consistent manner in the course of their diagnostic assessments. Such psychologists tend to rely heavily upon content manifestations. The content tends to be interpreted in libidinal terms. Of necessity, such psychologists are forced to ignore a thorough assessment of specific ego functions and the manner in which the ego operates to integrate the various aspects of psychological functioning. With such an approach, they are unable to adequately assess the quality of specific ego functions. The emphasis on the structural aspects of the test protocols, on the other hand, allows the psychologist to analyze the nature and quality of specific aspects of the functioning of the psychic structure in a systematic manner.

References

1. American Psychiatric Association, *Diagnostic and Statistical Manual of Mental Disorders (DSM-II)* (Washington, D.C.: 1968).
2. C. E. Osgood, G. J. Suci, and P. H. Tannenbaum, *The Measurement of Meaning* (Urbana, Ill.: University of Illinois Press, 1967); B. L. Whorf, *Language, Thought, and Reality*, edited by J. B. Carroll (Cambridge and New York: M.I.T.-Wiley, 1956), pp. 212–14.
3. G. W. Albee, "Notes Toward a Position Paper Opposing Psychodiagnosis," in *New Approaches to Personality Classification*, edited by A. R. Maher, pp. 385–95 (New York: Columbia University Press, 1970); R. D. Laing, *The Politics of Experience* (New York: Ballantine, 1967); T. S. Szasz, *The Myth of Mental Illness* (New York: Harper & Row, 1961).
4. G. W. Allport, *Pattern and Growth in Personality* (New York: Holt, Rinehart, and Winston, 1965).
5. S. Freud: *The Interpretation of Dreams* (1900), standard ed. (London: Hogarth, 1953), vols. 4 and 5; *Analysis Terminable and Interminable* (1937), standard ed. (London: Hogarth, 1964), vol. 23; *An Outline of Psychoanalysis* (1940), standard ed. (London: Hogarth, 1964), vol. 23.
6. S. Freud, *Analysis Terminable and Interminable*, p. 235.
7. S. Freud, *The Interpretation of Dreams*.
8. R. Waelder, "The Principle of Multiple Function," *Psychoanalytic Quarterly*, 1936, 5:45–62.
9. A. Freud, *Normality and Pathology in Childhood: Assessments in Development* (New York: International Universities Press, 1965), pp. 110–11.
10. K. Dabrowski, *Personality-Shaping Through Positive Disintegration*, (Boston: Little, Brown, 1967); K. Dabrowski, A. Kawczak, and M. M. Piechowski, *Mental Growth Through Positive Disintegration* (London: Gryf, 1970).
11. K. Goldstein, *The Organism* (New York: American Book Co., 1939); A. H. Maslow, *Toward a Psychology of Being* (New York: Van Nostrand Reinhold, 1968); A. H. Maslow, *The Farther Reaches of Human Nature* (New York: Viking Press, 1971).
12. S. Freud, *Beyond the Pleasure Principle* (1920), standard ed. (London: Hogarth, 1955), vol. 18.
13. C. D. Darlington, *The Evolution of Man and Society* (New York: Simon and Schuster, 1969); R. Dubos, *Man Adapting* (New Haven, Conn.: Yale University Press, 1965).
14. R. W. White: "Motivation Reconsidered: The Concept of Competence," *Psychological Review*, 1959, 66:297–333; also "Ego and Reality in Psychoanalytic Theory," *Psychological Issues*, 1963, 3(3):1–210.
15. S. Freud, *Instincts and Their Vicissitudes* (1915), standard ed. (London: Hogarth, 1957), vol. 14.
16. A. Adler, "Individual Psychology," in *Psychologies of 1930*, edited by C.

Murchison, pp. 395–405 (Worcester, Mass.: Clark University Press, 1930).
17. Maslow, *Toward a Psychology of Being.*
18. J. Lampl-DeGroot, "Symptom Formation and Character Formation," *International Journal of Psychoanalysis*, 1963, 44:2.
19. Dabrowski, *Personality Shaping;* and Dabrowski et al., *Mental Growth.*
20. E. R. Zetzel, *The Capacity for Emotional Growth* (New York: International Universities Press, 1970).
21. G. L. Borofsky: "Regression and Ego Functioning in Creative Normals and Psychotics," doctoral dissertation, Michigan State University, 1971; "Creativity, Normality, and Psychosis: Styles of Psychological Functioning and Their Relationship to the Theory of Positive Disintegration," *Proceedings*, 2nd International Conference of the Theory of Positive Disintegration, at Loyola of Montreal, Dec. 1972.
22. Borofsky, "Creativity, Normality, and Psychosis."
23. Dabrowski, *Personality-Shaping;* and Dabrowski et al., *Mental Growth.*
24. Borofsky, see note 21.
25. Lampl-DeGroot, "Symptom Formation and Character Formation."
26. A. Freud, *Normality and Pathology.*
27. For example, A. Freud, *Normality and Pathology;* E. H. Erickson, *Childhood and Society* (New York: W. W. Norton, 1950).
28. D. Rapaport, "The Structure of Psychoanalytic Theory," *Psychological Issues*, 1960, 2(2)1–158.
29. S. Freud: *The Ego and The Id* (1923), standard ed. (London: Hogarth, 1961), vol. 19; *New Introductury Lectures on Psychoanalysis* (1933), standard ed. (London: Hogarth, 1964), vol. 22.
30. J. A. Arlow and C. Brenner, *Psychoanalytic Concepts and the Structural Theory* (New York: International Universities Press, 1964).
31. Rapaport, "The Structure of Psychoanalytic Theory."
32. Arlow and Brenner, *Psychoanalytic Concepts*, p. 47.
33. Arlow and Brenner, *Psychoanalytic Concepts.*
34. L. Bellak, *The Schizophrenic Syndrome* (New York: Grune and Stratton, 1969).
35. R. L. Spitzer and J. Endicott, *Problem Appraisal Scales (PAS)* (New York: Biometrics Research, New York State Department of Mental Hygiene, 1970).
36. S. J. Beck: "The Six Schizophrenias, Reaction Patterns in Children and Adults," Research Monograph No. 6 (New York: American Orthopsychiatric Assn., 1954); also *Psychological Processes in the Schizophrenic Adaptation* (New York: Grune and Stratton, 1965).
37. Bellak, *The Schizophrenic Syndrome*, p. 793.
38. Ibid., p. 794.
39. L. Silverman and L. Bellak, *Revised Psychological Test Manual* (New York: Research Center for Mental Health, New York University, 1968), mimeographed.
40. Bellak, *The Schizophrenic Syndrome.*
41. Silverman and Bellak, *Revised Psychological Test Manual.*

42. Since the writing of this paper, an expanded and refined version of the work of Bellak and his coworkers has been published in L. Bellak, M. Hurvich, and H. Gediman, *Ego Functioning in Schizophrenics, Neurotics, and Normals* (New York: Wiley, 1973).
43. A. Freud, *Normality and Pathology.*
44. Beck, see note 36.
45. R. R. Holt, *Manual for the Scoring of Primary Process Manifestations in Rorschach Responses,* 10th ed. (New York: Research Center for Mental Health, New York University, 1968), mimeographed.
46. T. C. Kroeber, "The Coping Functions of the Ego Mechanisms," in *The Study of Lives,* edited by R. W. White (New York: Atherton Press, 1963).
47. O. F. Kernberg, "A Psychoanalytic Classification of Character Pathology," *Journal of the American Psychoanalytical Association,* 1970, 18:800–22.

Psychotherapy, Assessment,

and Clinical Research:

Parallels and Similarities

LEONARD HANDLER*

SOME PARALLELS MAY BE DRAWN AMONG CLINICAL RE-
search, psychotherapy, and personality assessment—parallels
that should have some relevance for a more comprehensive
view of human beings than we sometimes take in our profession. In many respects, psychotherapy, assessment, and research may be viewed as quite similar if we accept the premise
that a meaningful experiment must take into account the relationship between the subject and the experimenter, just as
effective psychotherapy must take into account the quality of
the relationship between the patient and therapist. We must
explore what I have come to call the "psychosocial interior" of
the research setting as actively as many of us explore the clinical relationship in the psychotherapeutic process, or in the
assessment process. Responses are not enough; it is important
to try to understand the expectations of the subject as he sits
in our research room and proceeds through our investigations,
just as it is important to try to understand the expectations and
beliefs of our patients toward us and toward our profession.

*The assistance of Drs. Howard Pollio, Norman Rasch, and Harold Fine in preparing
this paper is greatly appreciated, as is the assistance of many graduate students who
have contributed to the development and exposition of the ideas presented here.

I remember a patient I saw a number of years ago at Allen Park, Michigan, VA Hospital. He was an old man, of Polish descent, with little formal education. He was referred to the Mental Hygiene Clinic, where I worked as a trainee, because the hospital physicians had determined that his vague assorted aches and pains had no physical base, but were emotionally determined. "Sometimes," I told him, in a manner which was both too vague and too imprecise, "Talking about our problems helps to make us feel better." We continued to talk for another half hour, as the patient described his physical symptoms and I probed for alternatives. Suddenly he turned to me and remarked, "Well, I don't feel better yet!" Needless to say, our expectations were quite dissimilar.

I thought about this incident recently when I read an interesting piece of research by Warren and Rice.[1] These researchers trained low-prognosis clients (clients who ordinarily tend to drop out of therapy prematurely) with regard to their manner of therapy participation. For each client, these sessions involved four half-hour (outside of therapy) sessions, with an investigator who was not a therapist. Training consisted of "stabilizing" the client, assisting him to clarify any concerns he had about therapy, and encouraging him to introduce these concerns in the therapy session. The second part of the approach consisted of structuring the client, teaching him to participate productively in the therapy process. Warren and Rice found that attrition was reduced significantly by the training procedures, that total therapy involvement was increased, and that the therapy process was improved, leading to more constructive personality change.

This unique and creative approach, nevertheless, still merely attempts to alter the patient's expectations so they fit those of the therapist more closely. It will remain for others to consider the, perhaps, more unique adaptation of the therapist to the client.

The importance of understanding the expectations of, and our relationships with, the people with whom we work are nowhere better illustrated than in the hypnosis literature and in the body of literature on expectancy.[2] For example, Orne[3] has indicated that nobody who lived at Lourdes ever got healed there. According to Orne, Janet established that the percentage of people who got cured was directly proportional to the distance they traveled to the Lourdes shrine. The further one came, the higher the odds were for a miracle. By the dust on the traveler's shoes, Janet suggested, you could estimate whether or not he would get well.

In both clinical practice and in research efforts, we sometimes forget that our patients and subjects have thoughts, feelings, and ideas other than the ones we tap, all of which might determine to some large degree what results we obtain from them, or with them. This is especially illustrated in the manner in which some clinicians approach intelligence or personality assessment, where test responses per se are stressed, rather than the interactional processes that generate or shape these responses. Clinical psychologists, perhaps in their attempts to emulate physical and natural scientists, have been so thoroughly overconcerned with responses, or outcomes, that they have ignored process variables. So great is the concern with evaluating whether or not something works, either in psychotherapy or in research, that we lose sight of what is going on between patient and therapist, or between subject and experimenter. We tend to act as if our experimental operations, and little or nothing else, influence our subjects; we conceptualize them as mere reflex arcs, responding only to the "stimuli" we present to them. In similar fashion, we sometimes narcissistically view the patient as responding only to the content of our interpretations and not to the dozens of other cues and stimuli that impinge upon him—not only during the psychotherapy hour, but during the many hours of the week we do not actively share with him. This is not to diminish the importance and the possible impact of the therapist and the therapeutic hour. I am merely suggesting that other factors, perhaps of equal valence, may be operating for any one individual.

Timothy Leary sums up the issue with surprising clarity. When we study our fellow man we must treat him as what he is, a *human being*, and not as an object to be dissected, manipulated, controlled, predicted by scientists or clinicians. . . . The patient or subject should be seen and treated not as a passive thing to be done to but as the equal of the psychologist in the collaborative research. The patient, after all, is the world's leading authority on the issue at hand—his own life and the transactions in which he is involved. . . . Always get the viewpoint of the patient on every issue, question, and decision, and treat this viewpoint as equal to your own.[4]

I was naively surprised to find the following quote by Teichner, a physiological psychologist, in a review article:

In the presence of a stressor, behavioral and physiological measures may increase, decrease, or not change at all according to the nature of the ongoing regulatory activity and according to whether what is being observed is a controlling or controlled variable. It is not, therefore, a question of which physiological or behavioral event provides a more sensitive measure of stress or what pattern of increases or decreases occurs reliably, or whether a particular measure increases in the presence of a stressor while another one decreases. Instead, the organism must be viewed as a system and the ongoing state of the system must be known before the experimental conditions are applied. Furthermore, this approach asks that the system state be known for the individual since individuals may vary widely in regard to chronic capacities, activation levels, and bandwidths. Unless the individual is known in these ways, all that can be expected under stress are unpredictable individual differences in performance and in "patterns" of physiological response.[5]

Despite vehement criticism from a variety of sectors, much of our research is not person-oriented, Leary's and Teichner's admonitions notwithstanding. For example, I recently reviewed some sixty articles while preparing a paper on the relationship between personality test data and autonomic variables; most or all of these studies had really ignored the interaction or the relationship between subject and experimenter. The researchers seemed to know relatively little about the autonomic mediating mechanisms involved, somewhat less about the test responses they so carefully recorded in the experimental situation, and even less about the subjects they covered with electrodes. They ignored the subject's impressions of them, his feelings about the test situation, and the implications of these feelings for his personal reaction in the situation. They ignored the experimenter's relationship to the subject and the possible implications this had on his responses in the testing situation.

We seem to treat all subjects as if they are all the same, and lump them together merely because they find themselves at the same university or the same hospital at the same time. I found only one study that was an exception, since it emphasized the interpersonal relationship in the experimental situation. This is a study done by Weiner, Singer, and Reiser.[6] These authors administered the TAT and extensively interviewed hypertensive, duodenal ulcer and healthy subjects while continuous recordings of heart rate and blood pressure were being made. They found that merely looking at a TAT card and having a fantasy about it without verbalizing it did not elicit increases in blood pressure and heart rate. Verbal communication between subject and examiner proved to be a necessary condition for changes in heart rate and blood pressure to occur. Some degree of *interaction* between the subject and experimenter was a requisite for evoking cardiovascular responses. These authors make meaningful use of the experimenter-subject interaction when they indicate that the behavior of the hypertensive subject was consistently impersonal, distant, and wary, and that this was true on formal psychological testing, in clinical interviews, and in the laboratory experiment, where they seemed to insulate themselves from interacting with the experimenter. The hypertensive patients were found to be *less* reactive physiologically than healthy subjects, unless pressured to respond in a less distant and detached manner, whereupon they responded with *greater* physiological reactivity. The authors state:

It seems clear . . . that no single psychological factor is responsible for cardiovascular responses in man. The method reported herein therefore clarifies some aspects of the complicated field of psychophysiological correlations, and lends further credence to the belief that such correlations cannot be made except by taking into account the total experimental situation and various aspects of the interaction of the subject and the experimenter. . . . The nature of the interaction . . . is complex, as evidenced by the fact that the reaction is partly determined by the sex of the examiner and subject; by the habitual means of relating to others; by changes in attitude of subject or experimenter or both; and by ongoing processes in the subject, such as depressive mood states, which adversely influence response to the task in the interaction. . . . A simple and linear stimulus-response model is inadequate to explain the complexity of bodily responses coincident with psychological events. Furthermore, such a model has in the past implied that feelings such as fear and anger cause, direct, or produce nervous impulses affecting cardiovascular responses. Rather, we believe that cardiovascular functions may reflect (and in some instances be a measure of) complex, ongoing, psychological processes with distal and proximate time referents. Acute changes in response to laboratory manipulations probably represent the effects of experimentally superimposed psychological situations which modify ongoing processes rather than initiating discrete changes from a stable, nondynamic base-line state.[7]

Thus, the data demonstrate that physiological responses in these hypertensive subjects are related to the interaction of subject and examiner, rather than to the content of the communication or the intended nature of the stressful stimulus per se.

I first became interested in the manner in which data are influenced or distorted by the interaction in the experimental situation when I did a study on the Draw A Person Test[8] at Michigan State University. It concerned the relationship between GSR and figure drawing anxiety indices. I attached a polygraph to each subject and asked him to draw human figures. In the study, most of the drawings looked like they were done by backward patients in a mental hospital.

At that time the Psychology Department was housed in a large, double quonset hut, and I had a tiny, windowless, dimly lit room to use for my research. It was filled with a great deal of apparatus, including a rather imposing looking polygraph console. The walls were covered with sound-deadening materials, which gave the room the eerie quality of a padded cell, or at least, of an isolation booth. The subject entered the room reluctantly through two double doors, which I immediately proceeded to slam shut. He was asked to sit in a chair with double armrests, and I attached recording electrodes to the fingers of the nonpreferred hand. Then I turned on the polygraph. All we could hear in the room was the soft whine of the ventilation fan, the hum of the amplifiers, and the clicking of the time-marking pen on the ink-writing oscillograph. The subject sat that way for at least a half hour, for what I intended to be an adaptation period. I was so involved in collecting data that I did not recognize the fantastic stress situation created for all the subjects, who probably thought that, at the very least, they would receive a shock sometime during the experimental period. No wonder the drawings looked so bad.

Another area in which clinical psychologists emphasize responses, to the exclusion of process, is in their use of assessment instruments and procedures. Test scores or test signs have become associated with highly specific interpretations, in a rather inflexible manner. For example, clinical lore has labeled the functions supposedly tapped by each of the WISC and WAIS subtests; despite research evidence to the contrary, a single descriptive label is often assigned to a specific subtest by the interpreting clinician.

Clinicians often attempt a direct translation from subtest data to a discussion of the patient's intellectual abilities which are based on these labels, all without an understanding of, and without trying to use somehow, the existing interpersonal situation in order to provide more information about the patient's functioning. It is not uncommon to see reports that purport to describe a person's intellectual attributes and deficiencies by a mere listing of subtest labels. For example, Patient

A has "good judgment" and "good abstract ability" but "relatively poor visual motor coordination."

A number of studies have begun to focus on the influence of interpersonal variables in determining WISC and WAIS performance. Thus, Furth and Milgram[9] found that results on the Similarities subtest may be greatly influenced by the patient's ability and willingness to communicate rather than by any abilities in concept formation or any ability to abstract. Therefore, if a patient is relatively terse and unwilling to verbalize, he may well get a lower score on the Similarities subtest, and perhaps on the other verbal subtests as well. Weiner[10] found that subjects who are distrustful score significantly lower on the Similarities and Picture Completion subtests of the WAIS compared to the low distrustful group. One of my patients responded to Similarities items by saying "They're not alike," as I kept going down the list of test items. Finally, I realized that this man was quite suspicious, feeling that I was tricking him. I then made it a point to let him know that there really *was* a way which the pairs of items were alike. We went back over the items, and the patient did quite well.

It is not difficult to find solutions to the problems discussed if we attempt to design studies and approach patients in a manner that would help to explore the meaning of and the importance of the relationship or the interaction. According to this principle, good human research and good psychotherapy should be approached in much the same way. When I work with patients, we spend a good deal of time discussing the present relationship, dealing with the patient's expectations in the "here and now" situation. Although we become involved in the past, I am also quite concerned about present relationships and feelings.

In a similar manner, we are attempting to design studies that will illuminate the interpersonal processes in the experimental situation and in the psychotherapeutic situation. For example, we have now almost completed a study of a single patient-therapist dyad, where both therapist and patient were interviewed separately before and after each therapy hour.[11] The interviews were tape recorded so that they could later be evaluated by more objective observers, whose impressions were compared with those of the participants. In addition, both therapist and patient were asked to respond to each question as he felt the other would. Most of the data have not yet been analyzed. However, preliminary results include the following:

> Both patient and therapist started out agreeing that the sessions were very therapeutic. By the sixth session, the therapist was still positive, but less so. After the initial session, the patient's estimate declined; but by the sixth session, it returned to the original level.
>
> However, concerning the degree of emotional conflict in the sessions, the patient and therapist were at opposite ends of the scale at first: the patient rated the first session as very comfortable, and the therapist rated it as very uncomfortable. By the sixth session, both therapist and patient agreed it was very uncomfortable. Thus, even though the first session was rated as very therapeutic by both patient and therapist, they were quite divergent in their emotional reactions to it.
>
> When ratings made immediately after the session were compared to similar ratings made one week later, the therapist's agreement with himself was quite good. The patient's agreement with herself got consistently worse.

We are also attempting to determine whether experiments have different meanings for subjects than are intended for them by experimenters. In this respect, we are trying to determine whether private reactions, attitudes, and aims of the subject, separate from those of the experimenter, have an effect on his responses. It is probable, as indicated by Orne,[12] that subjects automatically expect a certain amount of deception by researchers and that they often develop their own hypotheses about the experiments. Therefore, as recommended by Orne, we are trying to arrange it so that every subject involved in our experiments will be interviewed and questioned extensively by a different experimenter soon after he completes his participation. We have developed a series of open-ended questions such as:

1. Have you ever been in a psychological experiment before? If yes, was it a particularly good or bad experience?
2. What are your personal feelings (attitudes) about the field of psychology?
3. What did you feel (think) about the experiment prior to actually coming over to be in it?
4. Were you in any special mood today unrelated to the experiment that you think might have influenced your behavior in it?
5. Were there any particular features of the experimental situation of which you were especially conscious?
6. Did you think that the purpose of the experiment was something different from what you were told? If yes, what *was* the purpose of the experiment?
7. Did you expect there would be deception? If yes, why?
8. What was your attitude toward participating once the experiment had begun?
9. Did you feel any particular emotions that were aroused by the experiment itself?
10. Describe your behavior in the experiment compared to the way you usually are outside of the experimental situation.
11. Did your attitude or feelings change significantly during the course of the experiment? If so, how did they change?

We plan to compare the results of this interview with each subject's performance in the experiment in order to determine what effect, if any, the expectations, impressions, and mood state had on the data.

In an effort to determine just what if any interpersonal factors affect the variety of responses obtained in the assessment situation, I often use an Inquiry and Testing of the Limits phase, somewhat similar to procedures employed with the Rorschach. Following the completion of the test, the patient is asked what he thought of each subtest, what he thought it was all about, what he thought it tested, how he felt while he was taking it. Then we go back over each item which was failed, and I try to give the patient a hint or a bit more information in order to determine what factor or factors determined his failure and what kinds of help he needs in order to function adequately. It is, of course, possible that the patient may not know the correct answer. However it is also possible that the answer may be in the patient's repertoire, but he has not offered it as a response; for one reason or another, he has offered an alternative, incorrect response, or no response at all. One method of differentiating between the two alternatives is to ask the patient to supply another possible response to the question. If this response is also wrong, the examiner might want to press further, making certain to be supportive and encouraging in order to maintain interest and motivation. A patient who offers correct responses to questions he initially got wrong would probably have potential for higher level intellectual functioning than a patient who cannot produce correct responses in any case. Compared with administration according to standardized procedures, patients with severe incapacitating emotional problems have shown large I.Q. discrepancies when tested with this method of "maximal facilitation."

When the examiner provides as many hints as necessary to insure success on an item, the number and types of hints provided communicate more information to the examiner than a mere statement that the patient failed the item. Different types of assistance could be offered, and the more effective types of hints could provide additional information concerning intellectual functioning. For example, a low score on Picture Arrangement might indicate difficulties with anticipatory planning, but there are other possibilities. However, if hints that provide structure in the Picture Arrangement subtest are effective, while those that suggest attention to details of the stimulus material prove ineffective, it would be possible to hypothesize that: (1) the patient's inability to structure situations will at times interfere with functioning; (2) the patient's ability to function will be enhanced if he is provided with minimal (or maximal, depending on the degree provided by the examiner) structure. A selection of one of these two similar alternatives depends in part on the initial level of performance on Picture Completion.

In this way, the examiner provides a host of miniature test situations that are potentially capable of reflecting the nuances of the patient's functioning. By *systematically* providing additional cues, the examiner can thereby make clearer, more explicit inferences from the patient's resultant pattern of functioning. The procedure also helps to establish rapport, and gives the patient a feeling that the examiner is a supportive person who is interested in helping him achieve at a maximal level.

Previous examples have emphasized active clinical intervention with patients and subjects. This last case example is somewhat different. The patient was a nine-year-old boy who achieved an I.Q. of 68 on the Stanford-Binet. This score was not consistent with my estimates of his general performance —e.g., his ability to read fluently and to ask sensible questions. An obvious thought disturbance was evident, and the child's thinking became more confused in the testing situation than when I observed him working alone in his classroom. Therefore, it was decided to allow him to take another intelligence test, but this time by himself. He was given the instructions for the Raven Progressive Matrices Test, and then I left the room. The child achieved at the 75th percentile, what is roughly equivalent to an I.Q. of 120. None of his previous I.Q. scores, or subsequent scores on examinations administered in traditional fashion, were above 79. The major importance of these findings is not that the child tests low or high, but that interpersonal relationships cause him to think less clearly and thereby interfere with functioning.

I have attempted to offer some solutions to the frequently very real division between clinical practice and clinical research by stressing that the focus in both situations must be on the *individual* being studied, and on the *unique* interaction between the human beings involved in this *unique* interpersonal situation. I doubt that many clinical psychologists would disagree with most of the premises set forth here. Yet, while we pay lip service to the interpersonal approach, our clinical research procedures (and in some cases our clinical application) remain inflexibly tied to simplistic and outmoded principles of "objective science." We decry the uselessness and triviality of much of the research published in our field, and yet we continue to produce these meaningless studies. Are we putting convenience and expediency in the place of proper conceptualization and understanding, or are we afraid to tackle and study real issues that face and try human beings? Are we afraid to do the "unpopular thing," to take risks by questioning established traditions, and to challenge the dominant logical positivism of our field? Perhaps the problem lies in many of the training programs that repudiate the quality and nature of human experience, and in the publish-or-perish atmosphere in which some academic training programs exist. Under such conditions, we should not be surprised to find dehumanized research and overobjectivity as dominant themes in our field.

References

1. N. Warren and L. Rice, "Structuring and Stabilizing of Psychotherapy for Low-Prognosis Clients," *Journal of Consulting Psychology,* 1972, 39:173–81.
2. R. Rosenthal, *Experimenter Effects in Behavioral Research* (New York: Appleton-Century-Crofts, 1966).
3. M. Orne, "Research in Hypnosis," teaching workshop, University of Minnesota, June 1966.
4. Timothy Leary, "The Diagnosis of Behavior and the Diagnosis of Experience," in *New Approaches to Personality Classification,* edited by A. R. Maher (New York: Columbia University Press, 1970), p. 213.
5. W. Teichner, "Interaction of Behavioral and Physiological Stress Reactions," *Psychological Review,* 1968, 75:282.
6. H. Weiner, M. Singer, and M. Reiser, "Cardiovascular Responses and Their Physiological Correlates," *Psychosomatic Medicine,* 1962, 24:477–98.
7. Ibid., p. 495.
8. L. Handler and J. Reyher, "Relationship Between GSR and Anxiety Indexes in Projective Drawings," *Journal of Consulting Psychology,* 1966, 30:60–67.
9. H. Furth and N. Milgram, "Verbal Factors in Performance on WISC Similarities," *Journal of Clinal Psychology,* 1965, 21:424–27.
10. G. Weiner, "The Effect of Distrust on Some Aspects of Intelligence Test Behavior," *Journal of Consulting Psychology,* 1957, 21:127–30.
11. J. Weaver, "The Process of Therapy as Seen by Therapist and Patient," doctoral dissertation (in preparation), University of Tennessee, 1973.
12. M. Orne, "On the Social Psychology of the Psychological Experiment," *American Psychologist,* 1962, 17:776–83.

Issues on the Interface
of Law and Psychology

ROBERT G. MEYER

THE EVERYDAY ACTIVITIES OF A CLINICAL PSYCHOLOGIST present constant legal ramifications. Yet, most of us are often unconcerned or ignorant about these issues, and this lack of concern allows control to pass to others. A couple of the most important issues are examined here, with the hope of pointing toward efforts that can be initiated.

A basic tenet in the American legal system is that the jury should hear all relevant data concerning a case. An important limitation comes under the term "privileged communication," which includes such things as confidential communications, trade secrets, and the rights against self-incrimination.

The difference between privilege and confidentiality should be noted. Confidentiality is not a legal concept; it is a code of professional ethics designed to prevent unauthorized disclosures of information by a psychologist without the informed consent of the client. Privilege is a rule of law that permits a witness to refrain from giving any testimony that he would otherwise be compelled to give (or allows one party to an action to prevent a witness from testifying) in order to protect a specific interest or relationship.

Typically, a privilege is considered to be personal in nature and therefore can only be asserted by the holder of the privilege (the one whose interest is protected), and not by any other party. Since a privilege can be waived by the holder, it is not an absolute bar to providing testimony.

The strength of a claim of privileged communication rests on two factors. First and foremost is whether or not such privilege adheres to all four of the standard criteria for claiming privilege. The second is the strength of the privilege in the history of law, and especially if it can be tied to one held at English or United States common law.

When a particular group claims privilege, it is traditional to analyze whether or not the validation of that privilege meets all four factors promulgated by Wigmore:

1. The communications must originate in a confidence that they will not be disclosed.
2. This element of confidentiality must be essential to the full and satisfactory maintenance of the relationship between the parties.
3. The relation must be one that in the opinion of the community ought to be sedulously fostered.
4. The injury that would inure to the relation by the disclosure of the communication must be greater than the benefit thereby gained by the correct disposal of litigation.[1]

It should be evident that, in the last analysis, this is a balancing process between the value gained by insuring the relationship versus the loss to society in not hearing all evidence that acts to protect its interests.

One could debate at length as to whether the practices of psychologists fit with these four criteria. However, Cross[2] has summarized the literature in the application of these criteria to both group and individual psychotherapy. He concludes that there is overwhelming evidence for a valid claim to privilege in these functions.

Most analysts are likely to agree that the Wigmore factors can be satisfied. However, in establishing a claim for privileged communication, the judicial decisions depend as well upon the second factor, the historical tradition of the claim. The definite problem here is that psychologists are virtual upstarts in their claim for privilege, at least in the perspective of law which stretches back into English common law.

It is sobering that Wigmore, the traditional authority on evidence, has placed psychologists in the category of "Sundry Confidential Communications," and not even very definitively there. He points out that the common law rule for privileged communications was balanced with the concept that "no pledge of privacy nor oath of secrecy can avail themselves against the claim for truth in a court of justice."[3] Thus, the concept of privilege can at any time be strictly construed, and this was most evident in the recent Supreme Court decision concerning journalists. When strict constructionism is in vogue, it is most likely to strike at a "sundry" claim.

By themselves, psychologists would come under the concept of "novel privilege," a variation of the sundry privilege, and would be considered as similar to the journalists or accountants. Let us also keep in mind that the 1937–38 American Bar Association Committee on Improvement of evidence strongly frowned on giving novel privileges and in fact wished to severely restrict most of the old ones.[4]

Yet psychologists do have privilege in many states. Incidentally, there is no evidence whatsoever for privilege being a constitutional right; rather, it must be established by statute.

Privilege has typically been obtained for psychologists by grafting their validation onto an already existing privilege. This has some advantages, depending on a particular privilege to which it is grafted.

Three existing traditional privileges have relevance to the present issue: the attorney-client, the physician-patient, and the priest-penitent privileges. Let us examine each of these as they relate to the confidentiality between the psychologist and his patient (or client?). Later, another privilege, that of husband and wife (spousal) will also be shown to have some relevance.

Psychologists have always been enamored of the medical model and have usually sought inclusion in the physician-patient privilege. It is ironic that of the three privileges mentioned, this may be legally the least desirable.

The prime irony is that the existence of the physician-patient privilege has actually never been accepted in either English or United States common law, and has been consistently denied in judicial decisions. However, in 1828, a New York statutory innovation established the privilege. It has since been accepted by other decisions, and is now incorporated in the Uniform Rules of Evidence, the authoritative source. Yet it still is highly restrictive and also has these established weaknesses:

1. As in the attorney-client privilege, disclosure to a third party waives the privilege. The implications of this point for group therapy will be examined later.
2. There is no provision in the physician-patient privilege for protecting disclosure of the fact that the patient was seen by a physician, but only for the contents of the communication. As future Thomas Eagletons might testify, this considerably weakens the privilege.
3. When adopting the physician-patient privilege, the psychologist automatically becomes bound to the semantic concept of "patient." This would restrict the privilege to situations in which the person is clearly defined as a patient, and many psychologists would feel this is a definite hindrance.
4. Of less importance, the privilege is held only by the patient, not by the physician. The physician can therefore be compelled to testify against his better judgment as to whether certain testimony should be made public.

In some states psychology has not been grafted onto the physician-patient privilege. This has occurred either because the state did not have a physician-patient privilege or because there was political pressure to exclude psychologists. Separate statutes have then usually been enacted establishing a psychologist-client privilege, and these have been tied to the attorney-client privilege.

The attorney-client privilege is considered to be the strongest existent privilege, which is not surprising since attorneys

make the laws. This privilege dates back to the reign of Eliza-
beth I, when it was defined, since that was the first time the
testimony of witnesses became a source of proof in jury trials.
Hence, there has never been any question as to its validity.

At first the attorney-client privilege was based on the oath
of the profession and honor of the attorney rather than in
consideration of the apprehensions of the client; hence, at that
time the attorney himself had the power to waive it. However,
in the 1700s this "point of honor" doctrine was repudiated, and
the privilege was definitely lodged in the client's apprehensions about disclosure, thus allowing the client to retain the
privilege of waiving it. Other more substantial weaknesses are
also in the attorney-client privilege:

> 1. As in the physician-patient statutory provisions, there is the
> problem of disclosure to a third party. Wigmore[5] puts it thusly
> "The presence of a third person (other than the agent of either)
> is obviously unnecessary for communications to the attorney as
> such, however useful it may be for communications for negotia-
> tions in the third person. It follows a fortiori, that communica-
> tions to the third person in the presence of the attorney are not
> within that privilege.[6]

Issue can be taken with the phrase "third person is obviously
unnecessary for communications." It could be argued that this
third person obviously is necessary to the group therapy process and therefore disclosure is not allowed. This will be examined later.

> 2. There is no provision in the attorney-client privilege for
> protecting either the name or fact of client visitation, only the
> contents of the communication.

Psychologists have not been tied to the priest (minister-peni-
tent) privilege as yet. It is unlikely that this will occur, though
this privilege has several advantages. The main disadvantage
is it does not have the traditional strength of the attorney-
client privilege. It is unclear whether or not the priest-penitent privilege held before the Restoration, but it was decisively

held not to exist in English or United States common law from that time forth. However, it is now established by statute in at least two-thirds of the states, as well as by judicial decisions.

Except for those few statutes that specifically tie the privilege to "confession" rather than "communication," the priest-penitent privilege has the advantages of being a broad concept. It is still not clear whether or not the name or fact of visitation has to be revealed, and this uncertainty is an advantage. Also, at least one decision has held that the privilege cannot be waived by either party alone, and this aspect could conceivably be applied to protecting the confidentiality of the group therapy situation.

The fact that one waives privileged communication by disclosure to a third person, which is found in both the attorney-client and physician-patient privileges, poses great problems in both marital and group therapy.

A judicial tradition has held that the physician-patient privilege is abrogated via disclosure in a marital consultation. For example, in 1933 in *Mullin-Johnson Co.* v. *Penn Mutual Life,*[7] the physician's treatment of the husband in the presence of his wife was held not privileged as to his wife's testimony.

However, in *Ellis* v. *Ellis,*[8] a recent Tennessee case, a different trend was voiced. In this instance, the wife attempted to use testimony of a psychiatrist who had examined both her and her husband in the presence of each other, as well as separately. The husband's attorney objected on the ground that it was based on privileged communication, and in response the trial court disallowed the testimony. The wife's attorney asserted that this was not covered by the physician-patient privileged communication statute. He argued that both parties were present during the examinations and thus confidentiality between the physician and patient was waived, in this case the physician being a psychiatrist.

The decision of the Appellate Court held that the husband and wife could testify as to statements made by each other under these circumstances. However, they also held that when a confidential relationship exists between a psychiatrist and a patient, communications are privileged, even though made in the presence of the other person.

If this decision is applied analogically to the group therapy situation, it would follow that while the therapist-individual group member communications would be privileged, all communications from one group member to another would be liable to the waiver of privilege. Since the majority of therapy groups[9] emphasize group interaction as opposed to constant therapist to group member interaction, it is obvious that virtually all information in the group could be made available.

Moreno[10] once spoke of extending the Hippocratic Oath to the members of the psychotherapy group. He suggested that pledges should be made within the group and that the members should be reassured that their verbalizations would thus be protected by the pledge made within the group.

In fact, each group member should be informed that this is a completely inadequate basis for such trust, though most group therapists and participants operate under the naive assumption that it is adequate. Protection will only emerge from statutory definition of privilege for group therapy, and ultimately by judicial decision.

Arthur Burton[11] has pointed out how widespread the phenomena of therapy groups has become and most authorities agree this is a trend that will continue. Group therapy is now being applied not only to neurotics and normals, but to such divergent groups as delinquents[12] and police officers.[13] Given this trend, it is imperative that some judicial definition be made of the limits of trust that a group member can realistically expect.

A reading of the standard physician-patient and attorney-client privilege statutes makes it clear that these are simply too narrowly drawn to provide for privileged communication in group therapy. Also, most authorities[14] agree that, on appeal, no definitive cases have established privileged communication in group therapy.

A few states have attempted to cope with this by statute. New York put in a "model law"; however, it now appears that it only protects disclosure by the therapist (only a psychiatrist); therefore, again not from one group member to another. Kansas, Illinois, and Connecticut have all passed laws; however, each has a particular substantial deficiency. California has the most modern and comprehensive law in this area. However, it has a vague phraseology by which the communication of one group member to another has to be construed as being channeled through the therapist in order to be privileged. Since these are the progressive states in this area of the law, it is apparent that communications in group therapy are simply not privileged in state courts at this time.

It should also be noted that the psychotherapist-patient privilege, which was proposed for the federal courts, and discussed in the following, would not have held any authority over the state courts.

The proposed Rules of Evidence for United States Federal Courts, which were to go into effect July 1, 1973, included an excellent psychotherapist-patient privilege. The relevant section of the Rules states that:

> 1. A communication is "confidential" if not intended to be disclosed to persons other than those present to further the interest of the patient in the consultation, examination, or interview, or persons reasonably necessary for the transmission of communication, or persons who are participating in the diagnosis and treatment under the direction of the psychotherapist, including members of the patient's family.[15]

This was a well-devised statute and apparently would have cleared up the confusion that has existed in previous attempts by the states. It seems obvious that group members are necessary for the transmission of the communication, since they are inherent in the group process. As in all legal statutes, nothing is in effect until a judicial decision has taken place and, as noted earlier, it would not have directly effected state decisions.

Unfortunately, these desirable rules will never be in effect. Congress first took the unusual step of voting to extend consideration of the proposed rules for an additional year, and they would have taken effect in June 1974. During the process of consideration, this proposed section on privilege was abolished. The rules as they are now written would have the federal court privilege reflect the particular rules of the state in which the federal court action is taken, a victory for decentralization if not for leadership.

These federal rules of evidence originally proposed did not include any group other than clinical psychologists and psychiatrists. Yet it is obvious that other categories of therapists, often with little experience or training, are in charge of many groups. Hence, attention must be directed toward criteria for the legitimization of other group therapists, the accreditation of their training, and eventually the decision of whether or not to cover them via the privilege communication statutes.

One can sit back and wait for events to happen, as they did, or one can become involved in the process. Conveyance of information to legislators is the first avenue to effect rules concerning privileged communication. At the state level, it appears that special efforts should be directed to writing new legislation specifically addressed to the problems of marital, family, and group therapy. This is now most important, since federal courts will be relying heavily on state statutes for definitions of privilege. Clinical psychologists should be aware of whether they are covered by statutes in their state, and whether their licensing law addresses this area. If new legislation is needed, the originally proposed Federal Rules afford an excellent model for these endeavors.

Other issues, similar to that of privileged communication, are on the horizon. Wexler[16] has noted that several behavior modification procedures, particularly the use of token economies on mental hospital wards, are on a crash course with the law. For example, can a patient be deprived of those pursuits and items (future reinforcements) that the law may construe as "absolute rights"? If the courts say they may not, our opinion becomes literally academic. Input initiated by those working in the area can have a significant impact on the development of the law. Without such input, the law will be defined anyway —however based on ignorance or a distorted vision.

References

1. J. Wigmore, *Evidence*, 3rd ed. (Boston: Little, Brown, 1940), vol. 8, p. 2380.
2. W. Cross, "Privileged Communication Between Participants in Group Psychotherapy," *Law and Social Order*, 1970, pp. 191–211.
3. Wigmore, vol. 8, p. 2286.
4. Ibid.
5. Wigmore, vol. 8, p. 2311.
6. Ibid., p. 603.
7. *Mullin-Johnson Co.* v. *Penn Mutual Life*, F. Suppl. (N.D. Cal., 1933).
8. *Ellis* v. *Ellis*, 472 S. W. 2d 741 (Tenn. App., 1971).
9. F. Stoller, "A Stage for Trust," in *Encounter*, edited by A. Burton, pp. 81–96 (San Francisco: Jossey-Bass, 1969).
10. Cross, see note 2.
11. A. Burton, "Encounter, Existence, and Psychotherapy," in *Encounter*, pp. 7–26.
12. C. Richardson and R. Meyer, "Techniques in Guided Group Interaction," *Child Welfare*, 1972, 51:519–27.
13. J. Driscoll, R. Meyer, and C. Schanie, "Training Police in Family Crisis Intervention," *Journal of Applied Behaviorial Science*, 1973, 9:62–82.
14. Cross, see note 2; also a personal communication from J. Nellis, 1973.
15. Federal Rules of Evidence, Rule 504, *Supreme Court Reporter*, 1973, 93:55.
16. D. Wexler, "Token and Taboo: Behavior Modification, Token Economics, and the Law," *California Law Review*, 1973, 61:81–109.

Part 2

Roles, Models,
and Settings

The Agony and Ecstasy
of Professional Role Change

DURAND F. JACOBS

MANPOWER STUDIES SHOW THAT THE RATE OF TRAINING new professionals continues to fall far behind the growing demand for health and rehabilitation services. The virtual certainty that all Americans will be included under some form of national health insurance during the seventies makes it inevitable that large numbers of quickly and lesser-trained technicians be marshaled to augment the efforts of each of the helping professions. These trends herald radical changes in the role of the professional psychologist.

New and broadly staffed psychological service delivery systems can likely add to the psychologist's service impact, personal status, and material rewards. However, to realize this promise, new delivery systems will almost certainly involve extensive use of paraprofessionals[2]—possibly to the extent where they substantially outnumber the professionals.

While some psychologists fear loss of autonomy and control, are anxious about possible usurping of functions by paraprofessionals, show concern about increased client vulnerability, and question whether such changes will produce a watered-down quality of services, my position is one that strongly supports rapid development and use of paraprofessional manpower.

At issue is the *social relevancy* of our professional activities and the *accountability* of the psychology profession for meeting the needs of large segments of society numbering in the tens of millions. In the face of this challenge, can we persist in the exclusive use of methods that were originally designed for application to people characterized by far fewer personal, social, and occupational deficits than the new target population of today?

If professional psychology is to take its place in tomorrow's large-scale human services system targeted on rapid, demonstrable improvements in personal, social, or occupational functioning, practitioners must become much more conversant with the various factors that constitute the social and physical environment of the client and hence which influence his resultant behavior. This may well require a new site of operations for the scientist-practitioner—a movement from the cloistered consulting room to the complex in vivo arena of the client's own residential, school, work, and community setting.

To provide timely and sufficient services at the site where the need for services originates and where the benefits of services will be realized requires a dramatic extension of our present system. It mandates a corps of support personnel to augment what the individual professional psychologist cannot possibly do alone.

The use of paraprofessionals in mental health services is not new. The first two-year program for training mental health support personnel was established at the Ft. Wayne Extension of Purdue University in 1966 by True and Hadley. By the end of 1971 130 Associate of Arts training programs were designed to provide direct psychological or social services to disturbed or disabled people.[3] Over 2,000 paraprofessionals had graduated from such programs. Seventy-two percent of the graduates obtained jobs in mental health settings, while 19 percent were continuing their education toward a BA degree. It is projected that by 1976 there will be over 11,000 persons with Associate degrees in allied mental health fields.[4] Similar programs are beginning to appear in four-year colleges, with the specific goal of preparing psychology technicians.

How are these paraprofessionals presently being integrated into psychological services?

Virtually all these programs emphasize the acquisition of interviewing skills for application in a variety of inpatient and outpatient mental health settings, family and welfare agencies, schools, correctional institutions, and so forth. Students learn to deal with children, the aged, delinquents, the mentally ill, drug addicts and their families.[5]

Many students in Associate and Bachelor degree programs are also trained in counseling and psychotherapy. Ordinarily, training follows the Truax and Carkhuff model (recently modified through the work of Kagan and Hinds et. al.)[6] wherein specific types of client therapist interactions are identified, and technicians are trained to become competent in their use.[7]

Learning theory and behavior modification techniques also are being taught in a rapidly increasing number of Associate of Arts programs. Graduates are hired in institutions, such as schools for the retarded, mental hospitals, rehabilitation centers, homes for the aged. Often this type of training is done on-the-job with persons possessing little more, and frequently less, than high school diplomas. However, this is hardly unusual in light of the findings of Margaret Rioch,[8] who trained a group of intelligent housewives to function quite effectively as psychotherapists.

A second area in which technicians are being used, particularly in the VA, is as assistants to counseling psychologists in vocational rehabilitation activities. Two psychology technicians have functioned quite effectively at the Brecksville, Ohio, VA hospital in this capacity.[9] They take employment histories, do job development and vocational follow-up on patients in their training and work settings, make referrals and act as liaison persons with community rehabilitation groups, and do employment interview preparation and initial vocational exploration with selected patients as directed by the supervising psychologist.

Some programs, usually but not exclusively at the baccalaureate level, teach the administration of psychological tests. Graduates are employed as psychology technicians. A typical employment setting is the Central Psychological Test-

ing Laboratory at the Brecksville VA Hospital. It is staffed by
two psychology technicians and one undergraduate aid. This
testing service responds to the individual requests from a staff
of fifteen doctoral level psychologists and eight to ten doctoral
students. In this thousand-bed, high turnover, psychiatric hospital paraprofessionals administer and score on a one-day-
service basis over 800 tests per month for approximately 180
patients, which cover virtually all staff needs for psychological
testing. The battery includes a range of twenty-five paper and
pencil personality, intelligence, vocational interest, aptitude,
achievement, and organic impairment tests, including the full
Reitan-Halstead Battery. The activities of the paraprofessionals are under the general supervision of a professional psychologist, who now finds less than 10 percent of his time required to oversee his well-trained and seasoned staff. The
hospital plans to add more psychology technicians and train
them to provide supportive and behavior therapy in both inpatient and outpatient programs.

At the present time approximately 400 psychology aides and
technicians are employed throughout VA facilities in similar
activities.[10] In addition, during the last two years VA has initiated collaborative training programs with local community
colleges for the training of mental health associates. The fifty
students now in these programs are being trained as "general-
ists." Upon graduation, they will be assigned to one or another
of the mental health disciplines for integration into a particular
delivery of services system.[11]

The outlook for continued training and use of these types of
support personnel, particularly within psychology, is clear and
unequivocal. It will increase. It is important to note that within
the VA the assignment of technical support personnel cannot
be justified in the absence of adequate professional supervision.

Paraprofessionals are used to extend the impact and continuity of comprehensive psychological services. Additionally,
these programs provide a full career ladder in the field of
psychology for those interested and able to advance themselves.

Movement in the direction of training and use of paraprofessionals among the helping professions is not without its critics. It is necessary that the public become better informed on what it can reasonably expect from each member of a service delivery team. There is responsible concern over how the professional in charge can remain ethically and legally accountable for the activities of all those he directs. Fears expressed by a few psychologists sound strangely like the "status panic" evidenced by psychiatrists who insist emotionally, but not logically, that clinical psychologists are not trained to take the responsibility for psychotherapy.[12] Our own experience has clearly demonstrated that well-trained support personnel contribute to all major aspects of psychological functioning. Meanwhile, professional psychologists have been freed to apply their unique skills in a much more effective manner. The closely coordinated work of the professional-paraprofessional team has greatly increased the total impact of psychological services in a more timely, responsive, and economical manner to far more patients than we ever have been able to serve before.[13]

How will these changes affect professional roles of practicing psychologists and the training of future psychologists?

The problems attending professional role change due to the influx of paraprofessionals go beyond the pragmatic question of "who will do what for whom," and a subsequent division of labor among the two groups.[14] A critical indicator of professionalism is that practitioners have a high degree of autonomy in the performance of their work. A key source of strained relations between professionals and paraprofessionals lies in the fear that paraprofessionals will usurp some measure of this autonomy, thereby blurring the unique professional role.

As any profession is subdivided so that its component skills can be learned and applied separately by paraprofessionals, the laity begins to acquire competence in skills that had been exclusively those of the professional.[15] As more talented paraprofessionals use a career ladder to gain increasing professional status, the profession begins to lose its gatekeeping functions over who enters the profession. This problem becomes acute as the overlap between professional and paraprofessional functions increases. Finally, paraprofessionals may institutionalize their skills into an identifiable package and seek independence from the parent profession.[16]

Doubtless we will be forced to grapple with these problems for some time to come, with no simple solutions in sight. However, strengthening the profession in the face of an influx of paraprofessionals must be accomplished with the assertion that the client and society are to be protected, not the profession. Client and community needs must remain the point of focus as professionals and paraprofessionals develop new roles together.[17]

The lowering of standards, which some psychologists fear so much as a consequence of subprofessional training, is more likely to occur as a result of the profession's unpreparedness than as the consequence of the use of subprofessionals.[18]

Professional psychology must capture the initiative from those who are thrusting paraprofessionals upon it. It must take a leadership, rather than a reactive role in identifying where and how supporting paraprofessional manpower can extend psychological knowledge and expertise to all those in need.[19] Professional psychology, not government nor disgruntled consumers, must become the prime advocate for the responsible inclusion of paraprofessionals in human service programs directed by psychologists.

Professional psychology must open the doors of its national and regional associations to its technicians and aids. It must provide space in its professional journals to its corps of paraprofessionals; it must write these people into its standards of practice and into its Code of Ethics. Professional psychology must not only provide direction but also give to its support personnel a voice and a meaningful participant role in professional affairs.

We must guard against discouraging paraprofessionals by relegating to them our least wanted tasks (e.g., clerical or low-level repetitive work, night work, dealing with troublesome or uninteresting clients). Rather, we must delegate functions that do no violence to our own core status and responsibilities, yet which provide the paraprofessional with meaningful roles and enhanced status—all while increasing needed high-quality services to the consumer. The psychologist must learn to control his envy of the paraprofessional's greater direct contact with clients and the reinforcements these bring, while he maintains a less visible supportive and overseeing role. This requires retraining the professional to develop a new self-percept based on expanding his professional role in areas where he has had little time to explore, to develop new knowledge and applications with his "found time," and to devise means for increasing his professional impact by creating still more functions for paraprofessionals.

Fears that the paraprofessional will fragment his services to the point where there is nothing left are ungrounded. He will still be called upon to deal with the more difficult cases. He will be required to assess the infinite variety of new problems that will arise from greatly expanded systems, and devise means for solving them.

This will necessitate basic changes in the preparation of future psychologists. For instance, methods training in test administration and most forms of individual and group psychotherapy, counseling, and conditioning may be de-emphasized and replaced by learning better to integrate such input gained from others into more comprehensive or complex methods of problem definition and solution. Supplementing this might be greater emphasis on program evaluation and environmental design. Most importantly, perhaps, is the need to sensitize and prepare future professional psychologists to assume a somewhat broader stance toward improving the human condition.

Even as we hasten to prepare ourselves and our students to make necessary improvements in psychological delivery systems, it is well to remember that such services deal mainly with repairing failures in social functioning. Most of these problems have their roots in early neglect, in extended experience with physical, social, and educational deprivation, and in prolonged exposure to conditions of environmental deterioration. Beyond a certain point there is a danger that remedial services alone can only be a patchwork quilt, never quite covering the problems that lie beneath—a superstructure built on sand. Basic improvements in man-environment relationships are mandatory if the nation's human service programs are to rest on a solid foundation.

Hopefully, those in the behavioral sciences, and psychology in particular, will see to it that long-range preventive actions are not overlooked in the current crisis for augmenting direct services. The behavioral sciences also must assume the initiative for translating the relevant dimensions and goals desired of human service programs into measurable terms. This will provide a necessary yardstick for holding "the helpers" accountable for the timeliness and efficacy of their respective efforts. Establishing objective outcome criteria finally will make it possible to evaluate systematically the relative benefits of different staffing patterns and alternate delivery system models.[20]

The challenge to professional psychology in the 1970s is to respond with a new mix of methods and manpower to meet the needs of an overwhelming and largely unfamiliar group of consumers. This is reminiscent of a similar crisis situation in the late 1940s, when clinical psychology came of age as the newest mental health profession in VA hospitals and clinics. The mission was to meet the needs of great numbers of returning veterans with physical, mental, emotional, and vocational problems. Between 1945 and 1955 clinical psychology developed its professional role. Then, as now, it was the tenor of the times, the nature of the setting in which we practiced, the needs of the major target population we served, and the extent of our skills and knowledge that structured our professional role. These dimensions have all changed radically over the past twenty-five years. However, changes in our professional role have not kept pace.

Today the new target populations to be served necessitate a wider diversity of treatment strategies and methods than we have ever been called upon to provide. They are in such numbers and scattered across so many different settings that we must augment our professional manpower with paraprofessionals and together seek a new mix of functions between us that will best serve those in need. It is from this condition of pain and promise that a new identity for professional psychology will emerge. To the extent that some APA historian may some day describe the 1940s as the adolescence of clinical psychology, he may view the 1970s as the time when it reached a new level of maturity.

References

1. Based in part on remarks made as Conference Director, 7th Annual Institute on Man's Adjustment in a Complex Environment, 1972 theme: "The Paraprofessionals: Who to Do What for Whom?" (Brecksville, Ohio, May 1972); and as a panelist at the APA Annual Convention in a symposium on "The impact of the paraprofessionals on changing role models in psychology," Hawaii, September 1972.

2. The term "paraprofessional" encompasses persons otherwise referred to as client-helpers, aids, associates, technicians, nonprofessionals, sub-professionals, and new professionals. By training, these groups range from clients-turned-helpers, with little or no academic and technical grounding, to those who have acquired academic credentials, from Associate of Arts to Bachelor's degrees or even at the postgraduate level (short of the Master's degree). Their experiential background ranges from simply being indigenous to the problem area to relatively unstructured volunteer participation to various levels of systematic on-the-job exposure. Supervision of paraprofessionals by those more highly trained in the service functions being offered may vary from minimal to maximal. Standards of practice for psychological services delivery systems, including paraprofessionals, are currently being prepared by the American Psychological Association. Meanwhile, guidelines recommended by the *APA Task Force on Standards for Service Facilities* in March 1970 have been included in the *Accreditation Manual for Psychiatric Facilities 1972* (Joint Commission on Accreditation of Hospitals in Chicago).

3. J. True, "National Status of Associate Degree Mental Health Programs," paper presented at 7th Annual Institute on Man's Adjustment in a Complex Environment, 1972.

4. Ibid.; also K. Skaggs, "Allied Health Education Programs in Community Junior Colleges," paper presented at 7th Annual Institute on Man's Adjustment in a Complex Environment, 1972.

5. A Wellner and R. Simon, "A Survey of Associate Degree Programs for Mental Health Technicians," *Hospital and Community Psychiatry*, June 1969, 20 (6): 166–69.

6. N. Kagan, "Influencing Human Interaction," I.P.R. Project, Erickson Hall, Michigan State University, 1971; W. Hinds, M. James, M. Gieszer, and B. A. Jacobs, "A Survival Manual for the Drug Center Volunteer," Governor's Office of Drug Abuse and Alcoholism, State of Michigan, 1972.

7. C. Truax, "The Training of Nonprofessional Personnel in Therapeutic Interpersonal Relationships," *American Journal, of Public Health*, 1967, 57:1778–79; C. Truax and R. Carkhuff, *Toward Effective Counseling and Psychotherapy* (Chicago: Aldine, 1967); R. Persons, C. Clark, M. Persons, M. Kadish, and W. Patterson, "Training and Employing Undergraduates as Therapists in a College Counseling Service," *Professional*

Psychology, May 1973, 4(2):170–86.

8. M. Rioch, C. Elkes, and A. Flint, "Pilot Project in Training Mental Health Counselors," PHS Pub. No. 1254 (Chevy Chase, Md.: National Institute of Mental Health, 1965).

9. Veterans Administration, "Psychology Aids and Psychology Technicians," Professional Services Letter No. 69–40 (Washington, D.C.: Department of Medicine and Surgery, May 20, 1969).

10. Personal communication from E. Ash (Chief of Training, Psychology Division, Veterans Administration, Washington, D.C.), May 16, 1973.

11. Personal communication from B. Pryor (Veterans Administration Education Service, Washington, D.C.), May 16, 1973.

12. A. S. Mariner, "A Critical Look at Professional Education in the Mental Health Field," *American Psychologist*, April 1967, pp. 271–81.

13. A. Pearl and F. Riessman, *New Careers for the Poor* (New York: The Free Press, 1965).

14. B. Barber, "Some Problems in the Sociology of Professions," *Daedalus*, Fall 1963, 92:669–88; D. F. Jacobs, "Purpose of the Insitutute," paper presented at 7th Annual Institute on Man's Adjustment in a Complex Environment, 1972.

15. M. B. Sussman, M. R. Haug, and G. K. Williams, "Paraprofessionalism and Rehabilitation Counseling: An Annotated Bibliography," working paper no. 1 (Cleveland: Case Western Reserve University, May 1971); G. S. Goldberg, "Nonprofessionals in Human Services," in *Nonprofessionals in the Human Services*, edited by C. Grosser, W. E. Henry, and J. C. Kelly (San Francisco, Jossey-Bass, 1969).

16. E. C. Hughes, "Professions," *Daedalus*, Fall 1963, 92:655–68; W. E. Moore, *The Professions: Roles and Rules* (New York: Russell Sage Foundation, 1970): A. Gartner, "Organizing Paraprofessionals," *Social Policy*, Sept./Oct. 1970, 1:60–61.

17. C. G. Wrenn, "Crisis in Counseling: A Commentary and (Possibly) a Contribution," in *Counselor Development in American Society*, edited by J. F. McGowan, pp. 234–38 (Washington, D.C.: American Psychological Assn., February 1965).

18. J. E. Gordon, "Project Cause, The Federal Anti-Poverty Program and Some Implications for Subprofessional Training," *American Psychologist*, 1965, 20:334–43.

19. L. E. Mitchell, "Nonprofessionals in Mental Health," in *Nonprofessionals in the Human Services*.

20. Jacobs, "Purpose of the Institute."

An Ecological Model
for Practicing Clinicians

JUDITH A. VAN EVRA

TEN YEARS AGO ECOLOGY WAS A WORD SO INFREQUENTLY used that it required definition in a proseminar lecture. Today, however, early grade-school children do pollution projects, wear ecosystem buttons, and read elementary portions of the vast literature on the subject. The ecological balance or imbalance between man and his environment has finally reached a point of high priority in the minds of thinking people.

Concurrent with the increased concern over the ecological balance has been the steady growth of community psychology, with its emphasis on healthy development and growth, and preventive programs to bridge the ever-increasing gap between demands for, and availability of, psychological services. It is becoming increasingly clear that the traditional one-to-one approach is inadequate, and various other models for today's psychologist have been proposed, including a problem-solving model,[1] a scientist-professional role,[2] a gatekeeper role,[3] the clinician as naturalist,[4] a free enterprise model,[5] a participant-conceptualizer model.[6] Ecological study of the reciprocal influence of people and their environment and the fluid balance between them has become increasingly apparent,[7] along with the rapidly growing literature on the study of communities and community mental health. With the exception of Kelly,[8] most of the ecological work of an applied nature seems centered on what might be called the "diagnostic" study of the community—or the complex relationships therein,—in a search for causal factors in later disturbances, or in an effort to plan comprehensive community services. Much of it is in the area of research rather than delivery of service, and often stops with the study of how the environment affects behavior, without going into its function in service delivery. Generally, the psychologist's role is still that of an expert who is expected to provide directly whatever help is required.

What I would like to suggest, as both an outgrowth of and modus operandi for, community psychology is an ecological model for the delivery of service; and my aim is two-fold: first, to suggest a more efficient way to deliver mental health services once problems arise;—and second, to suggest ways in which this model for service delivery can also serve an essential preventive function. The term "ecological" seems appropriate in that this model gives extensive consideration to a person's normal life situation and the natural roles he plays, as well as his balance with his surroundings. It strives for minimal disruption in that balance and places a greater emphasis on positive and healthy development and growth than on frustration, failure, conflict, and pathology. It also stresses prevention and helps to accomplish it. Finally, it makes more efficient use of the time and skills of professionals in various disciplines and settings.

REMEDIAL INTERVENTION AND PREVENTION

The Canadian Commission on Emotional and Learning Disorders in Children[9] cited one million children, or twelve percent, as needing help. In the United States, the National Institute of Mental Health estimated that nearly one and a half million children needed help in 1966, as well as an additional seven to ten percent in school surveys.[10] Clearly, the psychologist in his traditional role can help only a small percentage of those in need, and too often the help he can provide is necessarily temporary. The complex person-environment network of interactions and behaviors is disrupted by removing the person and treating him in isolation in the artificiality of an office or hospital. The client suffers the discontinuity of environments that change too quickly and too radically. In many instances, the persons most directly and naturally and logically involved with the problem on a daily basis,—e.g., parents, teachers, spouses,—are only minimally involved in the treatment and too often abdicate responsibility. The growing popularity of family therapy is a happy exception to this attitude. Hopefully, an ecological model can incorporate some of that more inclusive attitude, as well as the comprehensive knowledge of various systems and agencies required by an active community psychologist.

An even more efficient and effective use of a clinician's time is achieved to the extent that he can increase the skills of various persons in their natural roles (e.g., help parents become more effective parents, teachers more effective teachers) or increase the effectiveness of agencies or systems. Thus, the skill of the "front-line workers" can be increased through different kinds of intervention. The psychologist ideally becomes the consultant or problem solver; the parent or teacher becomes the "therapist" or "implementer" and retains responsibility for the child or client; and the latter remains in his natural environment. He hopefully benefits from a strengthened and healthier interaction, while the "consultees" gain new perspective and fresh insights into their roles. It is more than just better integration and coordination; it is a different kind of service in which the psychologist shares his skills and knowledge with laymen or persons in a variety of relationships with the client in order to effect change and promote growth. Thus, more people become more naturally involved, and the available help is extended significantly. This model appreciates the complexity of situations and allows for the separate handling of behaviors that differ according to setting as opposed to treatment in a clinic, where responses may or may not be like those at home or school. Too often, persons most directly involved are unfamiliar with community resources available and get little help with small problems. Seeking help often means a complicated referral and, in effect, turning a child or other person over to an agency with a result-ant loss of continuity and responsibility for continuous care. In our ecological model, these front-line workers have readily available professional resource persons on whom to call for information, advice, guidance, support, or other back-up con-sultation in the day-to-day playing out of their roles.This inter-facing of lay and professional persons means that the former remain involved, their capacity to help increases, and more normal development proceeds, with potential problems being identified much earlier.

One of the most important aspects to be emphasized is that the client's needs and his relationship with his environment are considered first. The focus is on the consumer of services and his needs. Dispositions are not made or services delivered for the convenience or perpetuation of existing systems or diagnostic categories, and functions and services are con-stantly reassessed. This combination of structure and flexibility allows for a smoother coordination of resources and a broaden-ing of services, and results in a more health-promoting, person-centered system. It also takes cognizance of the fact that inter-vention in one part affects the whole and, hopefully, allows for the anticipation and assessment of possible adverse effects of intervention for community resources or for functions of key persons as urged by Kelly.[11]

Thus, the psychologist's role is primarily consultative with his influence more often mediated indirectly, and is, to a much greater extent than previously, preventive. His functions in-volve less direct psychotherapy and more program planning, consultation and supervision, and education. Some of his many activities might include: conducting workshops for parents and teachers; disseminating psychological knowledge about development and child rearing, handling techniques, and learning principles; consulting with other community persons and agencies about their respective services and working out comprehensive and efficient programs to deliver those ser-

vices; designing screening programs in the schools and pre-
scribing early remedial or preventive programs; training
volunteers who are setting up new programs to help high-risk
groups or persons of varying cultural backgrounds or individuals who might not otherwise be helped; becoming involved on
school boards and committees to influence the type of cur-
ricula considered. The possibilities are infinite. Clearly, the
psychologist still needs a professional base of operations for
research and teaching, but this model does shift a significant
share of activity out of the office and into the community,
where his intervention is less disruptive and helps to implement changes there that can also be preventive. Further it provides more adequate linkage of "helping" facilities to "normal-
stream" institutions (e.g., education, recreation, family, and
work), as suggested by the Joint Commission (1970), and provides help to a person through his normal life experiences
without segregating him or damaging his self-esteem. This
approach improves his capacity for problem-solving, encour-
ages growth, and increases his self-confidence and self-esteem.

Thus, the practicing clinician in this model helps people to
grow and develop *in their own natural roles,* doing the things
they know most about. Psychologists must diversify; otherwise,
others will do what is needed, and psychologists will make a
less significant impact on the quality of life. As Gottlieb and
Riger suggest:

> the criterion of success of the mental health consultant is the
> degree to which the consultee (gatekeeper) is able to alter or
> improve his own role performance and, in turn, to enhance the
> future functioning of those potentially influenced by his gate-
> keeper role.[12]

If these aims can be accomplished, we will also effect a very
essential preventive function and help to reverse the current
unbalanced emphasis on treatment. In Canada, for example, in
1968, only five percent of the total health care budget of four
billion dollars was spent on nontreatment aspects including
training, research, statistics, and administration,[13] a staggering

testimonial to our neglect of preventive work. An ecological orientation, however, seems to lead more directly to preventive programs and intervention. Basic knowledge of the relationships and interactions between social structures and individuals and knowledge of the way in which maladaptive behaviors develop in different persons in varying environments lead to varying interventive and preventive proposals and usually involve multiple agencies and organizations.[14] Possible avenues for prevention have been alluded to previously. If, for example, rather than referring problem children to a psychologist, parents and teachers are enabled to retain and work more effectively with both normal and problem children in the home or classroom, perceiving and handling minor problems and thus preventing many more serious ones, they can also aid the child's growing self-reliance and independence by helping him "learn to learn," to learn how to approach and solve problems. Finally, families need to be exposed to the principles of healthy child-rearing practices.[15] They need to feel comfortable about their children's potential and see the positive, healthy aspects that blossom with affection. As Kanner states so succinctly, "Prevention is practiced by maintaining health, not by agitations intended to avert disaster projected into the future."[16]

IMPLICATIONS FOR TRAINING

Obviously, these kinds of role changes have significant implications for training, particularly for the clinical psychologist headed for clinical work and consultation. In the past, he has usually expected the community, or individuals in it, to come to him and has offered help within his frame of reference. However, today new ways of meeting the new kinds and greater number of problems are required. More knowledge of the reciprocal influence of people and their environments is necessary, as well as skills to maintain a healthy balance—both of which require a broad base from which to operate. Training should provide fairly extensive information and knowledge about social agencies, school systems, and the politics involved, community programs, the people in them and their background and training. A major emphasis on developmental concepts and learning theory is essential, as well as a sound base in supervisory techniques, teaching methods, consultative functions, and organizational dynamics.

What is urgently needed in training is an emphasis on efficient and productive approaches to problems, generalizable to problems in many areas, as well as specific diagnostic[17] and therapeutic skills. Wiens's "scientist-professional" model and Segalman's problem-solving model[18] emphasize and urge training and education in problem solving and scientific methodology. If these skills are then passed on to persons in key environmental positions for more effective delivery of mental health services, we stop perpetuating the more inefficient stop-gap approach that requires more and more psychologists and, increasingly, paraprofessionals in more traditional roles and psychological settings but which remains inadequate to meet the need.

Training of persons for this new role will also need to be multidisciplinary to prepare them for independent functioning in a variety of settings and problem areas. They will need to gain knowledge of fields such as economics, budget and finance, social work, psychiatry, architecture, politics, corrections, and planning, as well as knowledge of the people in those fields and their training. Practicums in various community settings and more interaction with people in the community will be necessary and helpful. Cowen's description of a training program,[19] including thirteen different projects, is illustrative of this notion and is recommended as an excellent example of the specific and varied kinds of training practices and experiences that would be relevant and helpful.

RESEARCH

Many of the old and familiar arguments for and against the naturalistic as opposed to the laboratory setting for research

arise again as this model requires more emphasis on the former, and several writers[20] have stressed the importance of
knowing about the natural distribution of psychological conditions and states outside the laboratory. Barker makes a strong
case in his behavior setting theory for the study of the natural
interaction of the variance within people and their environmental setting and the need to know about the ecological
context in order to study the developmental *process*, the
course behavior takes, rather than simply a behavior at any
given moment. We need, then, to relate this "diagnostic"
knowledge to service delivery and the most effective means of
intervention. Research can and should incorporate both aspects. Thus, as Kelly notes, behavior is evaluated in social
rather than intrapsychic terms:

> In the same way explanations of behavior change are not re-
> stricted to the interaction between an expert and a client but
> are viewed as taking place in multiple settings. A change agent
> becomes a person who alters behavior independent of formally
> designated helping roles. The social effectiveness of indigenous
> leaders under this model becomes as relevant a research topic
> as the efficacy of treatment institutions or treatment tech-
> niques.[21]

Psychologists working in laboratories may sometimes be
able to isolate variables for study, but this leads to an exclusion
of the community and its complex effects and interactions.
Lehmann[22] warns that we need to verify what we think is a
mini-social situation in a laboratory or office to see if there is
some relationship between it and what exists in the natural
state. We also need to take into account the effects of our
intervention on other parts of the system. If one is working
with persons in their natural roles, one can research the varying effectiveness of different kinds of approaches or techniques
in a natural context, where spurious or artificial results are less
likely and the difficulties inherent in laboratory-to-field gener-
alization are minimized. There is also the aspect of actual service delivery during, or as part of, the research, and thus an

opportunity to reunite the clinician's work with his research.

The possibilities and opportunities for psychologists in this model are endless. There are exciting and varied challenges to decrease the tremendous gap between the social effectiveness and equity of one-to-one work by professionals and that of broader-based consultative-preventive programs. The latter uses the psychologist's time and talents to greater advantage and in such a way as to effect more far-reaching change and growth with minimum disruption and imbalance. I would like to conclude with a quote from the 1970 CELDIC report:

> We want immediacy of help at the earliest possible moment of need. No longer should we tolerate the compounding of problem upon problem because we are too busy or too blind to make help immediately available to a child when a difficulty first arises. We must not continue our present emphasis on "mopping up" instead of "fixing the leak". . . . It requires that the specialist share the field with others with different training, with volunteers, and with families, helping these in turn to help the child.[23]

This, then, allows more effective and extensive application and points to a very diversified and challenging future for psychologists.

References

1. R. Segalman, "A Problem-Solving Model for Professional Practice: A Social Worker's View," *Professional Psychology,* 1970, 1:453–54.
2. A. N. Wiens, "Scientist-Professional: The Appropriate Training Model for the Mainstream of Clinical Psychology," *Professional Psychology,* 1969, 1:38–42.
3. B. H. Gottlieb and Stephanie Riger, "Social Interventions in the Community: Three Professional Roles," *Professional Psychology,* 1972, 3:-231–40.
4. H. L. Raush, "Naturalistic Method and the Clinical Approach," in *Naturalistic Viewpoints in Psychological Research,* edited by E. P. Willems and H. L. Raush (New York: Holt, Rinehart and Winston, 1969).
5. S. R. Sacon and A. R. Gruber, "The Community Psychologist as Private Entrepreneur," *Proceedings, 80th Annual Convention,* 1972, pp. 785–86.
6. P. E. Cook (ed.), *Community Psychology and Community Mental Health* (San Francisco: Holden Day, Inc., 1970).
7. R. G. Barker (ed.), *The Stream of Behavior* (New York: Appleton-Century-Crofts, 1963); R. G. Barker, "Explorations in Ecological Psychology," *American Psychologist,* 1965, 20:1–14; R. G. Barker, *Ecological Psychology* (Stanford: Stanford University Press, 1968); J. G. Kelly, "Eclolgical Constraints on Mental Health Services," *American Psychologist,* 1966, 21:535–39; J. G. Kelly, "Towards a Theory of Preventive Intervention," in *Research Contributions from Psychology to Community Mental Health,* edited by J. W. Carter (New York: Behavioral Publications, 1968); S. Lehmann, "Community and Psychology and Community Psychology," *American Psychologist,* 1971, 26:554–60.
8. Kelly, "Towards a Theory of Preventive Intervention."
9. *One Million Children,* report of the Commission on Emotional and Learning Disorders in Children (CELDIC report) (Toronto: Leonard Crainford, 1970).
10. *Crisis in Mental Health: Challenge for the 1970s,* report of the Joint Commission on Mental Health of Children (New York: Harper & Row, 1970).
11. Kelly, "Towards a Theory of Preventive Intervention."
12. Gottlieb and Riger, p. 239.
13. *One Million Children.*
14. Kelly, "Towards a Theory of Preventive Intervention."
15. L. Kanner, *Child Psychiatry* (Springfield, Ill.: Charles C. Thomas, 1972).
16. Ibid., p. 245.
17. Wiens, see note 2.
18. Segalman, see note 1.
19. E. L. Cowen, "Broadening Community Mental Health Practicum Training," *Professional Psychology,* 1971, 2:159–68.

20. Barker, *Ecological Psychology;* Lehmann, see note 7; Raush, see note 4.
21. Kelly, "Towards a Theory of Preventive Intervention," p. 59.
22. Lehmann, see note 7.
23. *One Million Children,* pp. 469–70.

Clinical-Adolescent Psychology:
A Need for Erudition and Application

ROBERT J. GREENE

THE WORDS "CLINICAL" OR "CLINICAL-CHILD" FLOW smoothly in writing and discussion. One stumbles with "clinical-adolescent" because it is not common, familiar, usual. This simple observation introduces my thesis: familiarity (i.e., study and application) within the special area of clinical-adolescent psychology is needed.

Professional psychological services for adolescents are anything but new or unusual. Yet, within clinical settings, adolescents are typically conceptualized and treated either as large children or immature adults. They are placed at the upper age level of the case load at child-guidance centers, at the lower age level at adult mental health centers, or are simply sandwiched in the middle at all-purpose mental health facilities. The same pattern, unfortunately, seems to hold for most clinical training programs. Brief note is made of the existence of this different species of "child" in clinical-child courses, a few comments are offered in adult-oriented courses or, more typically, no special attention at all is paid to the psychology of this specific developmental phase.

In most abnormal texts written for undergraduate use, one is impressed with the lack of significant reference to adolescent psychopathology. Except for excursions into problems of delinquency and some tangential consideration in conjunction with discussions of schizophrenia, attention paid to adolescent maladaptive behaviors has been almost negligible. Checking the indexes of major texts on clinical psychology usually provides reference to only a few paragraphs on adolescence. Clinical-adolescent publications appear relatively infrequently. This seems to be especially true for more prestigious outlets. In reviewing the contents of the more prominent research-oriented journals, one finds very few articles that can be identified as dealing specifically with adolescents. Moreover, in accord with traditional emphases, most of these few papers deal with problems of delinquency. Within these journals, the number of adolescent papers that have broad clinical applicability remains low.

A limited documentation of training gaps was provided by a brief survey conducted in conjunction with the writing of this paper. Twenty-two clinical psychology students at APA-approved internship facilities responded to a questionnaire designed to gather data about their training, interests, and knowledge of adolescent functioning. Only six students had taken any graduate course work dealing specifically with adolescence. Nonetheless, all (except one "undecided") reported that they planned to provide professional services to adolescents. Although no direct survey of psychology departments was conducted, a casual inspection of graduate catalogs leads to the hypothesis that a major factor contributing to not having had adolescent-oriented courses was the lack of class offerings in this area.

This state of affairs is especially disconcerting in light of the clinical uniqueness of this developmental period. Following an initial emphasis by Sullivan[1] and buttressed with more recent substantiation on the basis of accumulated clinical experiences,[2] it has been recognized that, within this segment of life, an exceptional opportunity is presented to reorient, reconstruct, and rectify the results of even serious states of psychopathology and maladaptive learning experiences.

DEVELOPMENTAL PSYCHOLOGY AND ADOLESCENCE

Much more attention has been paid to adolescence within the field of developmental psychology than within that of clinical psychology. Furthermore, commitments to developmental studies of adolescence are increasing. This can be seen in the call from the journal *Developmental Psychology*, under the editorship of Boyd McCandless, for "particular attention" to this age group. Most major general developmental texts have expanded their format to include discussions of adolescents.[3] In addition, for many years a number of specialized developmental texts have been devoted to adolescence. This library continues to be expanded and updated.[4] These books do not, of course, offer a consistent clinical focus. However, they are of great value to the clinician in providing a basic understanding of this developmental phase.

Developmental information on cognitive changes during adolescence, such as that outlined by Piaget,[5] is of crucial clinical importance. Indeed, any attempt to understand and assist in clarifying the thought processes of an adolescent would be less than practicable without being aware of the giant jump toward differentiation of thought from the external world and toward abstract thinking that has taken place at the onset of this phase. Elkind[6] has pointed out the powerful affective consequences of formal operational thought as related to the new-found abilities to: compare the possible with the actual; contrast how things are and how they might be, introspect, create a façade to mask feelings. Elkind[7] has also emphasized the frequent development of marked egocentrism at this stage of life. This results from a projection of concern about self. Again, cognizance of patterns such as these is basic for an accurate clinical understanding of adolescents and the formulation of intervention programs.

In addition to understanding specific facets of development, the clinician certainly needs to study critically the major theories of adolescence. A succinct and comprehensive review of central theories has been provided by Muss.[8] Especially important for the practicing psychologist is an awareness of widely divergent theoretical opinions and alternatives. Many clinicians seem to have been exposed to some of the more traditional theories that have suggested that inescapable psychological problems occur during adolescence.[9] However, there seems to be much less clinical awareness of alternative cogent theories,[10] which define adolescence as a transition period that need not be disruptive, chaotic, or distressing. Both sides of this theoretical dichotomy will be examined in more detail later. However, at this point, it is appropriate to note that the trend of developmental research data has been to add momentum to the challenge of traditional views. The time-honored perspective of the adolescent as a rebel who caustically impugns and rejects parental values in favor of peer values is being questioned. Value challenges may be common when addressing minor issues (e.g., hair and dress) but are atypical on major matters (e.g., career, marriage, life style).[11] In one study of more than 1,500 seventh, ninth, and twelfth grade students, responses to hypothetical situations clearly indicated that: "Where youth did opt in favor of complying with the wishes of others, they more often opted to comply with parental than peer wishes."[12] Similarly, Horrocks's summary[13] of studies of religious views concluded that adolescence does not bring with it great changes in religious beliefs and attitudes. Political changes also appear to be minimal during adolescence. In an intensive study of the development of political commitments, Easton and Hess[14] concluded that the truly formative years were the decade between three and thirteen. By the time the child enters high school, "His political orientation to regime and community have become firmly entrenched." The lack of political rebellion by youth has been confirmed many times in studies[15] that have determined that youth who are political activists are functioning very much in accord with, not in contrast to, their parents' beliefs and values.

Somewhere between the poles of theoretical disagreement lies the anthropological perspective. Since Mead's monumental lead,[16] the developmental-oriented anthropologists have successfully attacked many behavioral "universals" and "inherent" patterns. This holds for adolescent turmoil.[17] Nonetheless, Benedict[18] has argued that the discontinuity in our cultural treatment of adolescents does indeed increase the probability of psychological problems. This is most evident in relationship to responsibility, dominance, and sex role behaviors.

Augmenting the more established theories, viewpoints have appeared[19] that demand more attention. These perspectives, in accord with current psychological trends, provide basic formulations that argue for the need to include factors of rapid social change in attempts to understand adolescent adjustment. The immediate clinical relevance of some of the newer views is readily seen by examining specific theories that have focused upon adolescent conflicts and problems. Concepts such as the "breach of contract" hypothesis offered by Elkind[20] provide an orientation toward the understanding of seemingly senseless destructive acting-out by middle-class adolescents. Such views deserve much clinical consideration as a possible explanatory structure for family discord.

As a final note in this discussion of developmental psychology, the impact of dramatic physiological changes should not be ignored. The psychological ramifications of real and imagined physical deviancy during adolescence have been amply documented.[21] In addition to an awareness of general growth and physiological change patterns exhibited by adolescents, a general review of a text dealing with adolescent medicine, such as that by Gallagher, is suggested.[22] Gallagher outlines normal physical developmental patterns, and also offers a basic understanding of physiological problems confronted by young people. Such texts serve to sensitize the psychologist to possibilities of systemic problems that may contribute to disorders appearing to be completely of psychogenic origin.

PSYCHOPATHOLOGY AND NORMALITY IN ADOLESCENCE

Information from developmental psychology is a necessity for understanding behavior and cognitive functioning of the adolescent. However, perhaps of most importance for the practicing clinician is an accurate concept of normality in adolescence. Indeed, to assess the functioning of any individual and to formulate clear views of psychopathology, an objective reference base is essential. Yet, many clinical papers dealing with adolescent behavior have contributed to the development of widely accepted "normative" descriptions that have not been subjected to empirical examination.

One of the oldest and most pervasive views is that adolescence is inherently a time of marked psychological disturbance and turmoil. The formal direction for theories of inevitable adolescent psychopathology was provided by Hall's theory of recapitulation.[23] This resulted in his "Strum und Drang" viewpoint, which predicted inevitable disruption and problematic behaviors during adolescence due to the correspondence of this developmental phase to the time the human race was in a turbulent transitional stage. Psychoanalytic theory provided prestigious support for the concept of intense psychological problems occurring phylogenetically during adolescence. Libido expenditures required to deal with the upsurge of instinctual drives and with the reappearance of the Oedipal conflict were seen as resulting in a reduced resistance to hysterical and neurotic symptoms. Anna Freud's outline of adolescence[24] as a period of natural discordance and marked mood swings was expanded to the contention that signs of steady equilibrium during adolescence should be diagnosed as abnormal: "Where adolescence is concerned, it seems easier to describe its pathological manifestations than the normal processes."[25] According to Anna Freud, typical patterns included pathological overuses of the defenses of asceticism and intellectualization, and an overemphasis on the importance of friendships as a replacement of parents being abandoned through independence. Similarly, excessive aggressive patterns were viewed as necessary to avoid regressive tendencies toward dependency. Kessler concurred with this general orientation in observing that during the adolescent phase one might expect to see "disturbed behaviors (e.g., withdrawal, depression, rituals, hypochondriacal preoccupations, bizzare fantasies) which look like that of a psychotic patient."[26]

Lewin[27] was also a forerunner in presenting a "normal-conflict" theory. He conceptualized the adolescent as a "marginal man," existing in an unstructured social and psychological field. In Lewin's conceptualization, rapid changes in life space, which occur for all adolescents, result in stress, disorganization, and tension. Problematic behaviors follow.

In addition to the previously cited theories of inevitable psychopathology, Erikson's widely read opinions on youth[28] supported predictions of an unavoidable period of disruption. According to this theory, disruption is associated with the confrontation of the major adolescent task of establishing a meaningful identity while trying to avoid a continuance of the identity diffusion process. However, in Erikson's writings, it is clear that social resources could provide a supportive structure to minimize problems, but this is seldom accomplished. More frequently, in Erikson's opinion, condescension and fearful attitudes of adults contribute to more difficulties.

Recently, the theories forecasting inevitable psychological problems have been challenged by an increasing bank of data.[29] In accord with research cited previously, these projects indicate that the average adolescent is neither experiencing marked inner turmoil nor outer conflict with society or family. In fact, Douvan and Adelson's comprehensive investigation,[30] which included a sample of more than 3,000 adolescents, resulted in concern about the *absence* of levels of restlessness and conflict that might be necessary to enhance emotional growth. Masterson and his coworkers[31] have compiled data showing that adolescents exhibited a frequency of clinical psychopathology no higher than that found in the general population. In one of Masterson's projects, based on a comparison of more than a hundred adolescent outpatients with a control group, the conclusion was drawn that most authors have erred by making an overgeneralization from clinic clients to the general population.

The "low-conflict" empirical data are not without theoretical support. This can be seen in the formulations of authors who have argued that adolescence can indeed, without a violation of natural growth processes, be a relatively harmonious life segment. Spranger's "Value Heirarchy" theories[32] are in clear opposition to predictions of unavoidable problems during adolescence. Spranger does not see the young person at the mercy of either environmental or biological factors. Rather, from a phenomenological stance, he credits the adolescent with the strength to direct actively and to form his own growth. According to Spranger, the three patterns that may occur at this time are: (1) a growth process achieving personal goals, (2) a slow change resulting in the adoption of cultural values without basic personality alterations, (3) radical changes accompanying a shift in the adolescent's perception of self. The last pattern increases the chance for the experience of discord, but is not a necessary pattern nor does it guarantee maladaptive behavior.

The most comprehensive and flexible theory not supporting inevitable marked conflict is one constructed by Havighurst,[33] who drew upon (and credited) many other theorists (e.g., Freud, Rank, Williams), but incorporated only what he felt was most accurately descriptive of and supported by observations of normal and pathological development. His detailed analysis of the adolescent developmental process conceptualizes this period as entailing the successful mastery of a series of developmental tasks. These include:

1. accepting one's physique and accepting a masculine or feminine role;
2. establishing new relations with age mates of both sexes;
3. achieving emotional independence of parents and other adults;
4. achieving assurance of economic independence;
5. selecting and preparing for an occupation;
6. developing intellectual skills and concepts necessary for civic competence;
7. desiring and achieving socially responsible behavior;
8. preparing for marriage and family life; and
9. building conscious values in harmony with an adequate scientific world-picture.

In accord with some previously developed social orientation views,[34] this theory leaves room for psychological problems but does not lead to the prediction of a natural state of psychopathology. The orderly and nontraumatic successful accomplishment of the sequential developmental tasks leading to maturity is not unexpected.

Thus, theory and data combine into a clearly emerging direction. Recent research has contributed support to concepts of normal adolescence as not being synonymous with even transient states of psychopathology. The preponderance of opposition to low conflict theories is based mainly upon clinical impressions and studies of "problem" youngsters rather than samples from the general population. While the sufficiency of conclusive research has been questioned,[35] Weiner summarized his scholarly review of clinical and developmental data by stating "a heavy weight of contrary data and opinion argue strongly that these views [of adolescence as an era of disruption], whenever generalized to the adolescent population, are indeed a myth."[36] Thus, it seems that many of the stereotypes employed to describe the adolescent need to be discarded. Traditional conceptualizations of the "average" adolescent as a rebellious, nonconforming, value-rejecting individual who is in a natural "storm and stress" state of marked emotional conflict may lead the clinician astray from delivering effective services. Of central importance, inevitable psychopathology views probably promote errors in recognizing significant psychological problems that do exist.

Current Attitudes

A limited assessment of the current beliefs held by professional mental health workers is provided in the following data. This was gathered from a small sample (N = 27) of professional clinical psychologists and psychiatric social workers who responded to selected segments of the previously described questionnaire that was sent to psychology interns. The professional respondents reported spending an average of twenty-five percent of their time working with adolescents. Percentages of both professional mental health workers and clinical psychology interns endorsing each of the following views are indicated:

1. Most adolescents reject major parental values.
   (professionals, 26%; interns, 36%)
2. Adolescents exhibit more psychological disturbances than adults.
   (professionals, 63%; interns, 54%)
3. Marked conflict and disharmony in relationship to parents is a part of adaptive psychological adjustment during adolescence.
   (professionals, 96%; interns, 95%)
4. Most adolescents will "grow out of" symptoms of psychological disturbance.
   (professionals, 63%; interns, 54%)

These percentages suggest a significant endorsement of inevitable psychopathology theories. Yet, as we have seen, views of significant value rejection, marked parental conflict, and a high incidence of psychopathology are not supported by data. Data are also available that strike a strong blow to the application of "he will grow out of it" notions to symptomatic adolescents. A major project[37] that conducted two-and-one-half-year and five-year re-evaluations of seventy-five adolescents who exhibited psychological disorders found that approximately two-thirds of these young people still demonstrated moderate or severe impairment at the five-year follow-up. Real psychological disturbance exhibited by adolescents is not transient.

What, then, explains the questionnaire data from the mental health professionals and psychology interns? The response patterns may indicate marked disagreement with both data and theories supporting less problematic views of adolescence. Or, the response patterns may simply indicate limited knowledge of such theories and data. Given the limited training available in this field, this latter hypothesis is probably the more tenable.

From a practicing clinician's viewpoint, most perilous among the questionnaire responses is the large percentage who endorsed the "old and comforting empiricism . . . 'He'll grow out of it.' "[38] The consequence of this widespread belief by professionals may have a corrolary reflected in the statistics complied by Rosen et al.[39] These data provide documentation that, while adolescents constitute a large percentage of outpatient mental health referrals, they receive a low frequency of services beyond intake and diagnosis. Only about one-third of adolescents receive services following initial contacts. This is in contrast to approximately sixty percent of eighteen- to sixty four-year-old individuals receiving services beyond initial contact. Indeed, if one subscribes to a belief in spontaneous remission for most adolescent psychological disturbance, a strong argument can be made to adopt a laissez-faire position toward adolescents and expend clinical services for others. This may follow Kessler's diagnostic advice that, with adolescents, "it is much better to err on the conservative side and adopt a wait and see attitude."[40]

Patterns of minimal service and training have contributed to the conclusion that "the adolescent is a target population whose clinical and other service needs are especially acute at present."[41] A conservative summary of the adolescent's position relative to psychological services is that he is clearly "underserved."[42]

Current Trends

Thus far in looking at adolescence, we have seen a pattern of more extensive and systematic efforts expended by developmental psychologists than by clinical psychologists. We have also seen clinical opinions and service deficits that may reflect a lack of awareness of much relevant data. Plausible explanations for these circumstances are many: tradition, lack of interest, the absence of volumes of clinical data and literature, perhaps even the fact that problem adolescents who have often become experts at alienating parents and teachers are also experts at alienating clinicians. One might even hypothesize that Ann Freud's delineation[43] of the special difficulties encountered in working with adolescents (e.g., the adolescent's intolerance for frustration and immediacy of needs) has also been a deterring factor for some clinicians.

Happily, however, current trends indicate change. A body of theories, strategies, and techniques for dealing with adolescent populations is being built. While in still somewhat rudimentary stages, this area of specialization has an ample foundation and framework to warrant an emphasis in clinical training both for the neophyte clinical student and for the applied professional who may have been working without as full a complement of skills as might be developed from updated information.

A number of specific publications will be cited in following sections. However, a few immediate comments can provide an indication of current directions. One journal, *Adolescence,* publishes an increasing number of clinical and developmental papers each year. Our companion discipline of psychiatry has established a Society for Adolescent Psychiatry. This organization sponsors an annual convention devoted to information exchange on clinical issues and has also sponsored the publication of several clinical texts.[44]

In addition to many other specific areas of concern, the phenomenon of adolescent suicide has become a subject of increased interest. Perhaps this interest has been spurred by the recognition of the inordinately high ranking of this behavior as a cause of death for young people and the fact that the suicide rate among adolescents has been increasing over the past twenty-five years.[45] In any case, following surveys by Bakwin, Kestenbaum, and Teicher,[46] adolescent suicide has been examined in two original texts.[47] These studies provide a valuable exploration of both dynamic and demographic factors.

At this juncture, special mention is warranted by Weiner's recent book,[48] which is one of the most inclusive and scholarly works produced in this field. Weiner combines skills of academician and clinician in integrating data with recommendations for intervention. As much as any other single factor, the creation of this work provides a "sign of the times" in pointing toward an expanding focus on adolescence and pulling together an already noteworthy body of publications. Additional recent major works on adolescent psychopathology have been published.[49]

A brief overview of several areas that deserve special attention in the training of the clinical-adolescent psychologist will provide an indication of the scope and relevance of work in this area.

Psychotherapy

To work with the adolescent in psychotherapy "as if" he were a large child or immature adult is an invitation to failure. Such orientations, with predictably negative outcomes), in conjunction with misdiagnoses and deficiencies in accurate basic developmental information, may account for some of the professional patterns of avoiding extended contacts with adolescents. Again, clinically pragmatic literature that may serve as a corrective measure is becoming available.

Weiner[50] has outlined a number of necessary modifications of usual therapy strategies and techniques that he contends are requisite to achieve effective psychotherapy with adolescents. He emphasizes the need for openness, honesty, and a much higher level of activity on the part of the therapist. It has also been noted[51] that the therapist must immediately come to terms with the semivoluntary status of most adolescents who are referred for services and must circumvent the usual clinic delays in responding to the young person. Additionally, it should be mentioned that the therapist who is aware of the cognitive changes occurring during adolescence can capitalize on the newly developed cerebral capacities and interests by using "head" orientations such as rational-emotive[52] or transactional analysis.[53] Such approaches promote the development of independence and self-control and provide the conceptual tools to facilitate reaching these goals.

Providing one of the most complete original presentations

on treatment, Holmes[54] has enumerated a number of special positive factors exhibited by adolescents that contribute to therapy progress (e.g., interest in learning about self, curiosity, increased awareness of the future) as well as some counterforces (e.g., skepticism). Issues ranging from establishing the treatment contract to the use of extraverbal communication are discussed in detail, with a wealth of clinical illustrations.

Parents. Here a dogmatic rule needs to be attended to by student and practitioner: parents must be included in the therapy process. In most states, inclusion is automatic by law due to the fact that, as in Michigan (with the exception of drug abuse problems), psychotherapy services without parental consent are illegal. Thus, parents are automatically part of the therapy program and hold veto power at any stage in the proceedings. Desirable or not, parents are there, and data[55] indicate that parents' feelings of being uninformed or excluded have been a major factor in the premature termination of treatment. In Kaplan's words, "Parents insist on participating, and their interests and needs must be met."[56] Consequently, the question that requires consideration is not *whether,* but on *what basis,* parents should be included. For some clinicians,[57] the varied ramifications of parental influences constitute a greater problem than the adolescents themselves. For others, the concern is that substantial and permanent change cannot be achieved without family involvement. Weissman and Sigel[58] have recently added clinical data that suggest that a direct relationship exists between deviant behavior exhibited by adolescents and patterns of psychopathology exhibited by the mother. Focusing their treatment efforts on the mothers rather than the adolescents, they found that "mothers' problems with their adolescents improved, and many of the children's problems diminished."[59]

Planning parent contacts should depend as much on the maturational stage of the adolescent and on the receptivity of the parents to change as on any theoretical underpinning. Direct contacts need not be frequent nor specifically oriented toward family systems explorations and modifications in the case of the adolescent who has already progressed significantly into the establishment of emotional, financial, and structural distance from the family unit.

Confidentiality. Even more so than with adults, a breach of confidentiality with an adolescent client is an assured way to terminate therapeutic progress. By the time an adolescent arrives for mental health consultation, he has usually experienced a series of interactions in which adults have told other adults important information about him.[60] This frequently occurs in violation of implied confidentiality. The intent of such communication is usually good. The results are disastrous for the adult-adolescent relationship. As previously noted, parents must be involved, in some fashion, in the therapeutic process. This does not, however, necessitate open communication to them about material discussed in therapy. While formal writings relative to this issue are scarce, the author's experience is that parents, while openly expressing that they would "like to know," are understanding and acceptant of communication limitations. Often, interestingly enough, other professionals are less understanding and more demanding of information. Also, a typical comment from other professionals about an iron-clad rule of confidentiality is: "Yes, of course, but you do inform others if the youngster is taking drugs, or is planning to run away, or is stealing, or is . . ., etc., don't you?" No. The only justification in violating confidentiality (and even this is contested by some) is in the case of the therapist needing to share the responsibility when the adolescent communicates an unchanging suicidal intent that would be classified as highly lethal.[61] However, even here, the first alternative is to encourage the adolescent himself to communicate his feelings with other adults who are able to assume some responsibility for prevention. It should be explained to the client that this will circumvent the need for the therapist to do this. Thus, even in circumstances of potential suicide, the adolescent can be placed in a position where he has the option of retaining control of communication channels.

Group Work. The group as a therapeutic modality is being

given separate consideration due to some special attributes of this area relative to the adolescent. Positive indications for adolescent group psychotherapy, as well as specific group intervention techniques, have been outlined in a recent article by Greene and Crowder.[62] Factors, such as similar maturational and social conflicts, enhanced peer interactions and influence, and the alleviation of language barriers and suspicion aspects of the one-to-one setting were presented as most important. Rosenbaum[63] has reviewed much of the relevant literature dealing with adolescents in group treatment, and emphasizes the need for a "flexible approach" as most crucial. The flexible approach was defined as including the use of such techniques as control setting, active intervention, and the use of the environmental situation when appropriate. Ross and Anderson[64] argued for the use of cotherapists, and not merely because "two heads are better than one." Much more important, cotherapists were seen as promoting a pattern of guaranteed regularity of group meetings, with one therapist being available to cover in the absence of the others. An experience with maximum predictability and stability is thus established.

Uncritical endorsements of group treatment for young people ought to be evaluated in light of some unpublished preliminary data on therapy preferences that have been compiled by the author. Responding to a questionnaire designed to sample preferences of therapy orientations and settings, more than 230 high school students indicated that their first choice of therapy modalities would *not* be group psychotherapy. The overwhelming preference, 76 percent, was individual psychotherapy. Groups were a distant second, 20 percent. Family therapy was chosen by only four percent. Sex differences were negligible. In a limited sample (N = 96) of undergraduate college students, preferences for groups increased to twenty-five percent, but this still remained a considerable distance from individual therapy, 74 percent. Reflecting again on training needs, it is interesting to note that while both the mental health professional and psychology intern samples previously referred to were able to correctly identify the sequence of adolescents' choice, both ascribed a much higher preference for group psychotherapy than actually indicated by adolescents. Forty-one percent of the psychology interns and thirty-eight percent of the professionals guessed that adolescents would prefer group treatment.

From a broader perspective, the number of publications oriented to adolescent groups is reaching a volume that could easily justify attention as a training seminar in itself. Several books devoted to the psychologically disturbed adolescent in group psychotherapy are on the market.[65] The MacLennan and Felsenfeld text combines basic group methods with broad recommendations for group programs with adolescents. A multitude of settings are considered. While still judging the number of articles as "sparse," Lubin, Lubin, and Sargent[66] reviewed fifteen papers on group psychotherapy with adolescents that were all published in one year, 1971. This number of publications does, however, indicate some increase over that noted in Rosenbaum's twelve-year literature search[67] for papers on the treatment of adolescents with the technique of group psychotherapy (1956–1967). According to this survey, a low of four articles were published in 1967, with a high of eleven in 1966.

Behavior Modification. Authors writing in the area of behavior modification have paid little heed to the adolescent as a special entity. Certainly, behavioral intervention with adolescents does not require changes in either operant or classical theories. Nonetheless, even here, specific information about adolescents is valuable to help avoid subjecting the new clinician to unnecessary expensive learning by experience. For example, a crucial piece of basic information is the simple fact that the scope and control of reinforcers administered within the family and within broader adult social units become progressively restricted during adolescence. Often this constriction reaches the point where the "privilege" of residing in the home may be the only major tangible reinforcement left in the hands of the parents. With the exception of the inordinate amount of environmental reinforcer control seen within inpatient facilities that allows the construction of an extremely pervasive and powerful "reinforcer menu,"[68] the reinforcement limitations pose special problems that demand special consideration by behavior modifiers.

Also requiring special attention are adolescents' preferences toward psychotherapy approaches. The high school students sampled by the author were asked to indicate which of several therapy orientations they would choose. The most directive approach ("Tell you what you should do") was rejected by all except one student. A complex combination of insight and autonomous problem solving ("Help you understand why you are having problems plus help you think of your own solutions") was the preference of 84 percent. Here, also, the professional and intern samples were asked to guess which type of approach the adolescents would choose. As with the question on group, individual, or family therapy, most professionals and interns correctly identified the answer selected by the young people (67 percent of professionals and 68 percent of interns said that the adolescents would choose understanding plus self-determined solutions). They were also attuned to the near total rejection of the most directive approach (no professionals or interns selected this as the approach preferred by adolescents). However, whereas only six percent of the young people stated they would want a combination of insight plus directive advice, a much larger group of both professionals (18 percent) and interns (23 percent) guessed that this would be the adolescents' choice.

This preference data from students suggests that behavior modification approaches structured in a format of directive task-oriented advice may be rejected by adolescents before being given an adequate trial. If not, alternative approaches, alternative packaging, and presentation of standard procedures need to be considered.

In changing standard operating approaches, behaviorally oriented therapists have devised a few programs such as "contingency contracting"[69] that increase the adolescent's choices and accountability. While this procedure lacks some of the esthetic elegance of tighter S-R approaches, it has a pragmatic appeal for modifying problematic behaviors of adolescents who are experiencing difficulties within the home. This procedure also circumvents the paradox presented by more typical behavioral procedures that may aim at attempting to build a greater sense of independence and responsibility through increased external control of the young person's behaviors.

Inpatient. Little space has been allotted here to the discussion of work with the adolescent as a psychiatric inpatient. This area has, however, been explicitly examined in full texts.[70] and in numerous articles. These works emphasize the need for programs and treatment techniques specifically designed for the young person.

Assessment

Structured assessment of adolescents retains a high potential for investigation, despite the often emotional antitest sentiments expressed by many clinical psychologists. Perhaps a more rational and productive perspective of testing can be built in the area of adolescence due to the lack of intense previous involvement with this population. In contrast to other populations, broad promises, high expectations, and unrealistic demands for adolescent assessment have not occurred. Thus, the negative effects of overexpectation have been relatively minimal.

The pattern within the field of adolescent assessment is not dissimilar to that outlined in previous areas of consideration. Prior to the last decade, attention was slight with the exception of one or two major efforts that did not appear to elicit much response or follow-up. An example was Symonds's efforts in TAT-type testing.[71] Many psychological tests for children do contain notations of their applicability for adolescent age ranges (typically to age fifteen). Few, however, have specific norms, materials, or instructions for this early-adolescent group. What is to happen to the person who has passed age fifteen but has not reached adulthood is often left even more obscure.

Hirsch[72] provided a scholarly model for adolescent assessment in his extensive reporting of psychological testing of young people conducted as part of the Menninger Foundation's programs. This book presented a wealth of clinical data from psychoanalytic ego psychology and humanistic perspectives. Hirsch emphasized the crucial factor of using special testing techniques when working with adolescents. Creating a threat to autonomy (with resultant defensiveness) by providing either too little or too much psychological distance was an issue explored in some detail. A guarantee of sure failure within a testing setting was noted as a predictable result if the tester attempted to be "just another adolescent" in a nongenuine effort to win the adolescent's cooperation by feigning a rejection of adulthood. Despite the undeniable value of this work, Hirsch tended to perpetuate the picture of the normative adolescent as distressed, rebellious, and in a state of psychological disruption. This is illustrated in his remark ascribing "a good deal of truth to the statement it is 'normal for the adolescent to act in an abnormal fashion' " and his endorsement of "psychological upheaval" as "par." This viewpoint seems to have been developed in direct relationship to the absence of any significant body of data on other than clinic-referred young people.

Other major contributions in formal psychological assessment of adolescents have appeared in texts dealing with figure drawings[73] and Rorschach responses.[74] Both provided much needed normative data for these widely used projective techniques. Also, MMPI data and analysis directions are available in a book by Hathaway and Monachesi.[75] The user of this assessment instrument is provided with protocols from normal as well as problem adolescents.

Public Education

Adequate public education relative to adolescence necessitates a dual approach. Both facets have considerable potential payoff (from a primary prevention perspective), and both require special expertise.

Adults. The first consideration is to provide parents with

information about adolescents and adolescence. Usdin succinctly tied down a central problem stating: "Articles fed to
the lay press have nearly succeeded in building the state of
growth called 'adolescence' into a singular disease entity."[76]
Appropriate information would destroy myths and reduce
concurrent maladaptive responses toward youth by adults
(e.g., negative labeling and self-fulfilling negative expectancies). It would also assist the parents in recognizing psychological problems exhibited by young people and in obtaining assistance for them rather than continuing the prevalent practice
of judging behavior on the basis of its "nuisance value."[77] Educational programs can circumvent conflict by assisting the
broader social systems to understand and to accept the
changes exhibited by the adolescent.[78] Furthermore, these
programs could help parents confront their own anxiety stem-
ming from the separation and individuation of their children.[79] From a transactional analysis view, recognizing and
facilitating a change from a parent-child to an adult-adult relationship is most crucial.[80]

Perhaps more obvious, such directive interchanges can also
provide a medium to discuss and teach documented positive
factors in child raising, such as parental cooperation, explicit
limits, and consistency.[81] The ramifications of parental attitudes toward physical development also need explicit coverage in adult education. As substantiated by Schonfeld,[82] family
attitudes have the power to promote adaptive psychological
development in adolescents with body defects, as well as to
create a lack of security and anxiety on the basis of trivial
deviations. Often parents are not aware of the high vulnerability of their adolescent to even an imaginary deviation from the
norm. Among many possible entries into discussions of sex and
sexuality, a strong case can be built for a primary need of
parental instruction in providing the structure necessary to
counteract the attitudes experienced by adolescent females
toward menstruation. Even in our enlightened epoch these
attitudes and the concurrent self-concept attributes are negative.[83]

In addition to using the typical media channels for public

education (e.g., newspapers, television, PTAs, service and work groups) a series of well-publicized open group discussions about adolescent psychological development held at high traffic areas (e.g., shopping malls, factory cafeterias) would reach many adults missed by most media presentations. To augment live discussions, the use of low or no cost lay reading material is recommended. Carlson[84] has edited a helpful booklet that provides a broad coverage of topics ranging from "How adolescents evoke adult hostility" to "On being an American parent." This is available without charge. To expand professional knowledge related to questions with a high probability of being raised by the public, the psychologist might well examine publications similar to that compiled by Semmens and Krantz.[85] This work provides twenty-three original papers designed to promote an understanding of sexual, social, and moral issues of adolescence.

Adolescents. Providing adolescents with information about adults can also be of considerable value. Often, young people are honestly confused by what parents do and say (especially in regard to adolescents). Helping youth understand the anxiety frequently experienced by parents, and adults in general, generated by adolescents is recommended. To promote an understanding of parental anxiety, the following topics should be explored in detail in any educational programs directed toward the young person: (1) the concern elicited in adults by reading the portrayal of adolescents in popular media which emphasizes deviancy and sensationalism; (2) adult insecurities about their own value systems and the types of defense responses that occur when insecure values are challenged; (3) the fear of losing control of and separation from children; (4) difficulties inherent in the "sexual revolution" and the more open communication about taboo topics; (5) the overinvestment that many parents have in their children to reflect favorably upon them and to provide vicarious satisfaction of parents' needs.

In establishing communication channels between parents and adolescents, the hazards of: (1) not using "straight" language, (2) promoting major confrontations on minor issues, and (3) not rewarding parents for their efforts should be outlined to the young person. In the process of this education for understanding, the adolescent will become more sensitive to the needs, desires, and reactions of adults. Resultantly, the development of a more empathic relationship is promoted.

Also important for the young person is the presentation of basic individual differences information. Given appropriate data on normal growth curves and developmental patterns, special psychological problems such as those associated with the self-perception of deviancy could be reduced. Teaching increased acceptance of body types and variations could also result in more general adaptive changes by reducing problem behaviors of adolescents that follow the frustration and anxiety contingent upon any undesirable deviation from the norm.[86]

Research

As can be readily determined from the relative overload of clinical reports to empirical studies cited in this paper, the need is indeed present for more extensive examination of clinical concepts and services to the adolescent. To mention only a few, studies on self-concepts, interaction styles, thought processes, perceptions of psychological problems, preferences for therapy services, and patterns of psychopathology would be of great value to the clinician, clinical trainer, and trainee. Detailed research directions are suggested in the Report of the Joint Commission.[87] However, to gather data on "adolescence" employing the typical research sample of "college freshmen enrolled in an introductory psychology course" would probably promote as much confusion as clarification within this area. While some of such a sample are indeed within the parameters of this developmental phase (employing the upper-end definition of "executive independence" as the termination of adolescence,[88] many are not. Also, adolescent or not, the college student remains (even in the face of college education becoming less and less unique) not representative of the bulk of adolescents. Thus, research must focus on broader and younger populations.

This requirement presents a number of hurdles that do not seem to be confronted with zest by most researchers: going into the community; establishing working relationships with public school administrative heirarchies; discovering and communicating with out-of-school social groupings; depending upon and enlisting the cooperation of the adolescent himself. These are certainly impeding factors but by no means insurmountable to an invested researcher.

CONCLUSION

A major goal of this paper has been to present a wide range of information relevant to clinical-adolescent psychology; discussions have emphasized the ramifications for client services. The use of such information can be considerably expanded. One such expansion is into the psychologist's role as a professional resource person for others. Another expansion is into the training of paraprofessionals. It is clear that the vast majority of problem adolescents will *not* be provided services by people who have completed extensive clinical training programs.[89] However, even within roles of consultant, trainer of paraprofessionals, or researcher, the materials presented in this paper are meaningful. Briefly, these are: adolescents are different from children and from adults; the differences are significant; and specialization of clinical training and applied efforts to meet the needs of adolescents is necessary.

References

1. H. S. Sullivan, *The Interpersonal Theory of Psychiatry* (New York: W. W. Norton, 1953).
2. A. Bryt, "Dropout of Adolescents from Psychotherapy: Failure in Communication," in *Adolescence: Psychosocial Perspective*, edited by G. Caplan and S. Lebovici, pp. 293–303 (New York: Basic Books; 1969); B. R. McCandless, *Adolescent Behavior and Development* (Hinsdale, Ill.: Dryden, 1970).
3. P. H. Mussen, J. J. Conger, and J. Kagen, *Child Development and Personality* (New York: Harper & Row, 1969).
4. For example: J. Horrocks, *The Psychology of Adolescence* (Boston: Houghton Mifflin, 1969); E. E. Hurlock, *Adolescent Development* (New York: McGraw-Hill, 1967); McCandless, see note 2; D. Rogers, *Adolescence: A Psychological Perspective* (Monterey, Calif.: Brooks-Cole, 1972).
5. J. Piaget, *The Language and Thought of the Child* (London: Routledge and Kegan Paul, 1952).
6. D. Elkind, "Cognitive Development in Adolescence," in *Understanding Adolescence*, edited by J. F. Adams, pp. 128–58 (Boston: Allyn and Bacon, 1968).
7. D. Elkind, "Egocentrism in Adolescence," *Child Development*, 1967, 38:1025–34.
8. R. E. Muss (ed.), *Theories of Adolescence* (New York: Random House, 1968).
9. A. Freud, "Adolescence," in *Psychoanalytic Study of the Child XIII*, edited by R. S. Eissler, A. Freud, H. Hartmann, and M. Kris, pp. 255–78 (New York: International Universities Press, 1958): K. Lewin, *A Dynamic Theory of Personality* (New York: McGraw-Hill, 1935).
10. R. J. Havighurst, *Developmental Tasks and Education* (New York: Longmans, 1951); E. Spranger, *Psychologie des Jugendalters* (Heidelberg: Quelle and Meyer, 1955).
11. F. Elkin and W. R. Westley, "The Myth of Adolescent Culture," *American Sociological Review*, 1955, 20:680–84; D. Friesen, "Value Orientations of Modern Youth," *Adolescence*, 1972, 7:265–75.
12. L. E. Larson, "The Influence of Parents and Peers During Adolescence," *Journal of Marriage and the Family*, 1972, p. 73.
13. Horrocks, see note 4.
14. D. Easton and R. D. Hess, "The Child's Political World," in *Adolescent Development*, edited by M. Gold and E. Douvan, pp. 284–91 (Boston: Allyn and Bacon, 1969).
15. J. H. Block, N. Haan, and M. B. Smith, "Activism and Apathy in Contemporary Adolescents," in *Understanding Adolescence*, pp. 198–231.
16. M. Mead, *Coming of Age in Samoa* (New York: New American Library, 1950).

17. M. Mead, "Adolescence in Primitive and Modern Society," in *Readings in Social Psychology*, edited by G. E. Swanson, T. M. Newcomb, and L. E. Hartley (New York: Henry Holt, 1952).
18. R. Benedict, "Continuities and Discontinuities in Cultural Conditioning," in *Readings in Child Development*, edited by W. Martin and C. Stendler, pp. 142–48 (New York: Harcourt, Brace, 1954).
19. M. Sherif and H. Cantril, *The Psychology of Ego-Involvements* (New York: Wiley, 1947).
20. D. Elkind, "Middle-Class Delinquency," *Mental Hygiene*, 1967, 51:- 38–84.
21. W. A. Schonfeld, "Inadequate Masculine Physique as a Factor in Personality Development of Adolescent Boys," *Psychosomatic Medicine*, 1950, 12:49–54.
22. J. R. Gallagher, *Medical Care of the Adolescent* (New York: Appleton-Century-Crofts, 1960).
23. G. S. Hall, *Adolescence* (New York: Appleton, 1961).
24. A. Freud, *The Ego and the Mechanism of Defense* (New York: International Universities Press, 1958).
25. Ibid., p. 275.
26. J. W. Kessler, *Psychopathology in Childhood* (Englewood Cliffs, N.J.: Prentice-Hall, 1966), p. 261.
27. Lewin, see note 9.
28. E. H. Erickson, *Childhood and Society* (New York: W. W. Norton, 1950).
29. Elkin and Westley, see note 11; R. D. Hess and I. Goldblatt, "The Status of Adolescents in American Society: A Problem in Social Identity," *Child Development*, 1957, 28:459–68.
30. E. Douvan and J. Adelson, *The Adolescent Experience* (New York: Wiley, 1966).
31. J. F. Masterson, *The Psychiatric Dilemma of Adolescence* (Boston: Little, Brown, 1967).
32. Spranger, see note 10.
33. Havighurst, see note 10.
34. For example, A. Davis, "Socialization and Adolescent Personality," in *Adolescence*, National Society for The Study of Education yearbook (Chicago: University of Chicago Press, 1944), part 1.
35. M. F. Shore, reviews of *Adolescent Psychiatry* (1971); *Adolescence* (1971), *Teaching and Learning Adolescent Psychiatry*, (1971), *Report of the White House Conference on Youth* (1971), *American Journal of Orthopsychiatry*, 1972, pp. 884–87.
36. I. Weiner, *Psychological Disturbance in Adolescence* (New York: Wiley-Interscience, 1970), p. 10.
37. J. F. Masterson, "The Symptomatic Adolescent Five Years Later: He Didn't Grow Out of It," *American Journal of Psychiatry*, 1967, 123: 1338–45.
38. G. L. Usdin, "Adolescence: An Overview," in *Adolescence: Care and Counseling*, edited by G. L. Usdin, pp. 9–15 (Philadelphia: Lippincott, 1967).

39. B. M. Rosen, A. K. Bahn, R. Shellow, and E. M. Bower, "Adolescent Patients Served in Outpatient Psychiatric Clinics," *American Journal of Public Health,* 1965, 55:1563–77.
40. Kessler (see note 26), p. 261.
41. Joint Commission on Mental Health of Children, *Crisis in Mental Health: Challenge for the 1970s* (New York: Harper & Row, 1970), p. 120.
42. H. G. Whittington, "Delivering Community Mental Health Services to Children and Adolescents, *"Mental Health Bulletin* (Lathrup Village, Mich.: Michigan Society for Mental Health), 1970, 26:1–16.
43. A. Freud, "Adolescence," see note 9.
44. For example, S. C. Feinstein, A. Giovacchini, and A. Miller (eds.), *Adolescent Psychiatry* (New York: Basic Books, 1971–72), 2 vols.
45. A. Winickoff and H. L. P. Resnik, "Student Suicide," *Today's Education,* 1971, pp. 30–72.
46. H. Bakwin, "Suicide in Children and Adolescents," *Journal of Pediatrics,* 1957, 50:749–69; R. Kestenbaum, "Time and Death in Adolescence," in *The Meaning of Death,* edited by H. Feifel, pp. 99–113 (New York: McGraw-Hill, 1959); J. Teicher, "Why Adolescents Kill Themselves," *Mental Health Program Reports—4* (Washington, D.C.: U.S. Department of Health, Education, and Welfare, 1970).
47. S. M. Finch and E. O. Pozneinski, *Adolescent Suicide* (New York: C. C. Thomas, 1971); J. Jacobs, *Adolescent Suicide* (New York: Wiley-Interscience, 1971).
48. Weiner, see note 36.
49. J. G. Howells (ed.), *Modern Perspectives in Adolescent Psychiatry* (New York: Brunner-Mazel, 1972); M. Josselyn, *Adolescence* (New York: Harper & Row, 1971); D. Offer and J. F. Masterson (eds.), *Teaching and Learning Adolescent Psychiatry* (Springfield, Ill.: Thomas, 1971).
50. Weiner, see note 36.
51. B. W. MacLennan and N. Felsenfeld, *Group Counseling and Psychotherapy with Adolescence* (New York: Columbia University Press, 1968).
52. A. Ellis, *Reason and Emotion in Psychotherapy* (New York: Lyle Stuart, 1962).
53. E. Berne, *Transactional Analysis in Psychotherapy* (New York: Grove, 1961).
54. J. D. Holmes, *The Adolescent in Psychotherapy* (Boston: Little, Brown, 1964).
55. T. Hammer and J. Holterman, "Referring Adcolescents for Psychotherapy," *Clinical Pediatrics,* 1965, 4:462–67.
56. A. H. Kaplan, "Joint Parent-Adolescent Interviews in the Psychotherapy of the Younger Adolescent," in *Adolescence: Psychosocial Perspectives,* edited by G. Caplan and S. Lebovici, p. 315 (New York: Basic Books, 1969).
57. J. L. Schimel, "Parents of Problem Children," in *Adolescence: Care and Counseling,* edited by G. L. Usdin, pp. 119–29 (Philadelphia: Lippincott, 1967).

58. M. M. Weissman and R. Siegel, "The Depressed Woman and Her Rebellious Adolescent," *Social Casework*, 1972, 53:563–70.
59. Ibid., p. 576.
60. M. L. Meacham, "Counseling Strategies with the Adolescent," in *Adolescents: Readings in Behavior and Development,* edited by E. D. Evans, pp. 298–310 (Hinsdale, Ill.: Dryden, 1970).
61. N. L. Farberow and E. S. Schneidman, *The Cry for Help* (New York: McGraw-Hill, 1961).
62. R. J. Greene and D. L. Crowder, "Group Psychotherapy with Adolescents: An Integrative Approach," *Journal of Contemporary Psychotherapy,* 1972, 5:56–61.
63. M. Rosenbaum, "Group Therapy with Adolescents," in *Manual of Child Psychopathology,* edited by B. B. Wolman, pp. 951–68 (New York: McGraw-Hill, 1972).
64. E. K. Ross and J. R. Anderson, "Psychotherapy with the Least Expected," *Rehabilitation Literature,* 1968, 39:73–76.
65. I. M. Berkovitz (ed.), *Adolescents Group in Groups: Experiences in Adolescent Group Psychotherapy* (New York: Brunner-Mazel, 1972); MacLennan and Felsenfeld, see note 51.
66. B. Lubin, A. Lubin, and D. Sargent, "The Group Psychotherapy Literature 1971," *International Journal of Group Psychotherapy,* 1972, 23:492–529.
67. Rosenbaum, see note 63.
68. J. Shafer and S. V. Hansen, "Using Behavior Therapy with Selected Adolescent Patients," *Hospital and Community Psychiatry,* 1973, 24:30–32.
69. R. B. Stuart, "Behavioral Contracting Within the Families of Delinquents," *Journal of Behavior Therapy and Experimental Psychiatry,* 1971, 2:1–11.
70. P. G. Beckett, *Adolescents out of Step: Their Treatment in a Psychiatric Hospital* (Detroit: Wayne State University Press, 1965); W. M. Easson, *The Severely Disturbed Adolescent* (New York: International Universities Press, 1969); E. Hartmann and G. Adler, *Adolescents in a Mental Hospital* (New York: Grune, 1968).
71. P. M. Symonds, *Adolescent Fantasy* (New York: Columbia University Press, 1949).
72. E. A. Hirsch, *The Troubled Adolescent* (New York: International Universities Press, 1970).
73. M. Schildkrout, I. R. Shenker, and M. S. Sonnenblick, *Human Figure Drawings in Adolescence* (New York: Brunner-Mazel, 1972).
74. L. B. Ames, R. W. Metraux, and R. N. Walker, *Adolescent Rorschach Responses* (New York: Hoeber, 1954).
75. S. R. Hathaway and E. D. Monachesi, *Adolescent Personality and Behavior* (Minneapolis: University of Minnesota Press, 1963).
76. Usdin (see note 38), p. 13.
77. L. Kanner, "Emotional Disturbances in Adolescence," in *Counseling the Adolescent,* edited by A. A. Schneiders, pp. 173–81 (San Francisco:

Chandler, 1967).

78. E. J. Friedenberg, *The Vanishing Adolescent* (Boston: Beacon Press, 1959).

79. M. D. Schechter, P. W. Toussieng, and R. E. Sternlof, "Normal Development in Adolescence," in *Manual of Child Psychopathology*, edited by B. B. Wolman, pp. 22–45 (New York: McGraw-Hill, 1972).

80. T. A. Harris, *I'm OK—You're OK* (New York: Harper & Row, 1969).

81. R. R. Grinker, Sr., R. R. Grinker, Jr., and J. Timberlake, "Mentally Healthy Young Males (Homoclites)," *Archives of General Psychiatry*, 1962, 6:405–53.

82. W. A. Schonfeld, "Body Image Disturbances in Adolescents," *Archives of General Psychiatry*, 1966, 15:16–21.

83. G. Caplan, "Elements of a Comprehensive Community Health Program for Adolescents," in *Adolescence: Psychosocial Perspective*, pp. 372–86; McCandless, see note 2.

84. D. R. Carlson (ed.), "Adolescence for Adults" (Chicago: Blue Cross Association, 1970).

85. J. P. Semmens and K. E. Krants (eds.), *The Adolescent Experience* (New York: Macmillan, 1970).

86. McCandless, see note 2.

87. Joint Commission, see note 41.

88. D. P. Ausubel, *Theory and Problems of Adolescent Development* (New York: Grune and Stratton, 1954).

89. Caplan, see note 83.

Part 3

Therapeutic Modalities

and Innovations

Effective Therapist Interpersonal Skills: The Search Goes On[1]

KEVIN M. MITCHELL

DURING THE PAST DECADE, RESEARCH IN INDIVIDUAL PSY-
chotherapy attained a level of rigor and sophistication un-
matched during any previous period. Nevertheless, we have
failed to identify even *one* therapist variable that has been
shown to be related reliably to positive client outcome across
that heterogeneous array of therapists presently practicing individual psychotherapy in the United States. The result is that,
at this time, clinical training programs—whether in clinical
psychology, psychiatry, or social work—have nothing substan-
tive to offer trainees that relates directly and specifically to
training in individual psychotherapy.

The primary basis for these conclusions is a recently completed NIHM-supported study of the antecedents of effective
individual psychotherapy. The outcome data were generated
by a nationwide, reasonably representative sample of seventy-
five experienced psychotherapists, approximately half of
whom were in private practice and a majority of whom considered themselves to be primarily eclectic or psychoanalytic in
orientation.

Some general comments regarding the nature of client and
therapist variables are necessary prior to a description of the

study and presentation of those findings that relate selected therapist characteristics and client change. The purpose of this paper, then, is to examine in some detail those data relevant to the relationships between client change and the therapist interpersonal skills of empathy, warmth, and genuineness. Examination of those specific therapist variables—is based on the fact that, excluding the present study and only one other, the extant research regarding psychotherapy outcome strongly suggests that only these three therapist characteristics have been found to be related consistently to positive client outcome.

Client Variables

It should be noted that a substantial body of research provides data that have been viewed as indicating that a number of client characteristics, as well as client-therapist similarity along certain dimensions, are related to client change.

In the context of developing effective therapists, the only reasonable training strategy is that clients should be seen as "givens" and not within the purview of a training program. A more important reason for emphasizing therapist characteristics, however, is that perhaps the predictive and certainly the causal status of client variables as well as client-therapist similarity, measured before or during therapy, are open to question. Barbara Lerner, although focusing on psychotherapy with the disadvantaged,[2] provides some interesting data that suggest that such variables are not related *directly* to outcome. A reasonable alternative is that these are client personality characteristics or behaviors that therapists *believe* to be related to successful psychotherapy; and, therefore, therapist perception, or perhaps more to the point, therapist personality, is *the generic* variable in outcome research.

Therapist Variables

The review of outcome research by Luborsky et al.[3] is the most comprehensive one to date. Of approximately twelve variables that appear to be related *reliably* to outcome, these authors cite only two therapist variables—empathy and experience. Unfortunately, experience is a variable of limited value if one is interested in something more than merely *selecting* effective therapists, i.e., developing a program to *train* effective therapists.

In connection with empathy, the stance, or perhaps a better word is convenience, of calling certain variables "therapist" and others "client" deserves scrutiny. When a variable, for instance a demographic variable, is measured *prior to psychotherapy* it seems straightforward enough to ascribe it to a therapist or client. However, when the measurement occurs during the process of therapy, it seems to be much more difficult to talk about "purely" therapist or client variables. Perhaps all variables that are generated during therapy, to one degree or another, are interreactional in nature. However, a good deal of controversy exists on this point. For example, Truax and Mitchell[4] cite a number of studies that suggest that empathy, warmth, and genuiness are interpersonal skills possessed by the therapist-as-therapist and as-person. That is, these are interpersonal skills of the therapist that are exhibited to a similar degree across a number of different clients and in different interpersonal situations. In other words, these are fairly permanent personality characteristics as well as interpersonal skills. Van der Veen,[5] however, using some of the same data as Truax and Mitchell, but different statistical analyses, concluded that both therapist and client contribute to the levels of empathy, warmth, and genuiness exhibited in therapy. Clearly, research that gets at the issue more *directly* is needed. We must admit to some discomfort over the prospect of an important *clinical* issue being resolved on a strictly *statistical* basis. Ironically, in all these studies therapists were not asked if they responded differently to different clients.

Carkhuff and his colleagues[6] in a series of analog and quasi-therapy studies have reported the results of the experimental manipulation of clients' behavior on therapists' functioning. The data indicate that when an experimental "client" is instructed to do so, he can manipulate the levels of empathy, warmth, and genuineness offered by his "therapist." Although these studies clearly demonstrate that a client *can* influence his therapist's functioning, it has not yet been shown that clients do so in actual therapy.

On a purely intuitive level, it does not seem likely that a therapist is empathic, warm, and genuine totally independently of the person with whom his is purportedly involved in a relationship of some depth and intensity. Indeed, if these skills are relatively permanent personality characteristics of the therapist that were learned originally during early interactions with significant others and then expanded, amplified, and crystallized in subsequent interactions throughout his life, then they may be skills that are important to him and, consequently, more likely to change from client to client than characteristics that are less valued. In other words, whereas earlier the authors felt that relatively permanent characteristics of the therapist would not change appreciably from client to client, their present feeling is that if such characteristics, in addition, *are valued by the therapist* they may be *more* vulnerable to the vicissitudes of psychotherapy. Thus, the possibility we are most inclined toward at this time is that a therapist's *capacity* to be empathic, warm, and genuine is relatively fixed by the time he is an adult. But the degree to which he *exhibits* these skills is a function of both therapist and client.

The relative contribution of therapist and client to a particular in-therapy behavior is an important issue, particularly for those of us engaged in training therapists. Further research is necessary and, in that regard, perhaps the following observations might be helpful:

1. The most effective "therapist variables" may be those that are uniquely relevant to each particular therapist-client dyad. If this is the case, then it would be a mistake to continue to attempt to identify broad "therapist variables" that are effective in most if not all psychotherapy, or that are effective even for one therapist with most of his clients.[7]

2. However, if certain generally effective therapist characteristics exist, it may be of value to keep certain distinctions in

mind. Therapist variables may be categorized as attitudes, findings, personality characteristics, and behaviors, and these may be differentially related to variation with different clients. Furthermore, therapist variables may be learned or "inherent," and these also may be related differentially to variation as a function of the client as might characteristics that are learned early or later in life. The latter provide, incidentally, still a third among any number of possible classifications of "therapist variables."

3. One should distinguish between therapist variables measured before therapy, as opposed to during therapy. Among the latter, some variables more than others may be more a function of the therapist rather than the client, but very likely none are purely "therapist variables."

4. The distinction between a therapist's *capacity* to be empathic, for example, and the *actual* level of empathy he offers each client may be important.

5. Finally, therapists probably differ with respect to certain interpersonal skills regardless of the client. Thus, while each therapist may vary his level of empathy, for example, *within a certain range* as a function of the client, one therapist may be consistently higher with all his clients than another, all other things being equal.

With the understanding that, empathy, warmth, and genuineness are referred to as therapist variables as a convenience, the remainder of the paper is concerned with the relationship of these interpersonal skills to outcome in individual psychotherapy.

OVERVIEW OF THE LITERATURE REGARDING
EMPATHY, WARMTH, AND GENUINENESS

As mentioned, Luborsky et al.[8] cited empathy as a therapist variable that has been related consistently to outcome. Although the evidence is not as strong, a similar case can be made for therapist warmth and genuineness.[9] Truax and Mitchell[10] cite fourteen studies carried out between 1963 and

1969 in which the effect of empathy on outcome was investigated. In these studies, 24 specific outcome measures, of a total of 109, supported the hypothesis that empathy is related significantly and positively to client outcome, whereas no findings in the opposite direction reached statistical significance. With respect to warmth, twelve studies are cited in which 34 of 108 outcome measures supported the hypothesis that warmth is related significantly and positively to outcome, whereas, again, no findings in the opposite direction reached statistical significance. Finally, with respect to genuineness, eight studies are cited in which 20 of 88 measures supported the hypothesis that genuineness is significantly and positively related to outcome. With respect to genuineness, however, six outcome measures supported the hypothesis that genuineness was significantly and negatively related to client outcome.

Until very recently, the evidence indicating that therapist levels of empathy, warmth, and genuineness are related to client improvement appeared to be quite strong. Nevertheless, Matarazzo[11] and Meltzoff and Kornreich[12] questioned the validity of some of the studies. They suggested that, in many cases, the number of therapists was small; and, in an unknown number of instances, the therapists may have been aware of the particular hypotheses, and even associated with the research effort. Although it would be hard to document in retrospect, it appears likely that, at the very least, a substantial proportion of the therapists who participated in these studies were client-centered in orientation.

Two recent studies,[13] based on samples of therapists who were largely eclectic in orientation, would seem to offer support for the reservations voiced by Matarazzo[14] and Meltzoff and Kornreich.[15] Garfield and Bergin,[16] in a study of advanced level graduate studies in clinical psychology, found that therapist levels of empathy, warmth, or genuineness were not related significantly to outcome. The Mitchell et al. study,,[17] which will be described in more detail later, was based upon a nationwide, reasonably representative sample of seventy-five experienced psychotherapists, a significant proportion of whom were in private practice and a majority of whom were eclectic or psychoanalytic in orientation. The single most important finding was that therapist levels of empathy and warmth were not at all related differentially to client change, and therapist levels of genuineness were at best only modestly related. These results, in addition to those of Garfield and Bergin,[18] lead to the unavoidable, possibly uncomfortable, but preferably the exciting, conclusion that *twenty years of increasingly rigorous and sophisticated research has failed to identify any therapist characteristic that has been related reliably to client improvement when the study is based on a sample of therapists sufficiently heterogeneous in nature to be representative of those experienced clinicians presently offering individual psychotherapy in the United States.*

THE THERAPISTS

From the 1966 American Psychological and Psychiatric Association Directories, a large number of psychologists and psychiatrists were asked to participate in the NIMH-supported psychotherapy project. They were chosen randomly from both directories if they indicated that the practice of psychotherapy was a primary interest. Eventually 120 therapists (one percent of all those therapists who were asked to participate) and 258 clients contributed data of some kind to the project. We decided to include in the outcome analyses those cases that had pretherapy and posttherapy scores on at least *one* major measure: the Psychiatric Status Schedule (PSS), MMPI, or Q-sort. Included in the outcome analyses, then, were 75 therapists and 120 clients.

Demographic characteristics of the 75 outcome therapists included: 95 percent had a Ph.D. or M.D.; their median age was 42; and 49 percent were in private practice. Approximately 55 percent had had at least three years of supervised psychotherapy experience, and 44 percent reported that they tape recorded their psychotherapy either "frequently" or "routinely." Finally, with respect to *present* practice orientation, 36 percent referred to themselves as primarily eclectic, 34 percent were psychoanalytically oriented, and only 7 percent were client-centered.

Regarding representativeness of the sample of therapists in the outcome study, the 75 therapists were compared on a number of demographic characteristics with four groups of therapists who varied along a continuum that might best be described as willingness to participate in the study: (1) those who responded to the initial invitiation by indicating definitely that they would not participate (N = 80); (2) those who initially indicated that they might participate but subsequently did not (N = 47); (3) those who did not respond to the initial invitation to participate in the research project, but who did complete a second Biographical Information form (BI) sent specifically for the purpose of determining the demographic representativeness of the project sample (N = 60); and (4) those who did not complete either the first or second BI but who agreed to answer the items during a telephone interview (N = 61).

The five groups of therapists were compared on: (1) age, (2) sex, (3) marital stuatus, (4) paternal socioeconomic background, (5) present social class of typical client, (6) training orientation, (7) practice orientation, (8) number of years of supervised psychotherapy experience, (9) degree, (10) type of practice or setting, (11) amount of past tape recording, and (12) diagnosis of *typical* client. Only *age* (F = 3.53, p < .01) and *mean number of years of supervised psychotherapy training* (F = 2.42, p < .05) significantly differentiated among the five groups. The project participants, on the average, were younger than any of the other groups and indeed were four years younger than the therapists who initially indicated that they definitely would not participate. Such differences, however, must be viewed in light of the fact that the present therapists were experienced, and their median age was 42. In addition, 99 percent had an Ed.D., Ph.D., or M.D. The present therapists were also those who, on the average, had received the least amount of supervised psychotherapy training, but the largest difference between any two groups was less than one year.

The 75 outcome therapists also were compared on the same twelve demographic variables with the 47 therapists who, although they contributed some data to the project, were not included in the outcome analyses. Only one variable, *discipline*, differentiated significantly between the two groups of therapists. Of the therapists who provided at least one outcome case, 62 percent were clinical psychologists and 38 percent were psychiatrists. Of those therapists who did not provide at least one outcome case, 33 percent were clinical psychologists and 67 percent were psychiatrists.

It should be mentioned that, despite the fact that the present therapists appeared to be quite representative of the population of therapists from whom they were drawn as far as relevant demographic variables were concerned, they made up less than one percent of all those therapists who were asked initially to participate. No doubt, they differed alongsomedimensions that were not measured in the present study. One possible criterion for participating was that the present therapists were younger, therefore perhaps less involved in administration and, thus, more likely to engage in research.

THE CLIENTS

Demographic characteristics of the 120 outcome clients included: 80 percent were under age 35; 99 percent were white; 59 percent were female; and 80 percent reported an income of $7,000 or less per year. Diagnostically, based on the PSS, 37 percent were schizophrenic; 29 percent, neurotic; 13 percent had a sociopathic personality; and 16 percent were judged to be "normal." For 22 percent, the length of therapy was one to two months; and for another 22 percent, from three to six months; 28 percent were in therapy for more than six months but less than one year; while another 22 percent were in therapy for more than one year and up to as much as three years. In other words, 44 percent of the outcome clients were in therapy for at least six months and 22 percent for more than one year. Approximately 50 percent had 20 sessions or less; 43

percent had between 20 and 100 sessions; and 7 percent had more than 100 sessions.

Two kinds of client representativeness were of interest: (1) the degree to which the clients were representative of the population of clients seen in psychotherapy nationally from 1966–1970; and (2) the degree to which they were representative of the project therapists' case loads.

In determining the degree to which the *therapists* in the present study were representative of the population of therapists listed in both 1966 professional directories, four comparison groups were used. However, no such clearly appropriate *client* groups were available for the present quite heterogeneous group of clients.

Consequently, comparisons were made between the private practice and public clinic outpatients, who made up the largest single group of clients (72 percent), and the sample of outpatients reported by Strupp, Fox, and Lessler.[19] These investigators felt that the group they obtained was representative of all outpatients in the United States who had received psychotherapy during the late 1950s and early 1960s. Taking into consideration some qualifications that make the compairson a fairly gross one, the two groups of outpatients seemed to be reasonably similar in age, sex, marital status, income, and number of sessions. In addition, in terms of length of therapy, both in months and number of sessions, the present outcome clients were quite similar to those receiving psychotherapy in the United States during the late sixties.[20]

Whether or not the outcome clients were representative of their therapists' case loads presented additional problems. First, an examination of a random sample of therapist-client pairs included in the outcome analyses indicated that no therapist took more than two months to provide client data from the time he indicated his intention to participate by naming an independent psychometrist to actual participation. In addition, the 120 outcome clients were compared with the remaining 138 clients who were not included in the outcome study on the following demographic variables: sex, marital status, income, geographical location, diagnostic category, therapy setting, number of sessions, and length of therapy. Only two variables, *number of sessions, and length of therapy,* differentiated significantly between the two groups of clients (X^2 = 53.99, p < .001; X^2 = 45.93, p < .001, respectively). Such differences, however, would be expected on the bases of how the two groups were defined. However, they did not differ significantly on sex, marital status, income, geographical location, diagnostic category, or therapy setting. Consequently, while the conclusions must be seen as somewhat tentative, it would appear that: (1) the outcome clients were at least fairly representative of those clients receiving individual psychotherapy in the late 1950s and throughout the 1960s; and (2) they were also reasonably representative of their therapists' case loads except for length of therapy both in terms of number of months and number of sessions. However, it is impossible to tell if the latter represent "real" differences or if they are artifacts of how the present outcome clients were defined.

PROCESS AND OUTCOME MEASURES

This section includes a description of the outcome measures and more detailed definitions of the process measures of therapist empathy, warmth, and genuineness.

Outcome Measures

1. *Current Adjustment Rating Scale (CARS).* The CARS is a 14-item scale that purports to measure current functioning in a number of areas. It was developed initially by Miles, Barrabee, and Finesinger[21] and subsequently revised for the present study.

The CARS' brevity is a major reason for its inclusion, since therapists could complete it in less than ten minutes. The CARS was an important outcome instrument in the present study because it was completed by therapist, psychometrist, client, and friend of client, thereby giving us four perceptions of each client's pretherapy and posttherapy adjustment based on the same instrument.

2. *Social Ineffectiveness Scale (SIS)*. Psychometrists were instructed to complete the SIS based on information elicited from the client during the administration of the Psychiatric Status Schedule (PSS).

The SIS was initially constructed as a client outcome measure in connection with a series of psychotherapy research studies conducted at the Henry Phipps Psychiatric Institute, John Hopkins University Medical School.[21] It purports to measure seven active and seven passive modes of social ineffectiveness, as well as extent of sexual maladjustment. The SIS has been found to differentiate significantly between clients prepared systematically for therapy and those not prepared[22] and between clients who received only minimal therapeutic contact and those receiving traditional individual and group psychotherapy.[23] In each case, those clients who experienced more preparation or contact were significantly less socially ineffective after psychotherapy.

3. *Psychiatric Status Schedule (PSS)* The PSS is an open-ended but structured interview that was completed by the psychometrist. Seventeen symptom or *micro*-scales, indicative of particular symptoms as well as a validity check, have been established as well as four broader factors, termed *macro*-scales, based on specific clusters of the *micro*-scales: (1) subjective distress; (2) behavioral disturbance, (3) impulse control disturbance, and (4) reality testing disturbance. The PSS also provides scores on five innovative *role* scales: (1) wage earner, (2) housekeeper, (3) student-trainee, (4) mate, (5) parent, and (6) a summary role based on the five role scales. Finally, computer analysis also provides a diagnostic classification system that is quite similar to traditional psychiatric concepts.

Spitzer, Endicott, Fleiss, and Cohen[24] have reported reliability estimates for certain scales of the PSS. The *internal consistencies* of the four *macro* or summary scales ranged from .80 to .89; for the seventeen symptom scales, from .43 for agitation-excitement to .93 for alcohol abuse; and for the individual role scales, from .65 for parent role to .80 for student role.

In an earlier study,[25] which focused on the concurrent validity of the computer-based diagnoses of clients, agreement between computer and clinical diagnoses equaled the diagnostic agreement of two groups of clinicians given the same information. In addition, it was also demonstrated that these computer-derived diagnoses were in substantial agreement with diagnoses made by a third sample of psychiatrists functioning in a setting where they knew the clients well, as contrasted with the usual study where the criterion psychiatrists merely have to read a protocol or watch a "one-shot" interview.

4. *Psychiatric Outpatient Mood Scale (POMS)*. The POMS was constructed initially by Lorr et al.[26] to measure mood change during the week previous to the client's completing the scale. The scale used in the present study conforms closely to the third revision, first reported by Lorr, McNair, and Weinstein[27] as a measure of the *early* effects of drugs and psychotherapy. Lorr and McNair[28] used data based on Part II of the revised POMS to generate five factors: (1) Factor T, tension, anxiety; (2) Factor A, anger, hostility; (3) Factor F, fatigue, inertia; (4) Factor D, depression; (5) Factor V, vigor, activity, —as well as two tentative factors: Factor Q, friendliness; and Factor B, confusion.

In a review of studies using the POMS, Lorr and McNair reported that the first five scales have been shown to be effective in detecting changes over four- and eight-week periods of short-term psychotherapy with concomitant use of tranquilizers. In their view,[29] the POMS, Part II, ". . . represents a fairly sensitive measure of transient affective changes for up to twelve weeks. Not only drug and placebo effects are reflected but also early effects of psychotherapy, the relief of such complaints as undue tension, fatigue, and irritability."[30]

5. *Q-Sort*. Five different Q-Sort measures were generated from two client sorts-self and ideal.

In addition to the usual scoring of self- and ideal-self concepts, the sorts were scored by a method described by Dymond,[31] which yields both self and ideal "adjustment" scores.

It also was possible to compare clients' self and ideal Q-Sorts with the "expert" Q-Sort devised by Lewis.[32] The latter is an array based on the ideal sorts made by fourteen counselors at the University of Chicago Counseling Center.

The measures of self-concept employed in the present study, then, were as follows: (1) self-adjustment Q-Sort scores, (2) ideal adjustment Q-Sort scores, (3) the correlation between self and expert Q-Sorts, (4) the correlation between self and ideal Q-Sorts, and (5) the correlation between ideal and expert Q-Sorts.

6. *Minnesota Multiphasic Personality Inventory (MMPI).* The MMPI responses were analyzed in the usual manner using the K-corrected raw scores. In addition to scoring the traditional clinical scales and the sum of clinical scales, other scales used in the present study were: (1) *A*, which has been described as an anxiety or a general emotional upset factor;[33] (2) *R*, which has been related to the defense mechanisms of denial and rationalization and to a lack of effective self-insight;[34] (3) *ES*, an ego strength scale devised by Barron as a measure of latent personality strength and as a predictor of client response to therapy; (4) *SDS* (So-r), a measure of social desirability first devised by Fordyce[36] and revised by Edwards;[37] and (5) the revised Repression-Sensitizer Scale (R—S).[38]

Process Measures

Three sets of three raters each independently rated one of the three therapist interpersonal skills: empathy, warmth, and genuineness. The majority of the raters were female, otherwise unemployed, and in most cases wives of faculty or students. As has been the case in the earlier research using these scales, the raters were unfamiliar with psychotherapy generally and, in particular, with the hypotheses of the present study. Each rater was trained only on that scale she eventually rated and was accepted as a rater only if, within two weeks, the Pearson Product-moment correlation between her ratings of previously rated therapy segments and so-called "expert" ratings reached at least .50. For those who may be interested, both the scales and the rater training are described in more detail elsewhere.[39] For rating purposes, each case provided five three-minute segments, or fifteen minutes of psychotherapy, taken from each fifth portion of the therapy. The number of sessions representing each fifth of the total therapy was determined arithmetically, and the session closest to each one-fifth of case length was selected. An objection which might be raised quite legitimately is that five three-minute samples, or a total of fifteen minutes of therapy, is not enough to serve as a basis for rating fairly complex skills over the course of therapy which, in some instances, lasted for more than two years. Indeed, objections arose among the research staff, but time and expense dictated against increasing the number of segments. However, although the present report uses these ratings, a grant will be submitted to NIMH proposing, among other things, that additional ratings first be gathered on a random sample of thirty cases and, if the findings so indicate, additional ratings of all ratings of all cases will be taken.

We also have clients' and therapists' perceptions of these variables, taken at the end of the fifth therapy session. Although these data are quite interesting in their own right, they do not in any way contradict any of the conclusions reached in the present paper.

Ebel inter-rater reliability estimates[40] based on the mean of K raters (i.e., more than two raters) were: empathy, .67; warmth, .63; and genuineness, .79. These reliability estimates were quite high considering the restricted range of each of the process scores, a finding that will be examined in more detail later.

Pearson product-moment correlations between the tape ratings of three process variables indicated that they were fairly independent. Empathy and warmth were found to correlate significantly ($r = .42$, $p < .05$), but neither empathy and genuineness nor warmth and genuineness were *at all* related ($r = .10$; $r = .07$, respectively).

Table 1 shows the means and standard deviations of tape-rated empathy, warmth, and genuineness.

TABLE 1

Means and Standard Deviations of Therapist
Levels of Empathy, Warmth, and Genuineness.

Empathy		Warmth		Genuineness	
Mean	SD	Mean	SD	Mean	SD
2.3	.7	2.1	.3	2.3	.4

Clients were grouped into four quartiles, from lowest to highest, separately on the basis of each of the three scale scores for a number of analyses of covariance.

To make the outcome findings as meaningful as possible, it should be mentioned at this point that all three tape-rated process scores were lower and more restricted in range than scores reported in earlier studies. Only 14 of 120 clients received a mean level of empathy over the entire course of their therapy, which was judged to reach at least stage three, although empathy was measured on a nine-point scale; and only 20 and 13 clients respectively received at least levels of 2.5 on the five-point warmth and genuineness scales, respectively.

It is likely that the low scores and restricted ranges were at least in part responsible for the overriding lack of significant relationships between the three therapist measures and client change. However, the interpretation of these findings will be discussed further after the outcome data have been presented.

In the Results section which follows, it should be noted that our bias favoring therapist over client variables as the essential element in effective psychotherapy led us to restrict this paper to a presentation of those data relating the therapist interpersonal skills of empathy, warmth, and genuineness to client change. For clarity, it should be indicated that two different statistical models were used in examining the data: analysis of covariance and simple correlation. The size of the resultant N in most analyses mitigated against the planned use of both additive and multiplicative regression analyses.

RESULTS: I. RELATIONSHIPS BETWEEN
DIFFERENTIAL LEVELS OF THERAPIST EMPATHY,
WARMTH, AND GENUINENESS AND CLIENT CHANGE

Based upon *rater* levels of the therapist interpersonal skills, the 120 clients were divided into four quartiles (highest, high, low, lowest) separately on each of the three process measures. The cut-off points for selecting the different groups were based on inspection of histograms generated by the present data as well as data from previous research.[41] Three sets of analyses of covariance were computed: (1) with clients divided into *two* groups (higher and lower), that is, collapsing the four qualities into two groups on each of the process measures; (2) with clients divided into the four quartile groups; and (3) with clients who comprised the two extreme quartile groups, that is, the highest and lowest groups.

In view of the low magnitude (typically below 3.0) and restricted ranges of all three of the interpersonal skill measures, as a preliminary safeguard in advance of the outcome analyses, one-way analyses of variance were performed to determine if the groups of clients who had been categorized as described were significantly different from each other. In addition, chi-square tests were used to determine if the number of clients in each group was approximately normally distributed. Whether clients were cast into two groups of higher and lower, into four groups based on quartiles, or the two extreme groups of highest and lowest, separate one-way analyses of covariance indicated that the groups of clients so formed were significantly different from each other on empathy, warmth, and genuineness. In addition, none of the chi-squares was statistically significant, indicating that the number of clients in each of the groups described was approximately normally distributed.

Total Group

The total group analyses involved, then, three independent sets of analyses: (1) higher vs. lower; and (2) highest vs. high vs.

low vs. lowest, and (3) highest vs. lowest.

Higher Versus Lower Process Groups. Analyses of covariance were used to compare the amount of change experienced by the two groups of clients as a function of therapists' levels of empathy, warmth, and genuineness. The dependent measure was the difference score between the clients' posttherapy and pretherapy scores; the covariate was the particular pretherapy score. Based on all the subscales or items that comprised the six measures, 165 analyses of covariance were computed for each of the three interpersonal skill scores for a grand total of 660 analyses of covariance.

Before presenting the findings, mention should be made of the lack of control groups in the present study. In the early exploration of most "treatment procedures," it is necessary to compare "treated" to "untreated" control clients. This approach assumes that the treatment is a relatively unitary one, an assumption that seems quite untenable in the case of psychotherapy. The focus of the present study was not on "treated vs. untreated" clients but, instead, upon the *differential* effects of specified levels of the three therapist interpersonal skills. In this sense, the present investigation is analogous to pharmacology studies involving drug-response curves and to studies in experimental psychology of intensity levels of stimuli upon conditioning. In short, much of the present research was aimed at a parametric approach.

On the other hand, it should be clear that the change scores in the present study can be compared to other data concerning base rate expectancies for spontaneous recovery rates among hospitalized patients, outpatients, and counseling center clients.

When clients were divided independently into high and low *empathy* and *warmth* groups, in each case only approximately two percent of the analyses of covariance of the 165 items resulted in significant differences between the two groups. On the basis of the large number of analyses actually computed and the small number of significant findings, the significant differences should be seen simply as random occurrences.

However, with respect to genuineness, on more than two-thirds of the 165 outcome scores clients who received higher levels of genuineness from their therapists demonstrated a greater degree of positive personality change than clients receiving lower levels. All the nineteen statistically significant differences favored the therapists with higher genuineness. The number of significant differences, while not large, were above the expected random level of occurrence and, consequently, the differences between the two groups of clients on these nineteen items may be viewed as statistically and clinically meaningful. These findings favoring clients receiving higher levels of genuineness are of particular importance for two reasons: (1) in these analyses, neither therapist levels of empathy nor warmth were related to outcome; and (2) in *past* studies, genuineness generally has not been as strongly related to client change as have empathy and warmth. Thus, the present study is the first in which genuineness was found to be more strongly related to outcome than therapist empathy and warmth.

Comparison of the Four Quartile Groups and the Highest and Lowest Quartile Groups. When clients were divided into four groups, the proportion of overall significant differences for each process measure was: empathy, 7 percent, warmth, 2 percent, and genuineness, 5 percent. When the two most extreme groups on each of the three process measures were compared, the proportion of significant differences for each process measure was: empathy, 2 percent, warmth, 3.5 percent, and genuineness, 4 percent. Consequently, all significant differences based on these categorizations of clients appeared to have been random occurrences.

Neurotics And Psychotics

Higher Versus Lower Groups. As in the preceding section, tape ratings of therapist empathy, warmth, and genuineness were used to group neurotics and psychotics separately into high and low groups on each of the three process measures, using the same cutoff points as were used previously for all clients. Division into four quartile groups and the two extreme groups was not pursued.

A total of 465 analyses of covariance were computed separately for the neurotic and psychotic groups of clients. For both groups, only 51 of the total 928 analyses of covariance, or barely 5 percent were statistically significant. For the neurotics, the number of significant findings was 24 of 464 analyses, or less than 5 percent; and for the psychotics, 27 of 464 analyses, or slightly more than 6 percent. Again, it was concluded that the significant findings were likely random occurrences.

Comparisons Between Clients with the Greatest Positive and Least Positive Psychological Change: The positive and negative change client groups were formed by selecting from seven to fourteen clients from each end of the total distribution of change scores, with the stipulation that there be no overlap on the following nine client outcome scales: PSS Total Score, PSS Subjective Distress, PSS Summary Role, MMPI Ego Strength, MMPI Sum of Clinical, Q-Sort Self-Adjustment, and Overall Adjustment Scores from the CARS (Therapist), CARS (Client), and CARS (Psychometrist). Thus, the clients were classified separately on each of the outcome measures and then compared separately on levels of empathy, warmth, and genuineness received in therapy. None of the three therapist interpersonal skills differentiated significantly between those clients who changed the most in a positive direction and those clients who changed the least, or in a negative direction.

RESULTS: II. CORRELATIONS BETWEEN THERAPIST EMPATHY, WARMTH, AND GENUINENESS AND SELECTED OUTCOMES

Pearson product-moment correlations were computed between empathy, warmth, and separately, and the same nine change scores that had been used in examining differences between clients who showed the most and least positive change.

For all clients, empathy was significantly related to only one change score (MMPI sum of Clinical scales); warmth, to none; and genuineness, to three (PSS Total Score, PSS Subjective Distress, and Psychometrist [CARS]).

For neurotics, neither empathy nor genuineness were significantly related to any of the criterion change scores; warmth, to only two (MMPI ES, and PSS Total Score).

For psychotics, none of the three process variables was correlated significantly with any of the seven criteria change scores.

THE EFFECT: HOW MUCH DID CLIENTS ACTUALLY CHANGE

The nature of the design obscured an obvious question that occurred to us very late in the project and largely in the context of trying to come to grips with the lack of significant findings. Did the clients, in fact, change? Did we have an effect at all? It was decided to test for the significance of change from pretherapy to posttherapy by repeated measures analyses of variance. It should be noted, of course, that change that is statistically significant may not necessarily be of such magnitude to be clinically meaningful. In addition, since a control group of "no treatment" clients was not used in the present study, it can only be inferred tentatively that change was a function of psychotherapy. Clients were categorized diagnostically on the basis of the PSS and change on each of the 165 items was looked at separately. The majority of changes for the three client groups were in a positive direction: neurotics, 82 percent; psychotics, 90 percent; all clients, 94 percent.

In addition, the majority of differences were positive *and* statistically significant. Among the neurotics, 58 percent of all comparisons between pretherapy and posttherapy scores were positive *and* significant ($p < .05$), whereas only 3 percent of the differences were negative *and* significant ($p < .05$). The proportions of positive and negative change that were significant for the psychotics were 69 percent ($p < .05$) and 1.5 percent ($p < .05$), respectively; and for all clients, 78 percent ($p < .05$) and 2.5 percent ($p < .05$), respectively. When clients were designated as outpatients and inpatients, the results were quite similar. However, among normal clients, significant change occurred in a positive direction on only 29 percent of the items and in a negative direction on only 0.6 percent of the 165 items.

By and large, psychotherapy as practiced by therapists in this sample appeared to be at least modestly effective. In contrast to the standard median, 30 percent spontaneous remission rate most recently offered by Bergen and Garfield,[42] improvement rates in the present study ranged from 43 percent to 71 percent depending upon the outcome measure. However, it should be noted that these rates do not exceed the 72 percent spontaneous remission rate cited by Eysenck, although the latter as a base rate is open to serious criticism. However, in my judgment, 30 percent may be more accurate.

Consequently, it appears to be a reasonable, although tentative, conclusion that the psychotherapy offered by the present sample of experienced, *practicing* therapists, working in their natural surroundings, to clients who at least persumably were typical of their case load, was associated with at least modest client improvement.

DISCUSSION

The following outline is a summary of the more salient findings and some tentative conclusions based upon these findings. It should be kept in mind that these conclusions are based soley on those data regarding therapist empathy, warmth, and genuineness. A large amount of data relating to client and treatment variables has yet to be analyzed. Undoubtedly, some of these findings will make it necessary to qualify, and perhaps negate, at least some of these conclusions.

1. For some, perhaps the most important finding of the study, or its most significant consequence, is the fact that such an undertaking could be carried out by mail. Over the four-year period during which data were collected, more than 6,000 tape-recorded therapy sessions generated by 122 thera-

pists and 258 clients became available for research and training purposes.

2. In this regard, the present study is the largest and most comprehensive investigation of outpatient individual psychotherapy as it was practiced by experienced, largely private-practice therapists in the United States during the late 1960s.

3. The single most important finding is that empathy and warmth were not at all, and genuineness only modestly, related to client change. It would be quite reasonable to argue that the lack of significant relationships between these therapist interpersonal skills and outcome was due simply to the fact that the present therapists' levels of these process variables were decidedly lower than scores reported in earlier studies. An educated guess, however, is that the therapists in the present study, being for the most part eclectic or psychoanalytic in orientation and in private practice, do not value therapeutic skills that emanated from a Rogerian framework. This would account for the lowered and restricted range of scores. More to the point, however, this hypothesis suggests that, regardless of the scores these therapists might receive on scales measuring empathy, warmth, and genuineness, there are as yet untapped therapist variables that would be found to be more directly and strongly related to client outcome.

4. Until the present study is replicated, either or both of the above hypotheses would account for the present findings equally well. There is no escaping the *fact* that, on the tape-rated measures of empathy, warmth, and genuineness, the present therapists' scores were lower and more restricted in range than scores reported in earlier studies. However, the crucial point is the meaning to be attached to this finding. It would be perfectly reasonable, at this time, to view the data as suggesting that the present therapists were in some way deficient in therapeutic functioning. However, one would then be somewhat hard-pressed to account for the likely possibility that they also were modestly effective.

5. An alternative hypothesis, and one that we lean toward, particularly on the basis of the criticism leveled at the earlier

studies by Matarazzo[43] and Meltzoff and Kornreich[44] is that the earlier empathy, warmth, and genuineness scores were spuriously high and that the present data are more representative of current therapeutic functioning. If this is the case, then a number of alternatives present themselves with respect to these variables: (1) the *concepts* may not be relevant therapeutic dimensions for these therapists; (2) or one may retain the concepts and take the position that the present operational definitions of the concepts, the *scales*, were not particularly appropriate measures; (3) it could be argued that these variables are relatively more effective during certain stages of the therapy process than others; when mean scores over the entire therapy are used, the differential effectiveness of these variables mask whatever relationship they may have with client change; or (4) empathy, warmth, and genuineness are necessary but not sufficient conditions for change, at least with respect to the present therapists and clients, and thus, they are not directly or strongly related to change except if examined with other, as yet untapped, variables.

6. The third finding of some importance is that psychotherapy, at least with these therapists, is not "for better or for worse." While the present therapists may not have been any more than modestly successful, clearly they were not harmful.

7. In summary, then, there are no therapist in-therapy behaviors that have been related reliably and in a programmatic fashion to client improvement across those populations of therapists and clients currently engaging in individual psychotherapy. Until such behaviors have been identified and related to positive client outcome as described above, it makes no sense to talk in terms of effective and ineffective training programs. It might be shown that graduates of some programs effect client improvement consistently more than graduates of other programs, but until we know *what* skills to teach and *how* to teach them, there is no assurance that such (postulated) differences are related to training at all.

Notes and References

1. The data on which this paper is based were gathered over a four-year period (1966–1970), supported by a National Institute of Mental Health Grant 12306. Dr. Charles B. Truax was principal investigator during 1966–1968; and Dr. Kevin M. Mitchell, during 1969–1970. The authors are grateful to Dr. Richard C. Bednar, Jeffrey G. Shapiro, and Donald G. Wargo for their help in collecting the data.
2. B. Lerner, *Therapy in the Ghetto: Political Impotence and Personal Disintegration* (Baltimore: Johns Hopkins Press, 1972); B. Lerner and D. W. Fiske, "Client Attributes and the Eye of the Beholder," *Journal of Consulting and Clinical Psychology,* 1973, 40:272–77.
3. L. Luborsky, M. Chandler, A. H. Auerbach, J. Cohen, and H. Bachrach, "Factors Influencing the Outcome of Psychotherapy: A Review of the Quantitative Research," *Psychological Bulletin,* 1971, 75:145–85.
4. C. B. Truax and K. M. Mitchell, "Research on Certain Therapeutic Interpersonal Skills in Relation to Process and Outcome," in *Handbook of Psychotherapy and Behavior Change: An Empirical Analysis,* edited by A. E. Bergin and S. L. Garfield (New York: Wiley, 1971).
5. F. van der Veen, "Effects of the Therapist and the Patient on Each Other's Therapeutic Behavior," *Journal of Consulting Psychology,* 1965, 29:18–26.
6. M. Alexik and R. R. Carkhuff, "The Effects of the Manipulation of Client Depth of Self-Exploration upon High and Low Functioning Counselors," *Journal of Clinical Psychology,* 1967, 23:210–12; Carkhuff and Alexik, "Effect of Client Depth of Self-Exploration upon High and Low Functioning Counselors," *Journal of Counseling Psychology,* 1967, 14: 350–55; T. Friel, D. Kratochivil, and R. R. Carkhuff, "Effect of Client Depth of Self-Exploration on Therapists Categorized by Level of Experience and Type of Training," unpublished manuscript, State University of New York at Buffalo, 1968.
7. This suggestion was gratefully received from C. L. Winder, Dean, College of Social Sciences, Michigan State University.
8. Luborsky et al., see note 3.
9. C. B. Truax and R. R. Carkhuff, *Toward Effective Counseling and Psychotherapy* (Chicago: Aldine, 1967); C. B. Truax and K. M. Mitchell, "The Psychotherapeutic and the Psychonoxious: Human Encounters that Change Behavior," in *Studies in Psychotherapy and Behavioral Change,* edited by M. Feldman, pp. 55–92 (Buffalo: State University of New York Press, 1968); Truax and Mitchell, see note 4.
10. Truax and Mitchell, see note 4.
11. R. G. Matarazzo, "Research on the Teaching and Learning of Psychotherapeutic Skills," in *Handbook of Psychotherapy and Behavior Change* (see note 4).
12. J. Meltzoff and M. Kornreich, *Research in Psychotherapy* (New York: Atherton, 1970).

13. K. M. Mitchell, J. D. Bozarth, C. B. Truax, and C. C. Krauft, *Antecedents to Effective Psychotherapy*, final report, NIMH Grant 12306-04, 1973; S. L. Garfield and A. E. Bergin, "Therapeutic Conditions and Outcome," *Journal of Abnormal Psychology*, 1971, 77:108–14.
14. Matarazzo, see note 11.
15. Meltzoff and Kornreich, see note 12.
16. Garfield and Bergin, see note 13.
17. Mitchell et al., see note 13.
18. Garfield and Bergin, see note 13.
19. H. H. Strupp, R. E. Fox, and K. Lessler, *Patients View Their Psychotherapy* (Baltimore: John Hopkins Press, 1969).
20. H. Miles, E. Barrabee, and J. E. Finesinger, "Evaluation of Psychotherapy," *Psychosomatic Medicine*, 1951, 13:83–105.
21. R. Hoehn-Saric, J. D. Frank, S. D. Imber, E. H. Nash, A. R. Stone, and C. C. Battle, "Systematic Preparation of Patients for Psychotherapy. I. Effects on Therapy Behavior and Outcome," *Journal of Psychiatric Research*, 1964, 2:267–81; S. D. Imber, J. D. Frank, E. H. Nash, A. R. Stone, and L. H. Gliedman, "Improvement and Amount of Therapeutic Contact: An Alternative to the Use of No-Treatment Controls in Psychotherapy," *Journal of Consulting Psychology*, 1957, 21:309–15; M. B. Parloff, H. C. Kelman, and J. D. Frank, "Comfort, Effectiveness, and Self-Awareness as Criteria of Improvement in Psychotherapy," *American Journal of Psychiatry*, 1954, 111:343–51; A. R. Stone, J. D. Frank, E. H. Nash, and S. D. Imber, "An Intensive Five-Year Follow-up Study of Treated Psychiatric Outpatients," *Journal of Nervous and Mental Disease*, 1961, 133:410–22.
22. Hoehn-Saric et al., see note 21.
23. Imber et al., see note 21.
24. R. L. Spitzer, J. Endicott, J. L. Fleiss, and J. Cohen, "The Psychiatric Status Schedule: A Technique for Evaluating Psychopathology and Impairment in Role Functioning," *Archives of General Psychiatry*, 1970, 23:41–55.
25. R. L. Spitzer and J. Endicott, "Diagnosis: A Computer Program for Psychiatric Diagnosis Utilizing the Differential Diagnostic Procedure," *Archives of General Psychiatry*, 1970, 23:41–55.
26. M. Lorr, D. M. McNair, G. J. Weinstein, W. W. Michaux, and A. Raskin, "Meprobamate and Chlorpromazine in Psychotherapy: Some Effects on Hostility in Outpatients," *Archives of General Psychiatry*, 1962, 4:381–89.
27. M. Lorr, D. M. McNair, and G. J. Weinstein, "Early Effects of Chlordiazepoxide Used with Psychotherapy," *Journal of Psychiatric Research*, 1963, 1:257–70.
28. M. Lorr and D. M. McNair, "Methods Relating to Evaluation of Therapeutic Outcome," in *Methods of Research in Psychotherapy*, edited by A. Gottschalk and A. H. Auerbach (New York: Appleton-Century-Crofts, 1966).
29. Ibid.

30. Ibid., p. 577.
31. R. F. Dymond, "Adjustment Changes Over Therapy from Self-Sorts," in *Psychotherapy and Personality Change*, edited by C. R. Roberts and R. F. Dymond, pp. 76–89 (Chicago: University of Chicago Press, 1954).
32. M. K. Lewis, "Counselor Prediction and Projection in Client-Centered Psychotherapy," doctoral dissertation, University of Chicago, 1959.
33. G. S. Welsh and W. G. Dahlstrom (eds.), *Basic Readings on the MMPI in Psychology and Medicine* (Minneapolis: University of Minnesota Press, 1956).
34. Ibid.
35. F. Barron, "An Ego-Strength-Scale Which Predicts Response to Therapy," *Journal of Consulting Psychology*, 1953, 17:327–33.
36. W. E. Fordyce, "Social Desirability in the MMPI," *Journal of Consulting Psychology*, 1956, 20:171–75.
37. A. L. Edwards, *The Social Desirability Variable in Personality Assessment and Research* (New York: Dryden, 1957).
38. D. R. Byrne: "The Repression-Sensitization Scale: Rationale, Reliability and Validity," *Journal of Personality*, 1961, 29:334–49; "Repression-Sensitization as a Dimension of Personality," in *Progress in Experimental Personality Research*, edited by B. Maher (New York: Academic Press, 1964), vol. 1; *An Introduction to Personality* (Englewood Cliffs, N.J.: Prentice-Hall, 1966).
39. Truax and Carkhuff, see note 9; Truax and Mitchell, see note 4.
40. R. L. Ebel, "Estimation of the Reliability of Ratings," *Psychometrika*, 1951, 16:407–24.
41. Truax and Carkhuff, see note 9; Turax and Mitchell, see note 4.
42. Bergin and Garfield, see note 4.
43. Matarazzo, see note 11.
44. Meltzoff and Kornreich, see note 12.

The Creation of Meaning

Through Body Movement

ERMA DOSAMANTES ALPERSON

HISTORICALLY, A THERAPIST'S ROLE, GOALS, AND TECH-
niques, have been partly influenced by the dominant cultural
views of the day regarding the nature of man and of woman
and their relationship to their environment.

At present, we are witnessing the confrontation between
two ideologically opposing cultural forces, each of which is
reflected in the views of the adherents of today's various psychotherapeutic camps.

On the one hand, we have the older more established ideology born out of a culture that prizes pragmatic-materialistic
values. This perspective stresses man's "functional" value to
his society. From this vantage point, it becomes desirable for
man to be rational, in control of his emotions, and to adjust or
attempt to fit himself into his world as it exists, causing minimal
threat or upset among others around him.

On the other hand, we have the rebellious voice of the
humanists that began to emerge in the later 1950s and early
1960s from among a small group of psychologists and psychiatrists (namely, Maslow, Rogers, Gendlin, Perls, Szasz, and
Laing), who challenged the first ideology by suggesting that:
mankind's potential for self-directed creative behavior was being stymied; that human beings were partially educated and
only partially functioning entities by virtue of having lost con-

tact with their less rational, less conscious levels of experiencing.

As a force, humanists attack the dominant condition of our time—our obsession with control, analysis, and technological rationality. The therapeutic techniques that have emerged from this perspective tend to stress nonverbal modes of communication; they prefer touch to therapeutic distance; they stress sensation over analysis and phenomenological observation over theoretical explanation.

More specifically, therapists holding this view believe: that it is desirable for a person to become self-directed in her behavior and choices; that one's emotional states can be trusted to provide one with meaningful feedback about oneself and the world; that personal growth involves perceptual and behavioral change of the type that speaks directly from the person's experiential field of the moment; that the outcome or content of this change cannot be known in advance by another.

Therapists who hold this view also tend to adopt an inside-looking-out approach to the study of man's experience.[2] This approach makes the person the central source of her own experiential process. In therapy, the person becomes engaged in a self-discovering process—discovering what her experience is as it unfolds in her awareness. The function of the therapist becomes that of a facilitator, enhancing the person's optimal contact with the entirety of her own phenomenological experiential process.

Gendlin's work on the phenomenological experiencing process[3] has led him to conclude that basically two levels of experiencing can be distinguished. Both must be present and interact with one another, if personal growth and integration are to occur:

1. The first level, which he calls the *felt-level* of experiencing, includes all that one can experience when asked to focus on "the way it all feels".[4] It includes one's sensory and kinesthetic awareness, including emotional states. It is a body sense of a problem or situation. It is an implicit way of knowing one's

experience, since it is knowable only to the experiencing person.

> A body sense of a problem or situation is preverbal and preconceptual . . . it is not equivalent to any one verbal or conceptual pattern. To attend to it or speak from it is a further living and therefore a further structuring, a "carrying forward."
> . . . . Experiential body process is carried forward by action and feedback. As one acts, one perceives one's own acting.[5]

2. The second level of experiencing is the *symbolic level*. It flows directly from one's felt-level and permits the person an opportunity to conceptualize and verbalize her felt experience; thereby making explicit at least some portion of it. This level provides one with an opportunity to validate experience in the presence of others.

It is clear from Gendlin's work that neither the felt-level nor the symbolic level alone represents the totality of human experiencing.

Ornstein[6] believes that there is a physiological basis for the distinction between these two levels of experiencing. The right hemisphere of the cerebral cortex of the brain appears to be primarily responsible for our orientation of space, artistic talents, body awareness, and recognition of faces. It processes information more diffusely than the left hemisphere and integrates material simultaneously rather than in a linear fashion. The left hemisphere seems to be predominantly involved with analytic thinking, particularly language and logic. Ornstein believes that a complete human consciousness has to include both modes of thought.

At present, psychotherapists need to find more effective means of facilitating their clients' synthesis of both levels of their phenomenological process—the verbal with the preverbal, the conscious with the less conscious levels.

The problem with most verbal therapies of today that aim to promote personal growth and change is that they have failed to recognize that the felt-level of experiencing must precede the conceptual-verbal level. Furthermore, verbalization may not be the best method for contacting one's felt-level. Often, the very act of verbalizing about one's experience causes one to adopt the role of an observer looking at oneself, rather than being the active participant-creator of one's experience. Verbalization frequently serves to alienate us from our own experiential body process. According to Gunther,[7] verbalizing and analyzing our experience, leads us to filter out the uniqueness of each evolving event; we learn to see the world from a series of expectations, leaving little room for surprise at the unexpected or unknown.

The consequence of distancing ourselves from our experiential body process is that we literally cut ourselves off from the kinesthetic and sensory input on which we rely to know our various feeling reactions toward ourselves and others. Fisher[8] found that the more definite one's own body boundaries are, the clearer the person's sense of identity was likely to be. Laing[9] refers to schizophrenics lacking an awareness of their own bodies as "unembodied selves" to underscore the degree of estrangement they experience from their own experiential body process.

This body-sense dissociation, however, is not peculiar to persons we generally consider to be most regressed. Many clients seen today in outpatient clinics prove to be unsuccessful clients by virtue of their "externalizing" and "intellectualizing" attitudes. To be "externalized" is to be in a state of dissociation; not to see oneself as the source of one's own experiential process, but rather as outside of it and therefore not within one's control. To be "intellectualized" implies that the person has a cognitive or abstract understanding of her difficulties, yet lacks an emotional involvement with them. Both states of being simply reflect the person's own lack of connection with her own felt-level of experiencing, which is bodily derived.

I wish to explore a new approach to the realization of the "meaning" of one's felt-level of experiencing—a way that places the person in contact with her body in motion and allows emotional states, images, and ideas to emerge from this movement experience, which, can subsequently be conceptualized by the person through verbalization.

The earliest and most direct contact I can make with myself as the source of my experience is through my body. It is through the kinesthetic experience of my body and its way of moving that I have the only direct, immediate physical experience of myself from within.[10] I am able to interpret the muscular behavior of others through my own kinesthetic sense because I have experienced similar muscular reactions. Berger[11] calls this kinesthetic reaction to others' motor behavior, "kinesthetic empathy."

The distortions, tensions, and restrictions evidenced in my body reflect my psychological state of being of the moment.[12] Our bodies in motion confirm or betray our verbal communications. When our movements and words are in harmony, we experience ourselves as "in one piece"; when they contradict each other, we experience ourselves as dissociated.

The moving body is the center of our human experience.[13] How we move not only reveals what has been conceptualized and perceived by us, but our movements themselves, are capable of generating feelings, which are then transformed into images, percepts, memories, and concepts.[14]

Movement therapy concerns itself with the latter process of transformation, i.e., how we transform an ongoing continuous flow of energy and incipient body movement to felt-body movement to imagery to verbal communication.[15]

Movement therapy is founded on the premise that it is possible to discover the meaning of our felt experience by exploring fully our potential for "authentic movement" (movement that is involved and spontaneous) in the context of a relationship established with a movement therapist. Movement therapists are persons sensitized to a range of human movement experience (generally modern dancers with a psychological background). The expectation is that by becoming increasingly sensitized to internal and external stimuli as we move in space—at varying rhythms and at different levels of energy, alone or in relation to others, in stillness or in motion—our movement responses will begin to merge naturally with other modes of representation (e.g., images, memories), and the summation of these experiences will allow us to achieve a new integration of "meaning" from our experience.

I refer to therapists who emphasize the process of creating one's meaning from authentic movement responses, as "process-oriented movement therapists" to distinguish them from others interested in movement as a form of exercise or entertainment, or those intent on producing a specific outcome or product (e.g., the movement therapist who suggests to her client that she move within a set of prescribed images in order to reproduce the various Freudian psychosexual stages). The process-oriented movement therapist is interested in movement as a form of communication as well as a process for self-actualization. It is expected that the client will acquire an increased vitality, self-awareness, individuation, integration, and greater effectiveness in relating to her environment as a consequence of having gone through this process. The movement therapist is concerned with the creation of the conditions that will maximize her client's opportunity to create the content or "meaning" of her felt-movement experience.

In the early sessions, the therapist provides structured movement tasks through which the person may move, but leaves the client free to produce the content of her experience (e.g., the therapist may ask the client to explore abstract movement dimensions such as "open" and "closed," "up" and "down"). These tasks are geared to acquaint the person: with her own body and its various parts, to the numerous possibilities of moving in space and time with varying effort or energy qualities, also to the fact that she has a unique style of patterning her movement. In the process of becoming familiar with these aspects of movement, the person becomes sensitized to her own body as an instrument for obtaining experiential feedback. She becomes increasingly aware of her body as both the medium and the message; she not only receives but also reacts to her own kinesthetic and sensory experiences. The process is always self-directed; the client is free to ignore part or all of the therapist's cues. She can choose to move or not, in her own way and at her own pace.

Examples of the kind of structured movements tasks that the person may be encouraged to explore in movement might include:

(1) *Exploration of person's external space.* The client's attention is drawn to the space around her; as she moves, she may be asked to attend to how much of the space she uses, what the timing of her pace is, and the energy quality that emerges as she moves. If she is moving in a group, she may be encouraged to focus on how her movements are similar or different from others.

(2) *Exploration of person's internal space.* The client is encouraged to focus her attention inwardly and allow whatever thoughts, sensations, and images emerge and to flow freely without censorship.

(3) *Through self-controlled relaxation methods* intended to release residual muscular tension, the person is encouraged to achieve a state of relaxed-concentration that Rugg refers to as a state of "off-conscious." In this state, the person is relaxed, alert and in control of her actions (unlike hypnotic or dream states). Jacobson[16] believes that by learning to observe their own tension patterns and learning to relax them, clients can remove the "continuing causes" of their psychosomatic conditions and effect better use of the muscular energy available to them.

All these movement tasks are intended to achieve a heightened kinesthetic sensitivity and to extend the range and flexibility of the person's movement responses.

With time, the movement tasks provided by the therapist progress to make greater usage of the person's own imagination (e.g., the client may be asked to fantasy an object she cannot stand and to explore it through movement; she may be asked to focus on what she feels as she allows herself to move toward or away from the object). With time, too, the degree of structure initially provided by the therapist decreases and the person increasingly provides her own self-direction without need of any cues whatsoever from the therapist. The initial function of the therapist as a guide is transformed into that of an observer who intercedes only when the client is unable to move at all. At such a time, she functions to help the client move through the experience of being blocked.

Experientially the movement therapy process appears to be characterized by two distinctive phases.[17] During the first phase, the person becomes aware of her body and its increased reactivity to internal and external stimuli. She begins to realize that there is a relationship between her own energy level and her various feeling states. In addition, during the first phase, the person begins to try new, noncharacteristic movement patterns. The conclusion of the first phase is reached when the person can move freely and with involvement.

The second phase is marked by an almost totally self-guided movement process. As the person moves freely and with involvement, following her own impulse to move, she begins to contact tensions experienced as blocks. Because such a tension is experienced as uncomfortable or painful, it is disruptive of the flow of the felt-movement process. During this second phase the person experiences periods of being stuck. Her movement begins to meet with some resistance; this resistance is experienced as emanating from within herself. By allowing herself to move through such an impasse, the person is often able to gain fresh new insights about herself or herself in relation to others.

The following illustration shows how movement, imagery, and verbalization interact in a movement session to produce new meaning for the person:

Peggy is a hospitalized "paranoid schizophrenic" patient. In the sixth movement session, she broke into tears in the middle of a relaxation experience. When asked by the therapist what she was experiencing, she mentioned that her voices were commanding her to do something terrible, but would not mention what the something terrible was. The therapist encouraged her to express in movement, her experience with her voices. She started to tap the floor gently; soon the tap was converted into a pounding, which increased in intensity, until her whole body was involved in the action; she then proceeded to scream, making frightful noises while continuing to pound the floor. At the end of the session, the members of the group expressed surprise that such loud sounds could come from someone they had generally experienced as soft spoken and quiet; yet they were not rejecting of her. Two sessions later, she was able to acknowledge verbally that her voices were commanding her to kill the therapist; she admitted that at the time she had been angry with the therapist. To me, this indicated that she had begun to make the connection between her voices' commands and her actual experience with others.

The above illustration demonstrates how movement therapy, which provides a person with an opportunity to synthesize her felt-movement experience with subsequent imagery, memories, and verbalization, can promote perceptual and behavioral change. Hawkins believes that one possible outcome of the self-directed felt-movement process is the attainment of new integration and insight:

> When one is able to self-direct at the felt-level and can draw on imaginative responses, one then begins to combine the sensory data of the immediate response with the memory traces and builds a new kind of integration. I believe that it is out of this integration and forming that man gets insight and meaning from his experience in this world.[18]

I believe that the unique contribution of an authentic movement experience within the context of a movement therapy session is that:

1. It can acquaint the person with her physical self as the source of her felt-experiencing process.
2. It puts the person in touch with what her actual felt-experience is.
3. It allows the person an opportunity to express outwardly the intent of her actions in a safe, nonexplicit way.

I further believe that the verbalization that flows directly from such an authentic movement experience can enhance and extend the person's felt-experiencing outward by allowing the person an opportunity to make explicit her felt-reactions toward herself and others. In the process of sharing her felt experience explicitly, the person is able to validate her experience, clarify ambivalent perceptions, feelings, and actions, and acknowledge full responsibility for them. The end result is that the person becomes more fully integrated—having access to the totality of her experiential process: verbal and nonverbal, conscious and less conscious.

The potential significance of movement therapy for the field of clinical psychology is that it opens up a new avenue for the exploration of nonverbal levels of communication. These preverbal levels appear to represent less conscious levels of experience—the creative, the fantasy side of one's life. Movement therapy opens up the possibility for reaching individuals previously regarded as inaccessible to verbal psychotherapy. It also points toward a need for an interdisciplinary approach to clients, with perhaps dancers, artists, and psychologists working jointly to facilitate the person's greater awareness to the totality of her experiencing process. It further suggests, that we might consider for admission into graduate clinical programs, persons with strong backgrounds in the creative arts.

166

References

1. S. Keen, "Sing the Body Electric," *Psychology Today*, Oct. 1972, p. 56.
2. H. Rugg, *Imagination* (New York: Harper & Row, 1963).
3. E. T. Gendlin, *Experiencing and the Creation of Meaning* (New York: Free Press of Glencoe, 1962).
4. E. T. Gendlin, "Focusing," *Psychotherapy: Theory, Research, and Practice*, 1969, 6:5.
5. Ibid., p. 8.
6. R. Ornstein, *The Psychology of Consciousness* (New York: Viking Press, 1973).
7. B. Gunther, "Sensory Awakening and Relaxation," in *Ways of Growth*, edited by H. A. Otto and J. Mann, pp. 60–68 (New York: Viking Press, 1968).
8. S. A. Fisher, "A Further Appraisal of the Body Boundary Concept," *Journal of Consulting Psychology*, 1963, 27:62–74.
9. R. D. Laing, *The Divided Self* (Baltimore: Pelican Books, 1965).
10. E. G. Schachtel, *Experiential Foundations of Rorschach's Test* (New York: Basic Books, 1966).
11. M. R. Berger, "Bodily Experience and Expression of Emotion," *American Dance Therapy Association Monograph 2*, 1972, pp. 191–230.
12. W. Reich, *Character Analysis* (New York: Farrar, Straus, and Giroux, 1949); E. Jacobson, *Modern Treatment of Tense Patients* (Springfield, Ill.: Charles C. Thomas, 1970); A. Lowen, "The Body in Therapy," *American Dance Therapy Association Proceedings*, 1970, pp. 1–9.
13. V. Hunt, "The Biological Organization of Man to Move," *Developmental Conference on Dance*, 1966, pp. 51–63.
14. William James, *The Principles of Psychology* (New York: Henry Holt and Co., 1905), vol. 2, pp. 442–85; N. Bull, *The Attitude Theory of Emotion*, Nervous and Mental Disease Monograph No. 81 (New York: Coolidge Foundation Publishers, 1951).
15. E. Alperson, "Carrying Experiencing Forward Through Authentic Body Movement," *Psychotherapy: Theory, Research, and Practice*, in press.
16. Jacobson, see note 12.
17. Alperson, see note 15.
18. A. Hawkins, "Six Treatment Programs, I," *Proceedings of the First California Regional Meeting*, February 1972, p. 5.

Intervention of Mental Health Workers in Sexual Concerns of Students

RAYMOND S. SANDERS*

THERE IS LITTLE DOUBT THAT OUR SOCIETY HAS CHANGED IN its attitudes toward premarital sexual behavior.[1] This change is widely reflected on college campuses across the country. Not only are substantial numbers of students sexually active,[2] they also appear to be more involved with the issue of sex in regard to the quality of their interpersonal relationships.[3]

The openness of the sexual climate on the college campus has resulted in an increased awareness that students require special services and programs, encompassing the areas of medical treatment, counseling services, and educational experiences. Programs that have been developed were virtually unknown on campuses only a decade ago. Consequently, little has been written regarding an effective orientation to the implementation of these programs. However, our experience suggests that the clinical psychologist on the college campus is a unique position to provide innovative leadership, direction, and consultation to evolving programs.

On our campus at the Oregon State University, the Student Health Service, Mental Health Clinic, and Counseling Center, as well as several academic departments, have expanded the scope of their services to include assistance to students in re-

*The author gratefully acknowledges the writing assistance of Georgine E. Thompson and J. Mark Wagener.

gard to sexual matters. During the past six years mental health personnel have shared in the development of programs in pregnancy counseling, abortion referral, birth control education, treatment of sexual dysfunctions, and formal and informal educational experiences. Working with individuals and student groups has stimulated us to develop meaningful approaches to student sexuality that are compatible with the short-term, crisis intervention model that our service necessitates. As a result, we began to formulate an orientation toward the treatment of sexual concerns in a college population that varies from the more traditional orientation in which we were trained.

This is a description of the development and evolution of the functions of the mental health workers on our campus in regard to the sexual concerns of students and is a summary of our thinking in regard to the treatment of sexual problems within a college population. Also discussed is the development and application of therapeutic techniques which, when coupled with effective consultation and educational programs, have been found to be effective.

DEVELOPMENT OF PROGRAMS

The activities began with the development of pregnancy counseling and abortion referral programs. Prior to 1968 little attention was given to the pregnant coed by any of the student service agencies here. Although premarital pregnancies were being diagnosed at the Student Health Service in substantial numbers, no pregnancy counseling services existed. Several factors encouraged the staff of the Mental Health Clinic to become actively concerned about pregnant coeds. The consensus of our staff was that many of these women were significantly distressed by their pregnancies and most were unaware of the alternatives available. Also, our mental health staff was encountering female students attempting to cope with adverse physical and psychological reactions in response to illegally performed abortions. After therapeutic abortions were legal in Oregon, they were performed in substantial numbers. Fall term 1968 marked the beginning of an extensive program of pregnancy counseling and abortion referral by the staff of the Mental Health Clinic. Our program of abortion referral resulted in the investigation of what was known at that time about the impact of surgical termination of pregnancy on the lives and subsequent emotional adjustment of our students. Reviews of the available abortion literature suggested that information about the sequelae of therapeutic abortion was limited. Much of the information we found was speculative, obviously biased, or not applicable to a college population. Even less had been written about counseling techniques that might be implemented to reduce the potentially negative aftereffects that were hypothesized to result from therapeutic abortion. This served to stimulate our thinking, not only about the management of therapeutic abortion, but about developing an orientation toward the treatment of a variety of sexual concerns within a student population. It also served as the impetus to begin collecting follow-up data on the women with whom we were working.

The success and acceptance of our pregnancy counseling and abortion referral service resulted in the inclusion of the mental health staff in the birth control services emerging within the Student Health Service. This service began informally during the school year of 1968–69 and grew in scope with formal funding obtained through a grant from the Department of Health, Education, and Welfare for the school year 1971–72. A stipulation of these grant funds was that formal discussion groups of an educational nature be provided for those obtaining services. These groups have been conducted conjointly by a staff member of the Mental Health Clinic and a nurse of the Birth Control Clinic. Women requesting birth control evaluations are urged to attend a one and a half hour group session and, where feasible, are encouraged to bring their boy friends. The principal topics included in these sessions are: the methods and procedures of birth control, the psychology of effective birth control, and the psychology of sexual adjustment. Group interaction is encouraged, and every attempt is made to clarify areas of concern and uncertainty regarding sexual functioning.

During the school year 1971–72, 603 students attended these discussion groups. Student evaluation was highly favorable, with 598 reporting these sessions as positive experiences in terms of reducing anxiety about birth control methods, clarifying the role of sex within a relationship, and facilitating communication with their partners. On occasion, we have offered opportunities for these groups to continue meeting on a regular basis. The degree of acceptance has encouraged us to use group counseling in dealing with sexual concerns.

Our work with the Birth Control Clinic marked the beginning of our consultation services. This experience has had implications for our involvement with other campus groups. The limited number of professional mental health staff available on our campus for direct service has resulted in our developing relationships with a variety of on and off-campus organizations. Among the groups with whom we have contact are the residence hall staffs, the student-organized and operated Experimental College, Benton County Planned Parenthood Association, premarriage classes at the Catholic Church, local elementary and high school districts, the Division of Continuing Education, and the Benton County Crisis Service. The range of activities in which we engage with various groups is quite broad, including our attempt to provide for facilitation of referral, training in the management of crisis situations, and provision for educational services through in-service training. Through these activities, we are able to significantly influence a substantial number of on-and-off campus persons who are dealing with students displaying a variety of sexual concerns.

At the invitation of the Family Life Department, we became involved in the planning and implementation of an interdisciplinary course in human sexuality. While experts in the physiology of sexual functioning were readily available as speakers, expertise in the psychological aspects of sexuality was hard to find. Student questionnaires indicated, however, that the psychological aspects of sexuality were areas of great concern to them. They requested information on specialized topics such as abortion, sexual deviation, sexual problems of college students, and sexual inadequacies. Because of our experience in these areas, we were regularly asked to serve as speakers. Interactions between ourselves and the students within these classes resulted in our impression that college students experience a wide variety of sexual concerns. Not all of these concerns are of the magnitude that would necessitate a direct contact with a mental health worker but are sufficient to substantiate the need for educational intervention.

During the time that the activities described above were being developed, the requests for direct counseling services for sexual problems were steadily increasing. While we continue to treat a rather constant cross section of psychiatric sexual deviations (i.e., voyeurism, exhibitionism, transvesticism, fetishism, rape, and homosexuality), we heard increasing requests for treatment of a variety of sexual dysfunctions, including impotency, premature ejaculation, orgasmic difficulties, or deficiencies in sexual enjoyment. In addition, couples requested counseling on sexual technique or advice on the specific application of a sexual technique to a particular relationship. Other couples requested help in making sex a more meaningful part of their relationship, or in relieving a particular sexual inhibition. Substantial numbers of students requesting help for sexual concerns manifested anxiety about decisions regarding sexual involvement. Many of the individuals requesting these services were neither neurotic nor characterological. Rather, they were individuals whose sexual concerns were those of immature or sexually inexperienced people. Many were sexually involved for the first time and appeared frightened, yet intrigued, by their experiences. In addition, we saw many whose sexual difficulties reflected situational stresses of an interpersonal nature. We have continued to treat long standing or characterologically based sexual deviation with traditional insight oriented psychotherapy and have begun to develop more short-term and symptom-

oriented approaches applicable to this latter group of individuals. This has necessitated considerable revision of our orientation toward sexual concerns and the application and integration of a variety of specialized techniques.

SEXUAL PROBLEMS AND TREATMENT

The traditional treatment for sexual problems is an outgrowth of psychoanalytic psychotherapy, stressing the interrelationship of sexual impulses, ego defenses, and symptom formation. Considerable attention is given to the effect of early
experience in shaping the subsequent sexual behavior of
adults. Particular emphasis is placed upon those experiences
that are traumatic to the emerging ego of the child. When
these experiences are repressed, they find later expression in
sexual inhibitions, deviant sexual acts, or neurotic symptoms of
the adult. Inability to experience orgasmic satisfaction within
the context of an ongoing heterosexual relationship characterizes the neurotic individual. Long-term intensive psychotherapy is undertaken with the aim of uncovering the roots of the
neurosis, thus making the unconscious conscious and under the
control of the ego.[4] Growth results from emotional insight that
can be meaningfully translated and applied to life experience.
This is the tradition in which most of us were trained. However, it is not the only possible approach to sexual concerns,
particularly as they occur in college students.

In addition to the concerns identified by the psychodynamic
model, the problems of college students in regard to their
emerging sexual lives frequently involve fears of sexual experience based on inadequate information. Students face crisis
situations such as premarital pregnancy and are plagued by
sexual dysfunctions such as impotency, premature ejaculation,
or orgasmic difficulties. Rather than crystallized neuroses,
these concerns represent developmental crises. It has been our
perception that long-term psychoanalytically oriented psychotherapy applied to these kinds of situations serves to increase,
rather than decrease, anxiety. Further, it does not seem to be

effective in helping students cope with specific symptoms.

Our treatment approach to sexual concerns in college students makes the assumption that sexual behavior is an interpersonal skill. Sexual functioning can be facilitated by those activities which enhance such skills including practice, intrapersonal and interpersonal sensitivity, communication, progressive refinement, and shared commitment. A significant aspect of our treatment with college students involves the exploration and correction of unrealistic expectations regarding their sexual experiences. Misconceptions about sexual functioning contribute heavily to anxiety, apprehension, and self-doubt. Patients are urged against establishing performance criteria for their sexual experiences, thus becoming entrapped in situations involving success or failure. Rather, they are oriented toward focusing upon the interpersonal encounter in which they are involved.

Considerable attention is given in our counseling to help students implement concrete suggestions in regard to techniques of sexual intercourse. Suggestions for altering methods of foreplay and experimenting with positions of intercourse are given. We find that considerable facilitation of sexual functioning takes place when students are able to establish optimal conditions for sex to take place. Our recommendations are most effectively implemented when students establish conditions of trust and security in the context of relationships that are meaningful.

Our emphasis is one of working with couples to help correct sexual problems, since much of our counseling focuses on specific sexual behaviors and the relationship in which these behaviors occur. Every effort is made to resolve situational difficulties by involving both members of the relationship in joint counseling sessions whenever possible. Again, our focus is functional and supportive as opposed to emotionally insightful. Little emphasis is placed on determining the unconscious aspects of behavior. The typical course of treatment is short term and often highly educational in nature. Selected techniques are applied to specific sexual dysfunctions. For example, teaching the use of the squeeze technique as described by Masters and Johnson[5] has been helpful to male students in achieving ejaculatory control.

Overall, we try to provide a variety of experiences for our patients. Included in these experiences is the exposure to self-instructional or audio-visual adjuncts to therapy such as films, books, and tapes. To facilitate communication, we have recently been experimenting with the use of sexual instruction films such as those available through the Multi-Media Resource Center. It is our expectation that couples viewing these films and responding to them will be aided in a fuller understanding of both the interpersonal and technique aspects of sexual intercourse. In addition, we recommend exposure to a wide variety of educational experiences, both on our campus and in our community. These include premarriage classes, human sexuality seminars, health and hygiene classes, and the discussion groups available through our Birth Control Clinic.

We have consistently found it helpful to work with student groups, particularly when people within these groups are sharing common sexual concerns. The experience of finding others who are sharing similar feelings has had a facilitating effect. This has been particularly true with our work in the Birth Control Clinic, where the majority of female students requesting services are involved in making decisions about appropriate methods of birth control and most are involved in making sex a meaningful experience in their lives.

In situations where sexual concerns are of a more urgent nature, our technique changes to one of crisis intervention. This is particularly true of unwanted pregnancy. In these instances, premarital pregnancy is conceptualized as a crisis situation capable of generating intense feelings of anxiety, depression, guilt, and despair. Negative feelings and the conflicts associated with an unwanted pregnancy are assumed to have the potential to change an individual's self-concept and interpersonal relationships, and to impair psychological functioning. These emotional responses can result in the development of crystallized psychopathology and residual deficits in interpersonal behavior. However, if the emotional aspects can be resolved constructively, premarital pregnancy can potentially result in positive consequences of a growth facilitating nature.

Pregnant coeds with whom we work are actively discouraged from making impulsive judgments without total exploration of the possible alternatives. Of major concern in our approach to crisis situations of this type is the mobilization and involvement of significant other people. Joint counseling with girls and their families or girls and their boy friends is conducted when necessary or appropriate. On some occasions, we ask girls who have been pregnant and received services from us to discuss their experiences with those currently interested in obtaining an abortion. We stress the continued involvement of the physician who diagnosed the pregnancy, enlisting his services for the management of any physical problems. Occasionally, short-term hospitalization in the University Infirmary is instituted; and, when medically indicated, minor tranquilizers are provided to combat anxiety. The underlying emphasis in these situations is upon the use of the therapist-patient relationship as a supportive vehicle during the crisis period.

This approach to the problem of premarital pregnancy and abortion referral is well supported by our follow-up data.[6] Without exception, women within our sample retrospectively reported that their decisions in regard to abortion were appropriate. Although many women experienced short lived feelings of depression following therapeutic abortion, major physical or emotional aftereffects were rare. The impact of pregnancy and abortion upon significant relationships in a woman's life was consistently evident in our data. However, women in our sample reported that appropriate mobilization of important people in their environment contributed significantly to their own well-being. Our sample further reported that their sexual behavior subsequent to therapeutic abortion reflected a greater responsibility in the use of birth control. Not only was birth control being used more frequently, but women were relying upon statistically more effective methods. The conclusion of our research was that short-term crisis intervention psychotherapy can be effectively applied both to help cope with the immediate crisis and to reduce the potential for negative aftereffects.

IMPLICATIONS FOR TRAINING OF PSYCHOLOGISTS

Based on our experiences, we would urge the training in human sexuality be made an integral part of the graduate school experience for clinical psychologists and other mental health workers. Although each of us received our degrees within the past six years, initially none of us felt qualified to undertake the programs, consultation, and treatment that the emerging sexual behavior of the college student requires. The sexual counselor needs to be a credible source of factual information as well as an expert in the interpersonal, behavioral, and intrapsychic aspects of sexuality. We suggest that specific topics such as the anatomy and physiology of sexual functioning, conception, contraception, abortion, and venereal disease be included.

Because much of our treatment approach with developmental crises is symptom based, there is a need to be conversant with specialized techniques such as those of Masters and Johnson.[7] Also, considerable familiarity with psychotherapy adjuncts such as films, books, and tapes that can be used to stimulate communication and correct misconceptions; these also can serve to reduce the anxiety about sexual experience. The role of the therapist in these situations becomes one of facilitating interaction, increasing interpersonal sensitivity, and providing information. Particular attention should be given to behavior modification approaches as they apply to specific symptoms. Desensitization, discrimination training, modeling, behavioral rehearsal, mutual pleasuring, and sensory awareness training can all be adapted to the treatment of sexual dysfunction. Considerable attention needs to be given to adapting these already existing techniques for uses with couples and groups.

Inherent in the counseling of college students is the need to be able to relate to "normal" sexual concerns and the decision-making process that sexual expression requires. In those situations where sexual concerns are seen as developmental crises, the application of short-term and highly educational techniques appears appropriate and effective. This model is compatible with the needs of the majority of students who request services from us.

The ability to function in this frame of reference requires that the therapist divorce himself from the more traditional view that sexual dysfunction is inevitably symptomatic of internal neurotic conflict accessible only through long-term, insight-oriented psychotherapy. This in no way discredits the application of long-term therapy to neurotic or characterologically based problems, nor does it require that one no longer think in psychodynamically based terms. It does require that the appropriate techniques be applied to the particular needs of a given patient. With college students, we have found it more appropriate to maintain an orientation of facilitating adjustment rather than restructuring personality. We have found it important, however, to remember that a patient's initial presenting problem may not be his basic concern. Therefore, the decision as to treatment approach needs to be based on a thorough assessment of a patient's life situation. Simply because a patient presents himself for the counseling of sexual problems does not exclude the need for evaluation.

A requirement of all effective forms of psychotherapy is that the therapist be aware of his own shortcomings. This is particularly true in the area of sexuality. While the therapist need not be a paragon of sexual adjustment himself, he does need an awareness of those areas in which he is likely to distort, misperceive, or moralize.

As programs of sexuality become dispersed across the campus, the need to be a skillful consultant emerges. The psychologist with the background in the area of sexuality can expect that his services will be valued by a variety of campus agencies. We have found that our time is valuably divided between direct contacts with students and contacts with staffs of the other facilities. This suggests the need for a continued emphasis on a community orientation throughout the graduate school experience. While each of us felt competent as psychotherapists following completion of our formal training, our experience has been that we could have benefited from a better grounding in consultation skills. We would suggest that some attention be given to orienting psychologists toward working with organizations, program development, and program evaluation. This would seem to be a valid focus for postgraduate work for those who lacked this orientation, and which now may be incorporated in graduate training. In addition, we feel that a greater emphasis on group facilitation would have been helpful. Because of the necessity of providing group educational experiences, we have found that the use of encounter-sensitivity techniques, particularly in the form of group warm-up, has facilitated communication.

Because of his research background, the clinical psychologist is in a position to evaluate existing sex-related programs and influence their development through application and presentation of research data. Research facilitates interpretation of programs to the larger campus community. It is especially effective in dispelling notions such as direct confrontation with topics of sexuality or easy access to abortion is the promoter of promiscuity.[8] In this regard, research acts as a therapeutic tool to quiet the critics of various programs.

Finally, it is important that training not neglect the effect of changing mores on behavior, since these influence our interpretation of behavior and our treatment approach. With his research orientation, the clinical psychologist is in a unique position to investigate the effect of such changes on sexual functioning and thereby enhance the body of knowledge necessary for good clinical practice.

References

1. A. C. Kinsey, W. B. Pomeroy, and E. C. Martin, *Sexual Behavior in the Human Male* (Philadelphia: W. B. Saunders Co., 1948); Kinsey, Pomeroy, and Martin, *Sexual Behavior in the Human Female* (Philadelphia: W. B. Saunders Co., 1953); I. Reiss, "The Sexual Renaissance: A Summary and Analysis," *Journal of Social Issues,* 1966, 22: 123–37; I. Reiss, "Premarital Sexual Standards," in *The Individual, Sex, and Society,* edited by Broderick and Bernard (Baltimore: Johns Hopkins Press, 1969).

2. V. Packard, *The Sexual Wilderness* (New York: Pocket Books, 1968); M. Vincent and F. H. Stelling, "A Survey of Contraceptive Practices and Attitudes of Unwed College Students," *Journal of the American College Health Association,* 1973, 21:257–63.

3. Reiss, "Premarital Sexual Standards."

4. J. LeBolt, "Sexual Maladjustment and Its Antidote," *Treatment Monographs on Analytic Psychotherapy,* 1973, 4:2–9.

5. W. Masters and Virginia Johnson, *Human Sexual Inadequacy* (Boston: Little, Brown and Co., 1970).

6. R. Sanders, J. Wagener, and Georgine Thompson, "Counseling for Therapeutic Abortion," *Journal of the American College Health Association,* June 1973, 21:446–50.

7. Masters and Johnson, see note 5.

8. Sanders, Wagener, Thompson, see note 6.

Supervision as Personal Growth

HERBERT M. POTASH*

SEVERAL FACTORS LED TO MY DECISION TO SUPERVISE THE psychotherapy cases of interns in a group setting. Perhaps the most pressing issue was limited time. However, since the interns were novices, they would have similar experiences; and working in a group would enable them to profit from each other and gain a better perspective of themselves. Furthermore, in their placement at the Essex County Hospital Center, they would be doing group therapy exclusively. A supervisory structure that mirrored their own groups would maximize the prospects of transferring learnings from the supervisory group to their client groups. They would have a greater opportunity to observe how to run a group, and greater empathy might be generated toward their patients by their own participation as group members.

The first group began with three interns. We met once a week for a two-hour session. Subsequent group sizes have ranged from three to six. With one exception, there has been some continuity of membership in the group, since the placement of interns overlaps. This has been a distinct advantage insofar as the group climate has been set, and new members can fit into the ongoing format.

*The interns and staff of Essex County Hospital Center have provided the greatest impetus for this paper and deserve special mention.

Initially, the group followed a structured pattern, with weekly rotation of presentation by interns involving both video and audio tapes. Invariably with this group, and with most other interns I have dealt with, the first tape they made was not usable. Either they forgot to turn it on or the sound was too low or they sat out of camera range or the camera was out of focus. Looking back on my own experiences and that of my colleagues when we were supervisees, I recalled how we all made a similar faux pas, which led me to question what was behind the general resistance to supervision.

Before the interns played a tape, a frequent comment was, "I don't want to show this tape because it is terrible. Last week's session was great. If only I had taped last week." This statement is a good cue to the general set that interns bring to supervision. They see supervision as a situation that demands good performance. They fear that they might come across poorly and then be evaluated as less than perfect. This over-concern with evaluation coupled with the perception of psychotherapy as a performance situation seemed widespread among interns. They felt that school had prepared them to perform well; and now, having mastered a large body of knowledge, they were supposed to apply this knowledge as experts. They did not really approach supervision as a place to learn; or, if they did, it was with a great deal of ambivalence and guilt.

The interns' initial reaction to supervision reflected a complex of interrelated factors. Classroom experiences, perceptions of authority figures, their own sex-role identifications, underlying personality structures, and their conceptions of the nature of psychotherapy all affected their approach. Their comments at the internship's end were revealing. Almost all were uncomfortable in labeling their group experience as "supervision" because this word had negative connotations for them that seemed incongruent with their experience itself.

Dealing with interns' resistance to supervision requires an understanding of the aforementioned factors that contributed to their perfectionistic attitude. Because the interns' backgrounds were so diverse, generalities seem necessary, and I have focused on two of these factors: (1) the underlying personality structure and (2) the interns' conceptions of the nature of psychotherapy as affecting their response to supervision.

Typically, interns approach psychotherapy as an intellectual process. They place much emphasis upon techniques and search for the right versus the wrong way of doing things. In this context, psychotherapy becomes a form of role playing. It is approached much like intellectual material in the classroom. It is a new task or performance to be mastered. Since interns have a history of successful intellectual achievement, they use an intellectual approach to insure continued success. This approach to therapy is comfortable because it provides a structure that is familiar. The intern thinks that mistakes can be identified, that he can then learn what he did wrong and therefore prevent similar errors in the future. The amount of personal hurt would then be minimized. Furthermore, approaching therapy as technique and as role playing enables an individual to respond in a "proper controlled manner."

This conceptual scheme of psychotherapy implicitly demands that the client be open and revealing, while the therapist can assume an omnipotent and controlled stance. Often, in this case, the therapist is perceived as wooden and nonhuman. Openness is supposedly generated by therapeutic acceptance; yet acceptance is merely another technique in the therapist's bag of tricks. This becomes blatantly apparent when the white verbal middle-class intern is given a therapy group of black ghetto adolescents. The therapist has typically used suppression of hostility as part of his own life style, while much of the black teenagers' sense of identity has been derived from a continued defiance of authority figures. Usually, in this situation, the therapist "acts accepting," though he is seething over the group's behavior, while the group is enjoying pushing around another "weakling." The novice feels guilty because he is not really accepting and consequently believes that he is deficient in therapeutic warmth. He believes that warmth is a quality he should have at all times, even in situations where his client is unknown and hostile to him.

Another consequence of this technique-oriented approach is that the intern minimizes the nature of his client's uniqueness. He views patients as objects who are to be treated in pre-scribed manners through appropriate therapeutic techniques. Consequently, the rate of progress is seen as due to the thera-pist's skill, making the therapist responsible for curing his pa-tient. When the intern is doing his job properly, he expects the patient to show steady growth. Even though the interns know intellectually what resistance is, they tend to attribute the patient's resistance to their own failures. Each time the patient resists, the therapist re-examines what he has been doing in order to discover how he was wrong. He becomes vulnerable to massive degrees of self-doubt generated by his own errone-ous conceptions.

The novice is prepared for the patient who will not be good and grow according to the therapist's timetable. The intern needs to achieve by making the patient better, and thus he can safeguard his own self-esteem and feel worthy. If the client fails to improve, the therapist views himself as a failure. The greater the fear of failure on the part of the therapist, the more invested he is in the patient's growth, and the more implicit demands he makes on the patient. However, the greater num-ber of demands, the greater amount of resistance the patient offers; consequently, there is a reverberating cycle. The thera-pist is pretending acceptance but feeling angry; the patient is angry and not progressing. Because the therapist's own needs are disabling in this context, it becomes impossible for him to attend to and understand his patient's needs. Too much is happening within this inexperienced therapist for him to at-tend sufficiently to his patient.

An intellectual approach to psychotherapy is also congruent with the life style of many therapists. A prescribed set of be-haviors enables the individual to hide behind a façade. Intel-lectual skills can frequently be used as a cover for feelings that would make the individual uncomfortable. Consequently, even though the therapist allows himself to feel *for* somebody (sympathy and compassion), he cannot let himself feel *with* somebody in a manner that would necessitate the lessening or ultimate loss of intellectual controls. Using this format, the therapist can give from the vantage point of having control. When the client fails to take from him as the therapist believes he should, the therapist will first feel angry; but, since he considers his anger inappropriate, this anger is commonly turned into guilt. The feelings are "I am a failure, since I did not achieve." The client is relegated to a secondary role. He may be the cause of failure, and his lack of improvement may be the consequence of the therapist's errors; yet the trainee is too self-centered at that point to look beyond himself.

The definiteness with which the intern approaches therapy becomes applied to his attitude to the supervisor. The supervisor is viewed as an individual who can point out the intern's errors, make him feel guilty, and confirm his feelings of failure. The high degree of threat that supervision imposes, coupled with the intern's need to discover better and more efficient ways of treating patients, creates a great deal of ambivalence to supervision.

Interns are uncomfortable with all ways in which a supervisor might respond to them. When they are told that they have done a good job, they feel disappointed. Since supervision is supposed to be a learning experience, what have they learned if they are praised? Furthermore, they often do not really believe it when they are told they have done well. They call it an "accident," since they are very uncomfortable with positive feedback.

When supervision involves a discussion of his mistakes, the intern overtly accepts what is being said; yet there is much evidence that he feels deeply hurt. It is very common for the intern to add self-derogation to the supervisor's "criticism." He states that he really knew better, or was stupid to have said what he did to the patient. Frequently, there is a mushrooming effect, where the reaction is quite out of proportion to the issue under discussion, but this process may be internal rather than directly verbalized. The frequency of such reactions suggest that interns attach a great deal of meaning to being criticized, over and above the simple making of mistakes. The failure to be "perfect" reduces the intern's self-esteem. His feelings of being a worthy person are still highly dependent upon successful achievement. In this circumstance, it is almost inevitable that supervisors will be perceived as threats rather than as friends or resource persons.

For supervision to be effective, it seemed essential that I deal with the interns' attitudes to being supervised and the concomitant resistance they brought to the sessions. Interns felt they must be on guard, which seemed to be a long-standing pattern; yet to be effective in supervision, I must promote openness.

It seemed especially important that I reduce the interns' emphasis on technique and make their responses to patients real, believable, and expressive of their own feelings. Consequently, the focus became exploring the interns' personal reactions during their therapy sessions. My questions would frequently be along the lines of "Why did you say that? What were you feeling?"

As the supervisory groups developed and moved further into an exploration of interns' feelings, several common personality patterns began to emerge. While it is premature and probably erroneous to label these features universal among therapists, they were consistent among the different groups of interns that I have supervised.

Similarities in personality are to be expected insofar as professions attract people who have comparable need structures. A psychotherapist is typically seen as an expert in the field of interpersonal relations: a person with all the answers, who cares about and needs to help other people. Concern with making disturbed individuals better adjusted would then appeal to individuals with a strong sense of morality. "Good people" are unselfish, need to please others, and tend to be self-sacrificing. Despite our preference for more sophisticated terminology, we are "good people," since as therapists we basically help people do "right" as opposed to "wrong" things.

Only individuals who have a strongly developed conscience would be interested in a profession that demands a primary interest in helping others.

At the same time, therapists are uncomfortable in admitting their own moral nature. We speak of how important it is to be nonevaluative and nonjudgmental; yet social critics describe psychotherapy as the new religion. Therapists' dislike of Mowrer's description of neurotics as sinners, coupled with their own general discomfort in making moral judgments, has some elements of "the lady doth protest too much." It appears that therapists may be overcompensating for their strict moral codes. They help bad (inferior) people become (grow) good by helping them discover a better set of rights and wrongs, than the ones they used prior to treatment, upon which to lead their lives. This pattern becomes evident when working with interns whose morality is revealed in their overly strong sense of responsibility toward their clients. It is also indirectly expressed through their difficulty in responding to patients outside of sex-role stereotypes.

The development of this strict conscience seems to follow a particular developmental pattern. Through the course of childhood, the individual felt that he was only conditionally accepted by his parents, since he possessed several unacceptable qualities. He received an implicit message that these deficiencies could be overcome through hard work and effort (though he never quite succeeded). Being especially sensitive and wanting to avoid feeling vulnerable, he began to develop particular techniques to avoid further criticism. Paramount to this was the creation of a dominant conscience. In this manner, the individual now had a censor which would provide greater self-protection. Angry feelings, especially, had to go through a filtering process, so that they could be expressed only when justified, which means tinged with morality. Two of the many detrimental side effects that this produced were the restrictions in spontaneity and the overdevelopment of intellectual controls.

In those areas where censoring has been particularly effective, the intern becomes unable to recapture what his deficiencies are. He is, nonetheless, left with the feeling that if he were to lower his defenses and be himself, he would discover something horrible. He would not be accepted if he were really himself. Consequently, despite many past achievements, interns are very much in touch with feelings of their own inferiority. In fact, their need to achieve developed in order to keep people from knowing their weaknesses, and often they have greatly aware of this. Interns still disassociate their achievements from themselves. They view achievements as a technique they *had* to develop and feel; therefore, if they were to stop pushing themselves, the achievement behaviors would disappear permanently from their repertoire. The underlying feeling of being basically bad persists. If interns "push themselves hard enough," they might be perfect; and if, and when, that is achieved, then they might be "good." This conceptual scheme makes it impossible for them to accept or reward themselves. Each effective action becomes reduced to something that was expected, while each ineffective behavior is used as another piece of evidence to confirm their basic sense of inferiority.

The interns view much of their own behavior to be in the service of the needs for safety and self-protection. They achieve in order to hide their weaknesses and stupidity; they act in a "good" manner to hide their evil impulses; they care about others in order to avoid making enemies. With this range of feelings, it is no wonder that they feel terribly defensive and frightened by self-disclosure.

To help the interns see themselves more realistically, it becomes imperative to change this defensive pattern. Actually, interns are generally basically warm, caring, sensitive, and bright individuals who have a great deal to offer. However, their fears of self-disclosure keep them isolated; and, consequently, they fail to integrate their positive qualities into their self-concept. When they do accept themselves, they become tremendously effective in giving therapeutic service. Accepting the reality of oneself, for interns as for everyone else, is a most difficult thing to do.

By not accepting themselves, interns typically fall into a trap where they try to satisfy high achievement needs and the demands of a perfectionistic conscience. They must produce in order to feel competent. Adequacy is equated with inferiority, not with competence. Their internal demands are for perfection, and anything short of it is viewed as failure. Achievement situations are then full of threat, since the interns' self-concept will be reduced if they do not reach their level of expectation. Personal worth is measured by degree of achievement on a disproportionate scale. Only high degrees of achievement can minimally raise feelings of worth, while failure to achieve can result in serious lowering of self-esteem.

With a severely demanding conscience, all failure becomes attributed to personal weakness; and consequently their predominant emotional state is depression. Interns believe that it is inappropriate to blame others for mistakes, unless they can be sure it is really their fault. Consequently, they frequently feel depressed for short periods of time. The depression recurs, since it is impossible to fulfill the demands of an unrealistic conscience.

Yet given the interns' generally "good" behavior and seeming acceptance of the supervisory process, it is possible to go through the motions of supervision and to teach interns how to perform more efficiently without dealing with basic feelings and underlying self-doubts. However, the intern needs to integrate his experiences with his self-concept so that he will be freer and become more effective. As the supervisory process becomes therapeutic, the intern shows remarkable personal growth which becomes directly reflected in his therapy case load.

I have found a semistructured group format very effective in fostering learning and growth. Working in a group setting enables interns to discover how similar they are to their peers, which they find a great relief. Since the group contact is for supervision rather than psychotherapy, each individual can set his own limits as to how far he wishes to pursue self-exploration. In that context, the group process runs the gamut from tape presentations to discussions of their therapy groups to talking about themselves outside the work setting. We also focus on the ways in which they respond to each other and to me. In this regard, the group touches on both T-group and sensitivity group processes.

One notable consequence of group supervision, in my experience, is that when interns discover their own high level of defensiveness within the group, they noticeably reduce the demands they make on their own patients. Furthermore, their own group participation helps them learn the major difference between being therapeutic and being real. In the course of group participation, they grow to care for each other, and friendship patterns far outlast the internship experience.

For the groups to be effective, I have had to set the stage and be open and genuine. I have found that talking about myself and my own experiences helps enormously in lowering barriers, particularly when I share my deficiencies and mistakes. To the degree I can be myself, they can be themselves.

In closing, in many ways interns come to their first placement having learned too much rather than not enough. The numerous techniques that serve a host of personal needs, the high expectations they have of patients, the concern with being right rather than wrong, all cramp their therapeutic style and help to keep them overintellectualized. In that regard, I see supervision as promoting unlearning—taking away the rules and formulas that interns bring to the placement. I try to help them lower personal barriers, to look at themselves, and to see that what is there is genuinely likable. When they do this, what is left to do is to be themselves. I know of nothing more therapeutic than a genuinely caring human being.

Part 4

Training
for the Future

Implications of Humanism and Behaviorism for Training in Treatment

JOHN M. REISMAN

LESS THAN THIRTY YEARS AGO MORRIS KRUGMAN[1] SUR-veyed the field of clinical psychology in the United States and noted a recent development—clinical psychologists were becoming more and more interested in psychotherapy. When Krugman made his report, psychoanalysis enjoyed a position of pre-eminence in psychiatry and psychology.

During that seemingly halcyon period in academic circles, Dollard and Miller[2] tried to marry Hullian learning theory to psychoanalysis and there was "a new look in perception," giving forth studies on perceptual defense and subliminal stimulation. The major tenets of psychoanalysis were well known and had entered the public domain: unconscious motivation was important, and the early years of childhood had a significant bearing upon the behavior of adults. The ideal form of maturity described by analysts was a reasonable, judicious, socially useful expression of impulses. Although analysts spoke of the frustration of sexual and aggressive instincts, they saw some degree of frustration as essential for psychological growth and they believed in the need for instinctual forces to be delayed and subordinated to the demands of reality and the control of the intellect.

At the same time, the seeds of movements antithetical to psychoanalysis had already been sown and were beginning to grow. Two of these movements, humanistic psychology and behavior therapy, have attracted large followings and much popular interest. Despite the fact that they are often presented in opposition to one another, and although they do differ on a number of fundamental issues, they have at least four points of agreement that set them apart from psychoanalysis. These are worthy of our attention because of their implications for training in treatment.

Both humanistic and behavioristic therapists agree that a reconstruction of the past of a client is not necessarily relevant to his psychological treatment. A more forceful expression of this view is that an examination of the individual's past, not only may not help, but actually may impede, the progress of treatment. Stoller,[3] a leading representative of the humanistic movement in psychology, in his discussion of encounter groups stated, "These new groups are explosive because they concentrate on immediate behavior within the group, not on explanations of past behavior—that tempting search for a scapegoat."

In a similar vein, Wenrich, in his exposition of the behavior modification movement, declared:

> It may be that the single most important aspect of the behavior modification movement is its emphasis on an operationally defined, readily observed, and easily measured dependent variable: behavior. In making behavior the focal object of "therapeutic" attention, rather than "conflict resolution" or other "tinkerings" with the "mental" apparatus, behavior technologists have provided themselves with a most objective and sensitive indicant of their activities.[4]

A second point of similarity is that both humanism and behaviorism emphasize the modifiability of human behavior. While analysts talk of repetition compulsion, humanistic psychologists speak of growth, becoming, and self-actualization, and behaviorists speak of conditioning, teaching, and training. Both movements seem eager to try their methods in precisely those situations where other methods either have been thought inappropriate or have been attempted and found ineffective.

Accordingly, humanism and behaviorism radiate a feeling of hope, of optimism, of producing something better, which they have also translated into new directions for the reformation of American society, such as Esalen and Walden II. One supposes that an archaeologist digging in the debris of that new society would find, among the artifacts, textbooks on psychodynamics and some projective techniques.

A third similarity between these movements is that they do not promote intellectual values. Neither has as its goal the growth of reason. Unlike psychoanalysis, which feared the immediate discharge of impulses and which valued the anticipation of consequences and acting-out in thought, humanistic and behavioristic therapists emphasize doing and feeling over thinking. An action orientation is common to both movements. Innovation, experiencing, experimentation in the real world are preferred to contemplation and intellectual rumination.

The behaviorist defines reward and punishment, after the fact, as a stimulus delivered immediately after a response that either increases or reduces the future probability of that response;[5] thus, it is not possible to know what is a reward or a punishment until some action has been taken following a response. The cover of *Gestalt Therapy Verbatim*[6] describes the book as, "An action approach to deepening awareness and living fully in the Here and Now, as experienced in workshops at Esalen Institute." Not so surprisingly, while humanism and behaviorism are often conceived as polar opposites, a client with inhibitions about his body would receive similar treatment from a gestalt or a behavior therapist. The former might recommend participation in a nude marathon, while the latter might urge the client to stand in the nude and indicate parts of his anatomy. Of course, the humanist and the behaviorist arrive at their "anti-intellectualism" by traveling along very different routes. As opposed to Freud, who espoused a rationalist tradition, and whose rallying cry was, "Where id was, there shall ego be,"[7] the humanists are in the mainstream of romanticism; and the behaviorists, in empiricism. The one prizes spontaneity and human feelings, and the other has the control of behavior as its goal; yet both detract from the esteem of intellect, either by ignoring it or by glorifying intuition, impulse, and emotion.

Some years ago a favorite remark of speakers when commenting on behaviorism was, "First psychology lost its soul, and then it lost its mind." That observation has much in common with the slogan attributed to Fritz Perls, "Lose your mind, and come to your senses."

Finally, the behavioristic and humanistic movements share in their relative freedom from professionalism. Both discuss with enthusiasm the recruitment of nonprofessionals in providing treatment or reinforcement. They have encouraged the development of training programs that are brief and limited in scope, and yet few of these professionals seem to believe that "A little learning is a dangerous thing." Instead, the view is expressed that even with just a little learning, some people are able to help a great deal. This conviction has long been held by Rogers,[8] who has consistently stressed the importance of human characteristics, such as warmth and understanding, over intellectual attributes, such as theoretical sophistication and specific techniques. Gardner stated the value of nonprofessionals:

> The first working assumption is that almost every individual is capable of providing educative or therapeutic treatment for mentally retarded or emotionally disturbed individuals. . . . Evidence for the veracity of this assumption comes largely from the success of different nonprofessional therapy programs . . . from behavioral engineering to client-centered counseling.[9]

This belief in the effectiveness of nonprofessionals or paraprofessionals is very appealing, particularly to those who have not invested a great deal of time and effort in becoming psychotherapists. It contrasts markedly with the demands that are made by the American Psychoanalytic Association or by the faculties of many graduate schools in clinical psychology. Obviously, it has implications for training, as do the other points mentioned, and I would like to note just four of them.

The first is that the very existence of these methods has created a much greater diversity of treatment approaches available to the student than was the case just ten years ago, when there were at least twenty.[10] The superiority of one over the other of these approaches is a moot point, which still remains to be settled by research, and which will probably be answered in the form that this method is best suited for this client with this problem to be treated by this therapist.[11]

In the meantime, each year students are applying to graduate schools and training agencies, where, it seems safe to say, not all these methods are taught with equal vigor and skill. Students should be informed what the treatment methods are that are offered by a particular program, so that if by chance they have a preference for a specific method of treatment, they can be assisted in finding a school or agency that offers it.

Let us apply the concept of informed consent, which has been recognized in the ethical principles that guide psychologists in their research—"Openness and honesty are essential characteristics of the relationship between investigator and research participant"[12]—to the teacher and student relationship. It would require that students be given a definite statement of what they may be offered in the way of treatment philosophy and method at a given graduate school before they make application. Moreover, internship agencies and institutions would have to be equally clear.

While some schools and organizations do make explicit statements about their treatment policies and practices, many are content with vague descriptions of themselves as "psychotherapeutic" or "psychodynamic," or with no description at all. It is true that this is a matter that should be investigated by the student. But the investigative abilities of students should not be overtaxed in this area where schools and agencies can reasonably be thought to have a responsibility to declare themselves and where such a responsibility could easily be assumed by them.

A second implication can be derived again, from the sheer

diversity of treatment methods, as well as from studies into the attributes of effective therapists. It is that greater attention be given to the guidance of students into treatment training programs for which they seem most apt. The great amount of research that has been done on characteristics of therapists leads not only to the simple conclusion that much more needs to be done, but also that "there are no qualities of the therapist that are definitive, and it is preferable to speak, not of a good therapist, but of an appropriate therapist for a particular client."[13]

This means that studies should be conducted for the identification of therapist characteristics associated with effectiveness in the use of a given method of treatment. It seems safe to say that Rogerian therapy is best employed by those who have the ability to be empathic, but that this ability is not essential to the conduct of behavior therapy. It also seems highly probable that a student may show little aptitude or inclination for one treatment method—Could Anna Freud use a cattle prod as a noxious stimulus with children?—and yet be suited admirably for some other method. Therefore, what would seem to be appropriate is that the student be evaluated early in his career and counseled as to which treatment approaches would be best suited to him. The purpose of such counseling would not be to deter the otherwise qualified student from pursuing clinical psychology because his personality characteristics are unsuited to a particular method but to guide the student to those treatment approaches for which he seems most inclined. An implication of this implication is that there will be greater and greater heterogeneity among clinical psychologists in the coming years. Already the broad range of treatment approaches seems to be acting to promote acceptance of greater diversity among students than was known some years ago.

A third implication is that universities are becoming less able to train students in all methods of treatment. Linda Hess[14] in describing her experiences at the seventh annual meeting of the American Association for Humanistic Psychology indicates part of the problem:

> I had my belly massaged by a Catholic priest, groped through
> a ballroom full of 1,500 people with eyes shut, heard the latest
> research on out-of-body travel and the emotional life of plants,
> listened to a willowy brunette in underwear scream "NOOO!"
> while a psychiatrist pushed his finger down her throat, had
> conversations with hands, dialogues with eyes, embraces with
> strangers, fights with fresh acquaintances, discussions on new
> approaches to therapy, education, black-white encounter, tran-
> scendental experience, growth centers, communes . . . and that
> wasn't all.

Body contact, rage induction techniques, nudity, punitive
forms of aversive conditioning, sensitivity training, marathon
and encounter groups are controversial methods within the
profession. They arouse both the interest and the suspicion of
the public. By their very nature, many of these techniques
constitute an assault upon the individual. They attempt to
impose an effect, and the danger is that the imposition may be
greater than what had been intended.

From the standpoint of the university, there is always concern that it represent the highest standards of proper conduct
and that it maintain the confidence, trust, and support of its
society. I think it can be agreed that despite the liberality of
professional attitudes, there would be public reaction to any
report that teachers and pupils are seeing one another in the
nude at any state-supported school. It is also likely that in view
of the $170,000 in damages awarded to a woman who was
distressed by her experience with a "rage reduction" technique,[15] faculty members and administrations would be wary
of encouraging treatment practices along similar lines. While
these examples are perhaps extreme, they are intended to
convey the idea that some treatment methods that may seem
especially exciting and innovative may not be able to be taught
and practiced in a university setting.

Already the disparaging attitude of some psychologists toward psychotherapy and the squeeze upon training by being
crunched between the scientist-practitioner model and a rapidly expanding field of knowledge held within the vise of a

limited period of graduate school have produced a trend toward the development of professional schools and institutes. The restrictions upon what can be practiced within the university, brought about by the nature of the content and the time available for the host of treatment methods have enhanced the attractiveness of post-doctoral fellowships and workshops and compel us to consider what the university can and cannot offer.

The university cannot train the student equally well in every treatment method. With all the diversity that now exists and that is coming into being, no university conceivably has or could have the faculty to make possible such an offering. Some treatment techniques are not appropriate to the university setting. Some are too extreme in their anti-intellectualism or in their claims that they are offensive to the academic community, while some skirt the fringes of what is offensive to the public or professional codes of ethics.

This leads to a fourth and final implication, a consideration of what the university can offer for which it is best suited and unique—training in selected methods and procedures at various levels of education and an appreciation and awareness of horizontal and vertical continuities.

Vertical continuities refer to the historical development of ideas, practices, and organizations. For the individual a sense of personal continuity is thought to be essential in establishing a feeling of identity.[16] It seems reasonable to suppose that it is just as imperative for the members of a discipline to be mindful of the history of their profession in order to establish a sense of their professional identity and to perceive some orderliness and consistency in the developments within their field.

This specification of vertical continuities has often been neglected. At times it is assumed that its mention serves no useful purpose and that psychologists are knowledgeable about their history. For example, Albee in his presidential address to the American Psychological Association stated: "Clinical psychology has a very different history. I will not tire you with its recitation because it is so familiar."[17] Yet despite "everyone's"

familiarity with the subject, in that same address Albee referred repeatedly to the traditions of clinical psychology extending back some twenty-five years, when it could easily be
demonstrated that those traditions extend back some seventy-
five years.[18]

At other times, the mention of vertical continuities is
brushed aside because they obviously conflict with the purpose
of creating discontinuities. New methods and new techniques
are introduced usually by stressing how they differ from established practices, with an intent to demonstrate that what has
existed has outlived its usefulness and should be supplanted.
This has frequently been the manner in which humanism and
behaviorism have been presented. However, without the perspective provided by vertical continuities, the persistent dec-
laration of discontinuities fosters apprehension and feelings of
alienation and can lead to calls for fragmentation of the field.[19]

Moreover, an awareness of vertical continuities does more
than tell us where we have been. It is a mark of the educated
and mature professional who recognizes that his world can
profitably be broadened by extending it back and by giving it
a perspective and relatedness with the aspirations and efforts
of those who preceded him.

Horizontal continuities refer to commonalities among existing methods and ideas. Just as there seems to be a need to
assert differences, so too does there seem to be an inclination
to seek out similarities when the differences are recognized.
Some of these continuities may be quite superficial. A beginning is to point out that psychoanalysts, behavior therapists,
humanistic therapists, and practitioners of whatever treatment method are all human beings. Another obvious similarity
was mentioned by London[20] in his call for a reconciliation
between behavior therapists and others. He noted that all
therapists share the goal of helping their clients. Although
these continuities cannot be denied, it would be preferable to
identify those that are more definitive and not so inclusive.

The identification of structures common to a number of
treatment methods or the specification of sets of principles

shared by a variety of treatment approaches is a means of noting horizontal continuities that helps both to order and to unify the field and to communicate its nature to the student. For example, one principle of psychotherapy is that the therapist negotiate a purpose or goal for the meetings with the client.[21] Such a principle is a relatively specific commonality among psychotherapists, whether humanistic, behavioristic, or psychoanalytic, which makes clear their role and which aids the student to discern unifying threads that run through existing, novel, and ever-changing approaches to treatment.

The university is ideally suited for the identification and dissemination of vertical and horizontal continuities. Unlike a training school or institute, it is not supposed to be partisan to any particular point of view. It is supposed to render an impartial account to its students of many positions and to provide a framework by which a multiplicity of theories and methods can be organized into an integrated understanding. Happily, its very word origins proclaim that task. The word *university* comes from the Latin words *unus* and *vertere*, "to turn into one," and it is that turning into one which makes the training of the university special and worthwhile.

References

1. M. Krugman, "Recent Developments in Clinical Psychology," *Journal of Consulting Psychology*, 1949, 9:342–53.
2. J. Dollard and N. E. Miller, *Personality and Psychotherapy* (New York: McGraw-Hill, 1950).
3. F. H. Stoller, "The Long Weekend," in *Readings in Clinical Psychology Today* (Del Mar, Calif.: CRM Books, 1967).
4. W. W. Wenrich, *A Primer of Behavior Modification* (Belmont, Calif.: Brooks-Cole, 1970), p. 73.
5. N. H. Azrin and W. C. Holz, "Punishment," in *Operant Behavior*, edited by W. K. Honig (New York: Appleton-Century-Crofts, 1966).
6. F. S. Perls, *Gestalt Theory Verbatim* (New York: Bantam Books, 1969).
7. S. Freud, *New Introductory Lectures on Psycho-Analysis* (1933) (New York: W. W. Norton, 1933), p. 112.
8. C. R. Rogers, *Client-Centered Therapy* (Boston: Houghton Mifflin, 1951).
9. J. M. Gardner, "Innovation in the Delivery of Psychological Services in an Institution," *American Psychologist*, 1971, 26:211–14.
10. J. M. Reisman, *Toward the Integration of Psychotherapy* (New York: Wiley-Interscience, 1971), p. 21.
11. A. E. Bergin, "Some Implications of Psychotherapy Research for Therapeutic Practice," *Journal of Abnormal Psychology*, 1966, 71:235–46.
12. *APA Monitor*, Jan. 1973, 4:2.
13. Reisman, *Toward the Integration of Psychotherapy*, p. 92.
14. L. Hess, "A Note on the Climate," in *Confrontation*, edited by L. Blank, G. B. Gottsegen, and M. G. Gottsegen (New York: Macmillan, 1971).
15. *APA Monitor*, Sept.-Oct. 1972, 3:16.
16. E. H. Erikson, "Growth and Crises of the 'Healthy Personality,' " in *Personality: In Nature, Society, and Culture*, edited by C. Kluckhonn, H. A. Murray, and D. M. Schneider (New York: Alfred A. Knopf, 1971).
17. G. W. Albee, "The Uncertain Future of Clinical Psychology," *American Psychologist*, 1970, 25:1071–80.
18. J. M. Reisman, *The Development of Clinical Psychology* (New York: Appleton-Century-Crofts, 1966).
19. Policy and Planning Board, "Structure and Function of APA: Guidelines for the Future," *American Psychologist*, 1972, 27:1–10.
20. P. London, "The End of Ideology in Behavior Modification," *American Psychologist*, 1972, 27:913–20.
21. J. M. Reisman, *Principles of Psychotherapy with Children* (New York: Wiley-Interscience, 1973).

Reformulation as a New Direction in Psychotherapy

HAROLD B. DAVIS

INTRODUCTION

IN CONSIDERING THE PHRASE, "NEW DIRECTIONS IN PSY-chotherapy," we must keep in mind that *new* is a relative term. The social changes over two and a half decades, the revisions within the field based upon increased experience, the movement away from psychotherapy, and the changing of a generational gap all affect the place of psychotherapy in the culture or the concept of what constitutes therapeutic changes.

We are in a period when established institutions are being challenged—including the therapeutic community—with mixed feelings of powerlessness, boredom, and lack of commitment. These attitudes coalesce with a general anti-intellectual or pseudomeditative life style which, with valid criticisms, suggest that there is nothing to the psychotherapeutic process at all. Man must change institutions, not himself; he lives out himself, he does not analyze or change himself. The criticism of the psychotherapeutic process can be tested by Eysenck's research,[1] where the therapeutic outcome is considered in

I wish to thank H. Nechin, S. Gottlieb, and R. Kent for their helpful suggestions.

terms of specific behaviors. It can be used to illustrate that nothing happens in therapy when what should be criticized are the false claims of therapists and the idealized hopes of the patient. Disillusionment, not necessarily discouragement, is a by-product if not the essence of the psychoanalytic process.

THE CLINICAL MODEL

The Greek root of the word *clinical* means "of a bed" (sickbed or deathbed). In the medical sense, clinical can mean "occupied with investigation of disease in the *living subject by observation* as distinguished from controlled experiment." The dictionary defines *clinic* as a place "in which special problems are studied by *concrete examples* and expert advice or treatment is given."

The concept of clinical professor has always indicated one who practiced and taught via their experience of practice, whether it be medical or educational. All psychoanalytic practice, whether we deal with the problem as a disease[2] or not,[3] fits this definition. It is this clinical approach that is the essential ingredient of psychotherapy training and the one that creates the greatest difficulty of developing in a doctoral training program. The extent and limitations for this training will be discussed, although it is recognized that no program intends to be solely psychotherapy training.

The new clinical student embarking on a career in psychotherapy is presently introduced to the field with a marked disadvantage as compared to twenty-five years ago. Research, a method of investigation that he values, states that psychotherapy does not produce results. How can he have confidence, let alone faith, in a process whose logic is antithetical to the research process? Furthermore, the experiential aspects of psychotherapy lend themselves more to the language of poetry, art, ethics, and philosophy than they do to the logic of research methodology. Even where research does demonstrate positive outcomes—increased income, change in self-attitude—there is a disquiet about the extent to which psychotherapy can assuage the basic conflicts in a person's life and delimit the neurotic, that is, self-perpetuation of one's misery. Goals here do not refer to fulfillments of the patient's desire, often irrational, nor to the therapist's need to see success in order to justify his professional existence, but, rather, to the realization that the conditions of a person's life have changed in the direction of more emotional relatedness in some significant and meaningful way.

The reconstruction of one's life by a continuous inquiry into the persistent conflicts, the roots of these conflicts, and the aspects of the present personality structure that motivates a persistence of these conflicts is a potentially profound experience that may fundamentally change the way a person functions. To deal effectively with the process, the therapist must discern not only the issues in a person's life and relate to them effectively, but he must also become trusting to the patient. This ability or lack of ability to trust may account for the length of some treatment. Yet, on the therapist's side, he cannot develop trust merely by technique but, rather, by a demonstration of his sincerity in the task at hand. Knight in writing about Searles states that he "learned early in his work that all therapy, but probably especially modified psychoanalytic psychotherapy with schizophrenics, consists of a deeply significant emotional experience in *each* of the two parties to the therapeutic relationship, and that progress toward a good outcome requires ruthlessly honest self-awareness on both sides."[4] This ability to be honest to oneself whether or not one communicates this honesty to the patient is not a technique in any sense of the word. Certainly, clinical experience may be related to discovering what it is that is going on with the patient, but the lessening of the defensiveness and the ability to be relatively honest about oneself requires a courage in the therapist as well as in the patient. This type of courage is not readily trainable because it also requires a courage vis-á-vis acceptable standards of truth. The therapist may become like the child in the "Emperor's New Clothes," a metaphor used by Fromm[5]: capable of piercing the illusions of his culture.

How does a new therapist gain the awareness of the depth and scope of human experiences? How does he become aware of the scope of human possibilities, and therefore gain the awareness of what is possible for the patient—i.e., what are the present conflicts in the person's life and what are the possible alternatives open to the person? How does the new therapist learn to trust his own perceptions and awareness of the patient that tell him something that statistical data cannot produce? Thus, Reik's *Listening with a Third Ear*[6] is something that is alien to his academic training. Where does the new therapist come to grips with Erikson's statement[7] of the leverage of truth and the extent to which one human being can help another human being, knowing full well the limits and depths of this statement?

PROBLEMS IN PSYCHOTHERAPY TRAINING

The shifts in psychotherapy training over the past twenty-five years have not been basic ones, but rather extensions of a basic idea. Whereas in the late 1940s and the first half of the 1950s individual psychotherapy, particularly psychoanalysis or psychoanalytic psychotherapy, was the main mode of treatment, today we are exposed to many alternatives—e.g., client-centered therapy, rational-emotional, conjoint, family therapy, group therapy, behavior modification, and community mental health, especially with increasing dissatisfaction for individual psychoanalytic therapy. In addition, there are alternatives to legitimate therapeutic programs, such as sensitivity training, encounter groups, women liberation group discussion, which siphon off the emotional experience and provide people with a rationale or rationalization against psychotherapy, in addition to whatever independent merit they may have. After all, what brings people to psychotherapy are emotional upheavals or conflicts, and the need for basic concern no matter how these emotional needs are expressed or disguised via symptomatology.

In addition, the spoken word has lost its importance—witness the increase in TV, a medium that stresses action but where the use of words is frequently banal. A real loss of experience occurs when only words are used. The Aristotelian logic of language changes the nature of the experience and necessarily distorts it. Many patients are wary of words, if not actually mistrusting of them, because our society often prostitutes words.

Yet what we are left with are words and the necessity to become aware of their limitations. The limitations and dangers of intellectual constructions, particularly for psychologists who already are intellectualized, are well established. Nevertheless, the therapist intervenes with words, and the impact he makes is partly through his interpretations, confrontations, or reflections. Thus, a new therapist has to become aware of the actual and transferential impacts of what he has to say. Different therapeutic techniques reflect the implicitly different ways people relate to one another in addition to the explicit ways they relate via the words they use. The "therapeutic techniques" are aspects of human relationships. Thus, the different orientations—and there are differences to the different orientations—reflect different images of man or aspects of human relatedness.[8] These differences cannot be attributed only to technique. The product of psychotherapy is not one solely subject to techniques other than the implicit assumption of such a patient and therapist that life is simply a technical process: an alienated image that may be becoming more popular in our technological society.

Training in psychotherapy always existed with two aspects. One was the field experience (the practicum in doing), and the other was the reading of the literature. The readiness to do therapy, i.e., the maturity of the student, is not always taken into account. A clinician demonstrates his expertise by clearly delineating and developing the issues in the patient's life and helping the patient to deal with them. The new clinician learns through his own experience and through his observation of his supervisor, thereby gaining confidence in this approach. That this process may lead to identification by the student with the supervisor is to be avoided or at least recognized and appropriately handled. The student may, and likely will overidealize this skill, perhaps seeing it as magic, while not recognizing the dynamic links that make it feasible for the supervisor to see the connections better. The most likely reason the new student cannot make these connections lies in his learning style as well as blind spots.[9] The latter may well deal with specific blocks, but the learning style refers to the total way a person learns anything. In either case, it is a form of countertransference vis-à-vis the patient. I would suggest that the learning style, consistent with doctoral work, may be inconsistent with psychotherapy training. One learns by doing in therapy, not merely by intellectual knowledge. The style of learning in the living subject by observation or concrete examples is different from controlled experimentation. It is the starting point of experimental research to develop hypotheses for experimentation, and the psychotherapist-clinician has been a fertile resource for such hypotheses.[10] He has been the follower of the logic of discovery rather than the logic of justification.[11] But it is the latter that is necessary in experimentation. Certainly, science needs both, but emphasis on carefully controlled psychological experiments is abstract, if not irrelevant, to the therapeutic training and is certainly at variance with the clinical form of learning.

The cleavages in clinical psychology programs that have existed are due in part to conflicts, power, status, and so on; but the fact remains that the clinical psychologist as clinician has rarely been accepted in the psychology department. Over the past twenty-five years, we have witnessed eliminations of internships, a lessening of a commitment to practice, the development of professional schools and programs in medical schools, or postdoctoral programs in an attempt to find a more suitable setting for the training of clinicians, particularly therapists. These newer settings reflect a need to find an atmosphere more conducive to the clinical form of learning.

What skills does a psychotherapist need? First and foremost, he needs the ability to experience the inner state of another human being and at the same time remain sufficiently distant so that he can be therapeutically effective. The sufficient distance would prevent an identification with the patient or a merging with him. Too much distance, while affording some security to the therapist, and in some instances to the patient (those too afraid of closeness), may preclude empathy and recipathy.[12] This ability to comprehend the inner state of another varies in terminology and to some degree in meaning— e.g., Sullivan's participant observer,[13] Singer's nondefensive projection,[14] or Roger's definition of empathy[15]—but it is central to the therapeutic process. What experiences can develop this ability? On a most pessimistic level, I would say none. The student brings it with him, and thus selection factors are most critical here. And selection factors have to be open to the late bloomer or student who has had and resolved some crises, for he brings an awareness of human growth that cannot be taught.

One of the difficulties in training is that there is a differential rate in learning for clinical skill that does not mirror the academic schedule. Clinical skill depends upon the ability of the person to grasp the nuance via empathy and recipathy; and the learning style of academic psychology is inconsistent with this skill. It requires a reduction of both personal and achievement anxiety sufficient to permit this development, not necessarily the input of information or techniques. It is a skill, to use Toynbee's phrase,[16] that is part of a lifelong learning process. Different approaches, some traditional and some innovative, can be used to develop this skill. Certainly exposure of a student to different clinical settings with different populations is necessary, and role playing, listening to tapes, and such activities can be useful. The student needs to be exposed to the different orientations so that he may experience these differences and develop his own synthesis. Even if all roads lead to Rome, an unproved assumption, the roads do not go through the same terrain. Too often the technique of a particular orientation becomes the handmaiden of the procedure in that one learns to reflect, confront, or interpret as if this procedure will help the patient altogether. The therapist must be able to react, that is, use his self-awareness to comprehend and relate to the patient's symbolic communication.

Clinical theory is required to synthesize the data. Thus, the consistency of personality and the awareness of the basic themes of a particular person's life is important, and so is meaningful diagnosis. The new psychotherapy student needs to be aware of the defensiveness of individuals not in the intellectualized way learned in personality theory, but with an experience of that anxiety that has to be experienced as a person changes in life. This may require his own treatment.

Art forms and literature can help get at the inner experience, which of course is related to the behavior patterns. Yet psychotherapy is not an art form, but more likely a craft that we become increasingly more proficient with as we terminate with one patient and start with another.

One of the most important experiences for a new therapist is to become aware that: (1) some people can be helped by therapy and (2) that *he* can help some people. Research[17] show that most new therapists are not aware of the former because of their own defensiveness, particularly their tendency to resort to intellectualization. With regard to the latter, the psychotherapy training in a doctoral program is rarely of sufficient length to observe marked change in character structure. Secondarily, the kinds of change do not fit his learning theory. Could it not be done by any decent human being who can relate to a patient and listen patiently? Certainly the movement to BA mental health experts and paraprofessionals partly reflects this attitude. This leads to a number of clinical psychology programs and clinical psychologists de-emphasizing psychotherapeutic skills, and it leaves the new therapist uncertain and lacking confidence in the approach, more so than an initiate to another field whose problem is to learn skills, not question whether there is a justification to his field. Rarely in doctoral programs does a student get a chance to see the effectiveness of long-term treatment or to be exposed to a faculty who have made a commitment to clinical therapeutic practice. The student is thereby deprived of relying in a meaningful way on his elders, that is, to learn from their experience, not merely to acquire technique. Not yet able to learn from his own experience, and not able to find those to rely upon, there is a loss of purposefulness in this endeavor. For a therapist to gain confidence in his ability to help people and to realize what can be achieved, there is no substitute for the relatively successful treatment of one person over a relatively long period of time.

CRITIQUE OF TWO DEVELOPMENTS

Two "new" developments have become pronounced in the last decade: (1) community mental health and (2) behavior modification. The first reflects two processes or influences: the civil rights movement and black liberation illuminated the needs of poor people and questioned the relevancy of psychotherapy to their needs. In response, and with the infusion of money to doctoral programs, clinical psychology devised the community health program. The community or institution would be the patient or client to whom clinical psychologists addressed their skills. The hope was to reach more people indirectly, and it has some merit. All clinicians would like to extend the advantages of psychotherapy to a greater segment of our society. A clinician would like to try to his skills at resolving social conflicts. For example, Bard in his crisis intervention program at New York's City College has worked with New York City policemen to reduce family conflicts, but the work has been really tutorial and applied—that is, it has trained key people with skills of conflict resolution. In hospitals, we knew that the key personnel were aides and nurses, and group psychotherapy was planned for them. By reducing conflicts of the key personnel or by helping them better relate to those with whom they come into contact, we hoped to extend the benefits of our skill to more people. This might better be called indirect clinical practice than community mental health, for we know that this indirect factor occurs in psychoanalytic practice too. A teacher, who is in therapy, will as a result of her responding to changes within herself relate differently to her pupils. Similarly, people in key positions, such as administration, can do a lot of harm by neglect, especially when the motivation is resentment. Community mental health, when applied to institutional change, is doomed to failure when applied by psychologists qua psychologists. The nature of the social-political forces are such that no single group can effectively change the institutions: other groups whose values may be different also have political power. Nor do our clinical skills make us experts in social change. A clinical psychologist who wishes to be a social activist can only do so as an individual or as he reveals himself in the treatment process.

With regard to behavior modification, we are confronted with an interesting interaction between contemporary social forces and a treatment process rooted in psychological learning theory. But this approach clearly rests on manipulation (I do not mean this in the pejorative sense), and the goal is to instruct via techniques—a change in behavior *without* reference to inner states. This approach is in keeping with social attitudes in which people do not experience a sense of awareness and choice. It emphasizes a conditioning of the patient, not growth. The 1970 EPA Bulletin has two separate sessions on behavior modification that reflect the popularity of this approach. The search for new variations or techniques proliferate, but it appears that there is a running away from clinical practice of psychotherapy and what can be learned from this process, in particular via the development of choice and awareness. This running away reflects several factors, such as changes in our social attitudes and institutions as well as the inherent difficulties in being a clinician-therapist in our culture. These difficulties are the loneliness of the job, the need to face uncertainty, the devaluation of it via Bachelor and Master degrees or paraprofessionals. Also, our society looks for quick solutions, and work for a long period of time with a single person that produces nondramatic results is not valued. Yet, to the patient, the worth may be immeasurable. We arrive at a basic dilemma of values: what is worthwhile? Our society calls for quick solutions and something that is overt and demonstrable. That is part of our action-oriented society. While we must recognize that there may be some different approaches to different people, we ought to recognize, too, that when we deal with control or manipulation of behavior, we are dealing with social control and not treatment of a person. The patient has a choice of treatment; therefore, all forced treatment, whether behavior modification or psychotherapy, is an anathema. Nevertheless, behavior modification has been done essentially with populations who have no control over their fate.

REFORMULATION AS A NEW DIRECTION

Is it feasible to teach the nature of growth as applied to therapy? If we say yes, then it must be recognized that the form of training does not fit the usual sense. Therapeutic training that is restricted to a particular diagnostic category slots and treats an individual accordingly, which results in the treatment of an abstraction. The benefits may help an individual insofar as it helps deal with current issues in the person's life and insofar as he fits the slot. Yet a statement may be generally true but not most relevant at this moment for this individual.

The selection of new trainees needs to reflect the search for those who are open to the inner experiences and to empathy, that is, those able to see and ultimately learn the patterns of living and of growth. Within the training program we need to be able to *elicit*, not train, the responsiveness of the student so that he can constructively make use of his own awareness of personality and his reactions. Case material is a useful medium, but the approach is one of helping a student become aware of his blind spots and learning style in addition to didactic teaching. Video-tapes, observing behavior in classrooms, and similar activities can be used toward this purpose.

Analytic therapy still remains for those people for whom there are some options in life, and who feel the need to change themselves in some regard. Its implications for psychotherapy training still remain valid. We have learned that certain traditional treatment methods are not singularly effective, although they may contribute to the therapeutic process (for example, introspection). We have learned that dreams may not be as essential as before, that frequency of visits and certain rules concerning treatment will not readily be accepted in the present-day social order, or at least the patient will more readily express his resentment and not let it be readily dismissed as transference. We have learned to be less rigid in our approach and more honest in a self-awareness vis-à-vis the patient. We recognize that growth is not merely a function of frequency of visits.

Yet despite certain changes, the old remains very much true; transference, countertransference, empathy are still with us as viable aspects of the treatment process. The defensiveness of the individual, his avoidance of anxiety, and the consistency of personality are still crucial concepts. The importance of the self has been reintroduced as a crucial variable—for the maintenance of esteem. There are small increments and changes, but they make a difference in how a therapist relates to the patient, what in the communication he responds to and *what he does not* respond to, when he remains silent and when he speaks. A fruitful integration of the new and the old requires the recognition that there is no quick solution to this problem and that no specific technique that will do the trick. Since differences do occur in various approaches, the student has to sift and develop his approach and come to grips with his own orientation and ultimately take his stand. The new may be old—e.g., redefinitions of the concept of transference—and the old, new in that a new perspective changes the old so a new light is thrown upon it. The change may be subtle rather than clear cut, but the new integration makes for a substantial change in the quality of the therapeutic experience. It also is an inherent part of the clinical model—that is, where learning takes place in the context of the treatment of an individual. And it clearly is a learning that includes a revelation to a dimension of human growth and experience that is not as likely obtainable by other forms. A clinical psychology without therapy training is not viable, nor will it be feasible to have a meaningful psychodiagnostic or research program of a clinical nature without an appreciation of the therapeutic modality.

For some people whose lives have been particularly damaged by hurts and emotional cleavage, the changes that may take place may well be relatively short when compared to a lifelong problem—for example, a paranoid person who is helped to trust to some degree; a homosexual who becomes heterosexual by choice; a highly schizoid person who experiences some emotional relatedness, the ability to tolerate aloneness, and the reduction of massive dependency or symbiosis. The ability to choose the direction one wishes to go in life unencumbered by overwhelming irrational guilt or the capacity to experience guilt where justified. The general ability to make some alternatives in life—that is, not to be compelled by one's irrational strivings whether they be couched in the form of perfectionism or in the form of ambitiousness—require the goal of value and choice. The maintenance of these goals and values depend upon social forces that can also oppose them. What can be learned from these processes is crucial to a meaningful field of personality, abnormality, or personality change that are the keystones of clinical psychology.

References

1. J. Eysenck, "The Effects of Psychotherapy," *International Journal of Psychiatry,* 1965, 1:97–142.
2. David Ausubel, "Personality Disorder *Is* Disease," *American Psychologist,* 1961, 16:69–74.
3. Thomas Szasz, "The Myth of Mental Illness," *American Psychologist,* 1960, 15:113–18.
4. Harold F. Searles, *Collected Papers on Schizophrenia and Related Subjects* (New York: International Press, 1965), p. 17.
5. E. Fromm, *Sigmund Freud's Mission* (New York: Grove Press, 1963).
6. Theodor Reik, *Listening with a Third Ear* (New York: Pyramid Books, 1964).
7. Erik Erikson, *Ghandhi's Truth* (New York: W. W. Norton, 1969).
8. Maurice Friedman, *To Deny Our Nothingness* (New York: Delacorte Press, 1967).
9. R. Ekstein and R. S. Wallerstein, *The Teaching and Learning of Psychotherapy* (New York: Basic Books, 1963).
10. Robert R. Holt, "Yet Another Look at Clinical and Statistical Prediction: Or, Is Clinical Psychology Worthwhile?" *American Psychologist,* 1970, 25:337–49.
11. W. H. Reichenbach, *Elements of Symbolic Logic* (New York: Free Press, 1947).
12. H. A. Murray, *Explorations in Personality* (New York: Oxford University Press, 1938).
13. H. S. Sullivan, *Psychiatric Interview* (New York: W. W. Norton, 1953).
14. E. Singer, *Key Concepts in Psychotherapy* (New York: Random House, 1965).
15. Carl Rogers, *Client-Centered Therapy* (Boston: Houghton Mifflin, 1965).
16. A. Toynbee, Preface to *Campus 1980: The Shape of the Future in Higher Education,* edited by A. C. Eurich (New York: Dell, 1968).
17. Eysenck, see note 1.

The Continuity

of Training

JOANNE H. LIFSHIN

IN A COMMUNITY HEALTH CENTER, ISSUES ABOUT CLINICAL training regularly confront the clinical psychologist. Within a community setting, professional staff members must use both their theoretical and applied backgrounds in providing diagnosis, treatment, and in-service training, and in preparing community agency personnel to be primary care-givers. The range and focus of the psychologist's activities are limited by the overall orientation of the center, the needs of the community, and the background of the psychologist. The geographic location, hospital or community base, and relative activity of consumers of services in planning contribute to judgments on adequacy of training and how training will be used. This paper will focus on clinical training issues from three perspectives: preparation and continued training of staff psychologists, training of community-oriented students, and training of members of other disciplines, including paraprofessionals.

GENERAL DEVELOPMENTS IN CLINICAL TRAINING

Clinical training programs have changed to provide earlier exposure to clinical skills, as well as exposure to behavior therapy and community psychology. Core requirements have been reduced. By 1968–69 child-clinical training was more available than it had been in 1964–65.[1] The need for training programs to respond to consumer demands is now emphasized.[2] Specialization in terms of particular problems that lend themselves to interdisciplinary approaches is also recommended. Psychologists who are responding to changes in the broader social order, including greater student participation in the planning of training, are questioning the usefulness of the scientist-practitioner model. Schneider[3] notes the changes occurring in science and professionalism, observing that the role of the university in the broader community is changing. However, he is less pessimistic about the utility of the scientist-practitioner model than Albee[4] when the concept of science is expanded to include elements such as observation, description, and identification of natural phenomena, as well as experimental investigation and theoretical explanation. He further emphasizes that the roles of scientist and professional are not necessarily incompatible within the same individual as evidenced by several noted psychologists.

Criticisms of and alternatives to the traditional training of the psychologist as scientist-practitioner highlight the diversity of functions and settings that become the province of psychology. Knowledge available in other areas such as sociology, anthropology, and biology is necessary. The literature reflects a need to define the role of the psychologist that cuts through the diversity of activities and to develop approaches that will enable the student to meet evolving expectations when he leaves training. Increasingly, varied goals and capabilities of students are being recognized, and efforts are being made to make programs more flexible to enable students to capitalize on their interests and capabilities. One area that requires consideration in planning program changes is the extent to which earlier training in more traditional settings has prepared current staff members for innovation and what parts of the traditional training should be retained. The future may be expected to show the directions that will emerge from training planned by those psychologists whose own training has been less traditional, i.e., those psychologists trained primarily in behavior therapy or community psychology.

IMPLICATIONS OF TRAINING FOR A COMMUNITY MENTAL
HEALTH SETTING

Psychologists who choose to work in a community setting share common goals and experiences. Divergent views of community mental health appear, however, reflecting the broad range of activities that comprise community mental health centers. For example, one psychologist may relate almost exclusively to inpatient diagnosis and treatment, while another is engaged primarily in consultation with community agencies. Dialogue among psychologists highlights their differing needs for further education, and those aspects of graduate education that are most useful and those that are irrelevant. The diversity of expectations for psychologists from staff members of other disciplines and community agency personnel forces closer examination of identity as a psychologist. Decisions about use of staff time reflect decisions regarding role and function in this setting.

The psychologist in this setting shares with applied psychologists the need to seek knowledge of new developments in the field, thus preventing isolation and crystallization of practices that are of limited usefulness. The psychologist may explore new developments or expand knowledge in familiar areas to a different aspect of clinical work or for modification to the community mental health setting.

Careful consideration of the factors that impinge on the type of services offered precedes development of programs or introduction of new modalities of treatment. Community psychology can be viewed as an amalgam of many aspects of psychology, and programs introduced by psychologists typically encompass a range of areas to which the psychologists have been exposed. Resources that were readily available in another department or at least geographically obtainable to clients in graduate school may be unavailable or limited. If these services cannot be provided by other mental health disciplines, questions arise concerning the adequacy of the psychologists' current skills to develop them effectively, whether further education is necessary, or whether it is inappropriate for psychologists to enter a particular area. For example, it may be a relatively easy task to determine that special schools or classes for emotionally disturbed children are needed, but far more difficult to obtain these services or to develop alternatives. Current work on cognitive difficulties arose through identification of the need for services for children whose academic skills were severely impaired. The problem-solving and treatment skills of the psychologists working in this area are continuously evolving. Such children frequently show extensive ego deficits, and neither behavior modification in school nor child psychotherapy are sufficient in themselves to bring about change. Research, diagnostic, and treatment skills have all been required and have been modified in accordance with patient characteristics and factors specific to the setting. Knowledge of referral sources and consultation with care-giving agencies develop along with with specific projects. A review of courses available at the graduate level shows a wide variety that would aid in preparation for development of programs in any one area. However, preparation for program development in one area, such as cognitive difficulties related to ego deficits, can restrict one's awareness of related emotional and social difficulties and thus prevent a cohesive approach to the services required. The psychologist must be able to define goals clearly in reference to knowledge of what can be accomplished with the resources available and be prepared to redefine problems as new information is available.

The scientist-practitioner model is feasible in the community mental health setting when research data also contributes to the provision of service. Needs for observation, identification, and description of natural phenomena are highlighted when one seeks to obtain greater understanding and baseline data of coping mechanisms that enable individuals to function effectively in an economically deprived area. It is necessary to know whether or not nationally standardized assessment instruments are appropriate. A community such as Brownsville provides a rich natural environment for research, and extensive researchable problems are available. The extent to which research is feasible, particularly concerning experimental investigation, is considerably more restricted for the psychologist here than in the academic setting. Procedures for obtaining subjects require several levels of clearance in the center and in the community. Careful attention must be paid to providing service along with research. These safeguards of subject rights and demands for service are respected and are necessary. The traditional Ph.D. thesis or other student research does not prepare one for the development of research within an applied setting. One must be prepared to educate others about the usefulness of research data and the gains from systematic evaluation. The role of scientist-practitioner requires close cooperation among staff members and safeguards for completion of research aspects of problems. It would be useful for graduate students to initiate research projects in applied settings and to gain experience in communicating with personnel in service-oriented agencies about research while more experienced advisors are available for consultation.

IMPLICATIONS OF TRAINING FOR FIELD WORK STUDENTS AND INTERNS IN COMMUNITY SETTINGS

Due to the range of ongoing activities in a community mental health center, students can obtain differently oriented experiences consonant with their interests. School psychology interns and community psychology field placement students currently obtain experience at the Brookdale Hospital Community Mental Health Center. Arriving with varied levels of training, the students become involved in several ongoing programs. They can obtain exposure to inpatient, outpatient, crisis intervention, and consultation aspects of service. Experiences are structured so that students can assume differing degrees of responsibility in settings according to their levels of training. Students are quickly confronted with the problems—such as premature termination, disorganized families, lack of readily available resources—that are commonly encountered by the full-time staff. Supervision is provided for all students, and their level of training determines whether they are given primary responsibility for treatment, are involved in groups as cotherapists, or primarily observe and assist in program development.

When supervising psychologists consider experiences that can be offered in relation to students' expectations and goals, the major factor that contributes to planning is the supervising psychologists' own skills and orientation to clinical practice. The supervisors provide direct or indirect models. However, each supervisor must view his skills objectively and evaluate the extent to which he can enhance the student's current professional development. Students whose orientation to community psychology diverges widely from clinical psychology may benefit more from training in settings other than Brookdale. Supervisors can, however, through expanding their knowledge and exploring other resources within the setting, make a broad range of experiences available to students.

TRANSLATION OF CLINICAL SKILLS TO MEMBERS OF OTHER DISCIPLINES

Psychologists have been actively involved in in-service training and consultation with psychiatric residents and members of other mental health disciplines. Extensive training is directed toward paraprofessionals, who are an integral part of the delivery of services. Paraprofessionals contribute knowledge of the community and are often vocal spokesmen of consumer demands. Establishment of working alliances becomes a crucial part of the training process. Assessment of the paraprofessionals' level of prior training and ability to use various approaches contributes to effective training. Using videotaped group sessions as illustrations and working with paraprofessionals as cotherapists have been particularly effective. The professional who is presenting didactic material or supervising paraprofessionals becomes adept at translating complex concepts into common-sense language and in illustrating terms while assisting the paraprofessionals gain theoretical and practical understanding that will enable them to contribute more effectively to team efforts.

IMPLICATIONS OF COMMUNITY MENTAL HEALTH EXPERIENCES FOR CLINICAL TRAINING

Experiences within the community mental health center emphasize the need for a dynamic approach to training in which preparation for continuous professional growth and transmission of evolving skills to others is predominant. Clinicians must be prepared to respond to broad social change and consumer demands for training relevant to the contemporary social order. Experiences of community psychologists have emphasized the need to expand the scope of clinical skills, to adapt diagnostic and treatment skills to emerging needs, and to forego cherished criteria for delivery of services. Diagnosis and treatment assume quite different dimensions when the demand for service far outweighs available staff; prevention and treatment of identified problems both become primary goals. Innovative approaches may be zealously developed with the expectation that the outcome will be the same as that yielded by more cautious approaches. Reflection of outcome frequently indicates that goals must be modified, and innovative approaches can only come from understanding of available resources and knowledge of goals. Experiences in a community mental health center heighten awareness of social problems, the effect of community developments on community residents, and the impact of shifting governmental policies on individuals who are dependent on government-financed agencies for basic economic and health needs. The frequency with which shifts occur in social conditions mobilizes caution in training toward solution of particular problems or particular approaches. Knowledge of personality, the effects of maturation and environment on human development, and the ability to apply knowledge in a variety of settings become basic areas of expertise which withstand social change.

In view of waning financial expectations for community

mental health centers, one is acutely aware of the folly of preparing specifically for this type of setting. In common with other applied settings, however, this setting has the source of extensive information about individuals and a broad range of clinical problems. In this setting, psychologists' efforts are typically directed toward consultation, education, and outpatient treatment; the division between these areas is frequently ambiguous. Activity directed toward prevention and treatment of identified difficulties can gain from academic and other applied settings as well as make contributions to them. The psychologist has many opportunities for professional growth in the community setting in addition to that attained through other sources.

Psychologists in community mental health centers frequently play a key role in program development and evaluation. Dialogue among psychologists results in awareness of the continuity of services. An overview of the impact of services can prevent premature expansion or termination of projects. The psychologist who is training paraprofessionals, community agency personnel, and students can provide an effective model of awareness of similar programs, assessment approaches, and ways to adapt new skills in particular settings. The models one observes in graduate training contribute extensively to a psychologist's ability to fulfill this role effectively.

In conclusion, clinical training cannot be viewed as an isolated experience. Clinical training can prepare the clinician through observation of models and direct experiences to practice clinical skills in which he has acquired expertise and to judge when further training is necessary. He can assess outcome and combine assessment with service commitments. Training must be continuous and available for translation to others. The content and methods of transmission to others is continuously evolving. New developments may be expected to occur as human development is viewed from new perspectives and research procedures evolve to encompass new content areas. The pursuit of new developments, however, requires knowledge of personality and application of this knowledge to maximizing others' abilities to use their resources.

226

References

1. W. L. Simmons, "Clinical Training Programs, 1964–1965 and 1968–1969: A Characterization and Comparison," *American Psychologist,* 1971, 26:717–21.
2. H. M. Preshansky, "For What Are We Training Our Graduate Students?" *American Psychologist,* 1972, 27:205–12.
3. S. F. Schneider, "Reply to Albee's 'The Uncertain Future of Clinical Psychology,'" *American Psychologist,* 1971, 26:1058–70.
4. G. W. Albee, "The Uncertain Future of Clinical Psychology," *American Psychologist,* 1970, 25:1071–80.

Attitudes of Clinical Psychologists Toward Training Issues

MARK H. THELEN

THELEN AND EWING ANALYZED THE ATTITUDES AND PREFER-
ences of academic[1] and applied[2] clinical psychologists concerning current training issues in clinical psychology using
univariate procedures. The present study, a multivariate extension of these two studies, was undertaken to identify and
describe attitude *patterns* of clinical psychologists toward issues pertinent to professional training. These issues included
content (e.g., research and therapy), type of degree (e.g., Ph.D.
and Psy.D.), and social relevancy (e.g., of personality and clinical theory). These attitude patterns were presented separately
for an extensive sample of applied and academic clinical psychologists.

METHOD

The Samples

The population from which the sample of academic clinicians was drawn included all academic clinical psychologists in
the 72 APA-Approved Clinical Training Programs who were
receiving some part of their salaries through the psychology

*The author is most grateful to Linda Cohen, James Clark, Steve Dollinger, Andrew
Lester, Steve McColley, Dennis McGuire, and Steve Paul for their help with this
project.

department or from departmental grants in the spring of 1969. as To insure that every department would be represented in the sample, the clinicians were chosen by stratified sampling. This resulted in a total sample of 239 academic clinical psychologists, of whom 179, or 79 percent, returned the questionnaire.

The sample of applied psychologists was drawn from the 1969 Division 12 membership of the APA. It consisted of 664 psychologists who, as best could be determined from the APA directory, held an advance degree in clinical psychology and were not primarily involved in the training or teaching of psychology students, except perhaps interns. Exclusions (e.g., because of retirement or because their primary job was instruction) and a 79 percent rate of return of the questionnaire resulted in a usable sample of 401 applied clinical psychologists on which the analyses are based. The primary employers of the 401 respondents were as follows: state 36 percent; private practice, 32 percent; federal, 16 percent; college or university, 14 percent; other, 2 percent.

The Questionnaires

The questionnaires were designed to assess the attitudes of applied and academic clinical psychologists toward current professional issues. Some items used for the survey of the academic clinicians had to be adapted because they were not suitable for the work situation of the applied clinicians. Therefore, some items on the questionnaire for academic clinicians related to the respondent's *own clinical training program* as opposed to *training in psychology nationally* for the applied respondents. This distinction applied to ratings of actual training emphasis, ratings of training emphasis which ought to be, and ratings of the adequacy of training. Also, one set of items was included on the survey of applied clinicians that had not been obtained from the academic clinicians. We assessed the applied respondents' support for two types of degrees and three different departmental settings for training clinical psychologists.

Analysis

A full description of the original survey forms and samples appeared in 1970 and 1973.[3] To comply with data processing restrictions, only slightly over half of the items in the original questionnaires were included in the present analysis. It was necessary to modify the original survey response data in order to carry out the present analysis. All four-point scales used to indicate item preferences were collapsed into two-point scales. For example, liking for therapy originally rated as (4) very considerable, (3) considerable, (2) some, and (1) little was collapsed to (1) considerable, very considerable, and (0) some, little. These two response options for each item were then treated as separate items and *henceforth* will be referred to as items. In this way each question on the questionnaire was made into two items, and the number of respondents who endorsed each item was determined. Therefore, we could expect an unequal N across items, since responding to a given item always precluded responding to its counterpart.

The data were analyzed using hierarchical classification by reciprocal pairs.[4] Items are classified into reciprocal pairs such that item i is highest (in number of respondents) with item j, and j is, in turn, highest with i $(i \leqslant j)$ where i and j represent different items chosen by the same respondents. Established reciprocal pairs are then treated as if they were single items. Just as two single items may come together to form a pair, so may reciprocal pairs in combination with other items or reciprocals come together to form clusters. The pair formation process proceeds hierarchically. The item pair with the largest number of common respondents is classified first. The item pair enjoying the smallest number of common respondents is classified last.[5] The strength of the association is determined by the number of respondents contributing to a reciprocal pair or cluster.

RESULTS AND DISCUSSION[6]

One attitude pattern revealed by the analysis of the data is that what the respondents like is what they think ought to be. This is apparent for both the academic and the applied groups; however, it appears more prevalently among the academic group. For the latter, there is an association: between liking research and the perceived emphasis on research in the respondent's own program; between liking therapy and advocating an emphasis on training in therapy; and between liking diagnosis and advocating an emphasis on diagnosis. In addition, the analyses clearly showed an association between liking consulting and advocating an emphasis on consulting. Also, an association between low regard for the use of diagnosis and a belief that diagnosis ought not be emphasized in the respondent's own program was obtained. Among the applied clinicians, the analyses indicated that the respondents who like therapy also believe that therapy ought to be emphasized in training. If this phenomenon holds in day-to-day decisions, it follows that academic clinicians are promoting training goals for clinical psychologists corresponding with those activities which they themselves favor. To the extent that the preferred activities of academic clinicians are different from those of applied clinicians, applied clinicians are likely to be dissatisfied with the training priorities of academic programs.

The responses to items pertaining to social relevancy[7] tended to be consistent across areas for both the applied and the academic respondents. For example, if a given area—such as personality and clinical theory—was considered by an individual to be low in social relevancy, it was likely that the areas of applied clinical skills and personality and clinical research were viewed as low in social relevancy. It may be that the respondents did not make clear discriminations between these areas of psychology, or perhaps they simply felt that each of the areas was similar in regard to social relevancy.

The analysis revealed associations between attitudes pertaining to type of degree and location of training programs.

The respondents' attitudes toward type of degree or structure/location of program appear to be categorical, so that support of, or opposition to, a given factor often appears to outweigh other factors. Although there is evidence for this among the academic respondents, the evidence is most clear among the applied respondents. The analysis of the applied respondents indicated clusters of attitudes: (1) in support of an autonomous department, whatever the degree label; (2) in support of an interdisciplinary department, with little concern for the degree label; and (3) in opposition to a Psy.D. degree whether it is in a psychology department, autonomous department, or interdisciplinary department.

Another interesting point may be inferred from the data. The applied clinicians who support the value of consulting in clinical training also appear to support research emphasis and the Ph.D. type degree. We found that those who see current training in consulting as inadequate also tend to support the Ph.D. type program. Also, there was an association between a high liking of consulting, and a cluster of items that included an item indicating that research training ought to be emphasized. For the academic clinicians, an approximate counterpart of this association pattern also was found. Again, consulting activities were seen as being de-emphasized and inadequate, but there was support for Ph.D. programs that give considerable attention to science training. It appears that, particularly for applied clinicians, notions about training and activities in consulting are very much intermingled with ideas about the importance of research and training in research. In part, this may stem from the operant-oriented practitioners who have a consulting orientation and also support research.

In summary, the attitudes of clinical psychologists toward issues in clinical training are interrelated. Further, there appear to be generalized attitudes which may preclude discriminative deliberation about the various issues in clinical training. Perhaps we need to reason about the issues in clinical training, less in terms of our personal taste and more in terms of a detailed deliberation of the issues involved.

Notes and References

1. M. H. Thelen and D. R. Ewing, "Roles, Functions, and Training in Clinical Psychology: A Survey of Academic Clinicians," *American Psychologist,* 1970, 25:550–54.
2. M. H. Thelen and D. R. Ewing, "Attitudes of Applied Clinicians Toward Roles, Functions, and Training in Clinical Psychology: A Comparative Survey," *Professional Psychology,* 1973, 4:28–34.
3. Thelen and Ewining, see notes 1 and 2.
4. L. L. McQuitty and J. A. Clark, "Hierarchical Classification by Reciprocal Pairs of Course Selections in Psychology," *Education and Psychological Measurement,* 1968, 28:659–89.
5. The hierarchical process of classifications sorts items into pairs, clusters, or both and sequentially removes them from the data pool. As a result, the emergence of an interrelationship between first extracted and later extracted items is not possible.
6. Figures that depict the results in detail may be obtained from the author upon request.
7. Social relevancy was defined for the respondents as, "the pertinence, applicability, or transferability of current psychological concepts, knowledge, or skills to the present or foreseeable major social crises of our society."

Choice Points, Dilemmas, and Polemics in Psychology Departments*

JAMES F. ALEXANDER

IT IS CLEAR THAT FAMILY THERAPY IS AN ACTIVE AND GROWing endeavor. In graduate psychology programs, a major growth of interest in family therapy can be seen. For example, in our recent survey of ninety-five directors of clinical training, fifty-three of the fifty-nine respondents indicated at least some involvement in family therapy training. Of greater importance is the fact that forty-four percent of the departments have a formal program (often including a separate academic course and practicum training section), and forty-nine percent of the family programs have been initiated within the last three years (reflecting impressive recent growth of family therapy as both a philosophy and set of techniques for change). To some adherents of the family approach, it is disturbing that seventy percent of the programs devote less than fifteen percent of their training to family therapy. However, this small percentage is neither surprising nor alarming in light of the facts that: (1) family therapy is of fairly recent origin; and (2)

*Portions of this paper were presented at the National Conference on Training in Family Therapy, sponsored by the Philadelphia Child Guidance Clinic, November 1972. The author wishes to thank Drs. James Stachowiak, Ted Jacob, and Irv Altman for their comments and assistance.

234

CLINICAL PSYCHOLOGY

most graduate psychology programs are in the business of exposing their students to a wide variety of techniques and philosophies.

Thus, while some trainers see the expansion of family therapy training as the major issue we face in the near future, I would like to raise an entirely different set of issues.

These issues relate to all of graduate training in clinical psychology, and seem to both reflect and cause a pervasive sense of uncertainty, dissatisfaction, and need for change. While some of these issues (e.g., problems with the "scientist-professional" model) represent natural developmental trends in clinical psychology, others represent powerful new pressures for change brought on by major shifts in funding patterns, a new emphasis on subdoctoral training, the demand to be more responsive to community needs, and so forth.

We can respond to these issues by ignoring them (and having our fate decided by state legislators, university administrators, and NIMH), or by "riding along" and making both conscious and unconscious decisions as we go. However, it is hoped that in explicating the issues, we can move us toward the process of making active decisions and developing strategies for the future. In the process, we might turn some of these dilemmas at least into polemics and choice points, and maybe ultimately into a new sense of direction and growth.

BUDGET CUTS AND REALIGNMENT OF FUNDING PATTERNS

To start out on a gloomy (and hopefully overpessimistic) note, stories of budget cuts already planned or occurring continually arise, administrators are warned of "lean years" to come, and persistent rumors abound of even more severe cuts in the future. Simon,[1] for example, warns of budget realignments, with professional training funds decreased and subdoctoral (MA, BA, AA, etc.) training funds increased. Recent reports of the Committee on Graduate Training in Clinical Psychology warn that training funds may be entirely phased out or changed to a loan program, and state mental health directors have been told to anticipate ultimately a complete reversal in the ninety to ten ratio of university training funds to "continuing education" funds funneled through local nonuniversity agencies.[2] These trends, if truly forthcoming, have ominous implications. Local agencies, to which we send many of our "products," have already expressed a desire to have more input in university training, and cite the new funding patterns in suggesting they may eventually have much to do with the very selection process through which we bring students into our graduate programs. Further, much of the support we currently enjoy for trainees, faculty positions, clinic personnel, secretaries, training equipment, and the like may not be forthcoming in the future.

We have several potential directions to pursue in dealing with this issue. We can, for example, become more sensitive to the agencies representing the employment market, hoping to retain positive ties and somehow continue enough financial support to meet our needs. While this may be a reasonable strategy, unfortunate examples of this type of approach can already be seen in graduate programs where the faculty seriously devalue the utility of traditional diagnostic techniques, yet graduate students are still prompted to take diagnostic courses because without them they would not be employable. At best, this can produce a schizmatic training experience for students; at worst, it can produce serious and divisive polarities.[3]

Another alternative is to prepare to get out of the training business entirely. Since the majority of clinical faculty in a recent survey ranked research as their most important activity and clinical practice as last,[4] we might follow the advice of many of our hard-nosed colleagues and leave professional training to professional schools. I feel this would be a most unfortunate alternative, but it has recently received increasingly vocal support, particularly in conjunction with the movement toward independent professional schools.[5]

A third alternative is to do a better job of training along the lines of the scientist-professional model, moving entirely to applied clinical training, or incorporating new models into our training concepts. We will come back to this issue in a later discussion of training models.

PRIVATE PRACTICE MODEL

A second major issue results from the fact that even in many of the "progressive" settings (university, community mental health and child clinics, etc.) training in the private practice model of therapy still predominates. That is, service personnel are trained in the application of change techniques to clients who walk in the door (be it via referral, court order, etc.), yet there is increasing pressure to develop techniques of intervention and prevention to meet the needs of a large segment of the community presently not receiving services, or receiving services only when circumstances become dire.

Recent programs in crisis intervention, short-term marriage counseling, and management of aggression training for police responding to family disturbance calls, early childhood education programs, prevention-oriented programs through schools and churches, service and information centers in areas of heavy minority population density reflect a new emphasis in this direction. Such programs have recently received a great deal of publicity but still represent only a small portion of the total emphasis in graduate training.

In highlighting this point, I do not mean to imply we should necessarily de-emphasize our more traditional philosophies and techniques. But in terms of manpower needs and areas of expertise, it may be more efficient for Ph.D. level professionals to operate as program designers and evaluators, researchers, consultants, and trainers, leaving the application of the time-consuming one-to-one direct contact to other professionals and subprofessionals.[6]

Though many will disagree with this proposal, it should at least be considered in light of the recent survey by Stein et al.,[7] which indicated academic clinical psychologists have less training and experience in direct clinical application than other clinical psychologists, yet do the bulk of the training of budding clinicians. Unless one wishes to argue that experience has no relationship to expertise, these data suggest that the "applied" aspects of Ph.D. training may be inefficient at best.[8]

TRAINING IN TRAINING

No matter what direction we take in the future, it is imperative that we pay more attention to the training process per se. Most Ph.D. programs now allow some opportunity for advanced trainees to supervise, but relatively few have formal training in training and supervision. With trainees destined for university settings, this deficiency is just as ludicrous as is the lack of formal training in teaching; and most of us end up teaching like we were taught, supervising like we were supervised. If we decide to innovate, we must do so generally based on faith and intuition, which are notoriously unreliable and inefficient. Thus, at the very least, we must formally supervise supervision, perhaps with advanced students to the extent of spending as much time on this activity as we do on training in therapy per se. Further, at least some of us must develop and evaluate formal supervision models. Examples might be evaluating the effect of different supervision vehicles (direct observation, individual sessions using audio-tapes, etc.). We should also evaluate the proper focus of supervision: the trainees' interpersonal skills (à la Truax), the transaction between therapist and the family or client, or target behavior in the family/client. Of course, no supervision focuses exclusively on one of these dimensions, but important differences in relative focus do exist. It is probably true that a different focus is appropriate at different trainee levels (beginning vs. advanced) and with different intervention techniques (e.g., a highly structured operant program vs. a relationship-oriented or existential approach), but these issues must be emperically examined.

Finally, if we decide to follow the previously mentioned suggestions of Simon[9] and Milgram,[10] we will see a great increase in subdoctoral and paraprofessional training. The crea-

tion and evaluation of training models would also then become
imperative; otherwise many of our graduates will find themselves thrown into this activity with few guidelines available.
In this era of "community control," such a deficiency could
operate to reduce even more our impact and usefulness.

TRAINING CONTEXTS AND THERAPY MODELS

One often overlooked issue is the context within which
training occurs, and how this context may strongly influence
the nature of training. Although quite oversimplified, I would
like to discuss different types of training contexts and implications of each.

Case Management Model. This approach, more likely to be
found in larger clinics, involves family therapy, and perhaps
even several types of family therapy, as only one of several
possible treatment approaches. Patient populations are relatively more heterogeneous, and diagnostic/case management
issues are an important part of a student's training. Trainees,
too, are more likely to receive diversified training, using a
variety of approaches with a variety of clients. The advantage
of this type of training is obvious. The disadvantages are few
but important: (1) evaluation of the relationship of assessment
and intervention to outcome, and their interaction, is difficult;
and (2) given the usual time constraints, training in any given
approach is inevitably going to be less extensive.

Specific Training Model. In contrast to the above, some
training programs (such as the Parsons and Alexander delinquency program, Patterson's work with delinquents, Bach's
fight training, etc.) involve a generally more homogeneous
population, use fewer techniques, and assessment decisions
are generally less complicated (e.g., evaluation of specific deficits). In this context, trainees generally receive more intensive
training in a more limited range of skills (such as L'Abate's
Family Enrichment Programs, Truax's facilitating conditions,
and specifics of Parson's and Alexander's delinquency program). This is especially true once these programs become well

known, i.e., clients self-select themselves and other agencies begin to refer just one "type" of client.

Because of these limits, evaluation is generally easier (note that most adequate therapy process and outcome studies generally involve more clearly defined and specific techniques than the diverse hodgepodge we are often forced to use in the clinic situation). However, the obvious disadvantage of this type of training suggests it should not constitute the entirety of a student's experience. In light of the prior discussion of subdoctoral and paraprofessional training, these more specific (in terms of techniques and client problems) programs seem to be a natural direction for training at this level.

In summary, it is suggested that Ph.D. level trainees should experience at least some experience in the decision/alternative techniques model; both because they are ultimately more likely to be in positions of clinical decision making and also are more likely to be involved in program initiation. Specific programs, perhaps manned primarily by less than Ph.D. level professionals, can on the other hand be learned in considerably less time, resulting in more service.

EMPIRICAL EVALUATION

A somewhat separate issue, which I would offer as a fact, not as a point of discussion, concerns training in empirical evaluation of clinical interventions, assessment approaches, supervision models, and so forth. Our business is a serious one, involving human tragedy, suffering, and hopelessness. (I insert this somewhat melodramatic note because real people can get lost in such "professional" issues as funding, role models, and so on).

However, because our clinical training ultimately translates into seeing families in distress, we absolutely must make certain we are, in fact, helping. I do not intend to languish in the old "cure rate" problem, but the evidence clearly points to the fact that therapy may not always be helpful, and at times may actually hurt people. We must deal with this issue at the training level: deriving an understanding of what techniques work, with which clients, when administered by which therapists.

Trainees, for example, must at least experience a program that includes a formal on-line evaluation (if not a formal research design). And it will not do to rely upon reports of success in other locations, for differences between clients and therapists, seriously limit the generalizability of most therapy outcome studies. Each training facility must struggle with this issue, and the clinical faculty involved in training must involve themselves in this evaluation, if for no other reason than to provide adequate role models for trainees.

ROLES IN GRADUATE TRAINING

The issue of role models brings us to my final point. One implication of my remarks is that we should, at the same time: (1.) spend more time training in different intervention models; (2.) develop and evaluate formal supervision models; (3.) incorporate community and paraprofessional programs into our training experiences; and (4.) perform both basic and applied research functions.

And, given only a little time, many other items could be added to this list. However, we cannot simply ignore these demands, pointing to our already overtaxed training time and resources. Ross,[11] for example, emphasizes that if we simply drift to the primarily applied end of the scientist-professional continuum, practitioners so trained will be obsolete within ten years. If, however, we swing heavily to the scientist end, particularly in light of the tremendous service pressures and demands to be "relevant," we face further budget cuts and loss of students.

Must we, however, become super scientist-professionals (the impossible dream?). Broskowski[12] suggests a different model: the research and development approach used so well in several other fields. The goal of this type of training would be the creation of "middlemen" clinical psychologists with the ability to interface the basic research endeavors and the applied fields. Such Ph.D.'s would systematically conduct and use relevant research to develop procedures and techniques for solving or preventing problems. These procedures would include those enumerated above (i.e., supervision, paraprofessional training, etc.). As Broskowski points out, such a development would not be dissimilar from the role traditionally served by the engineering profession. Many engineers typically perform neither basic research functions nor direct application. Instead, they translate the data from basic research fields (such as structural physics) into techniques able to be used by contractors.

One clear advantage of having at least some clinical psychologists trained in the research and development model is that it allows others to specialize in basic research or direct application without having to fit (uncomfortably, as is usually the case) into the scientist-professional model.[13] However, without this middleman we cannot afford to let clinical psychologists gravitate to one of the ends of this continuum. Already we have experienced the powerful schisms this process generates.[14]

CONCLUSIONS

Despite the existence of powerful pressures to change, my systems orientation reminds me that as systems we will tend to resist change. Yet if we fail to retain vitality and growth, including the development of new training models to meet new pressures, we are likely to emerge from the upcoming "lean years" as an obsolete, irrelevant, and poorly financed discipline. The suggestions represent only a few of numerous possibilities we might consider, but the main point is that we do have to seriously consider something.

Whatever model, or models, we adopt, we must bring our student selection and faculty promotion criteria into line with these models. Graduate programs deciding to emphasize applied professional activities would be foolish to continue to base student selection primarily on formal academic criteria such as MAT"s, GRE's—criteria that are probably at best only minimally related to the helping process. Similarly, programs emphasizing basic research or Broskowski's R and D model may want to emphasize criteria other than the intense humanistic (defined, for my purposes, as heavily applied and often antiscientific, or at least impatient) orientation held by so many of our applicants today.

The criteria for faculty promotion (allocation of space, etc.) must also be brought into line with program goals. Programs emphasizing applied training must provide release time for clinical faculty and include excellence in applied training in promotion criteria. Faculty initiating new programs such as paraprofessional training and interdisciplinary community projects must receive additional departmental support, and so on. Only if faculty are rewarded for attempting new directions of growth and excellence will they attempt such growth.

This issue, of course, must be resolved at the department (not subdiscipline) level, and our history is replete with difficulties in interfacing many of the facets of clinical training with the experimental philosophy held by many of our colleagues. However, in the process of developing new training models we may create programs that are more palatable to our experimental colleagues and, at the same time, provide them with potential strategies for dealing with their own problems (budget cuts in basic research programs, demands to be "relevant," and so on).

Notes and References

1. R. Simon, "The Paraprofessionals Are Coming! The Paraprofessionals Are Coming!" *The Clinical Psychologist*, 1971, 24:3–6.
2. Personal communication from R. Grow.
3. For a more complete discussion of problems encountered when applied training occurs in graduate departments dominated by a somewhat antagonistic experimental/research orientation, see P. J. Rothenburg and N. J. Mateluf, "Toward Professional Training: A Special Report from the National Council on Graduate Education in Psychology," *Professional Psychology*, 1969, 1:32–37.
4. P. T. Adler, "The Scientist-Professional Model and the Professional School: Some Shibboleths Re-examined," *The Clinical Psychologist*, 1970, 23:13.
5. A. L. Kovacs, "A School for Professional Psychology in Our Time," *The Clinical Psychologist*, 1970, 23:2–3, 8.
6. N. A. Milgram, "Society Is Waiting for Paraprofessional Manpower—Will Clinical Psychology Do Its Part?" *The Clinical Psychologist*, 1971, 24:1, 15.
7. D. D. Stein, M. L. Goldschmid, H. N. Weissman, and J. Sorrells, "The Relationship of Clinical Training and Practice to Clinicians' Sex, Age, and Work Setting," *The Clinical Psychologist*, 1969, 22:137–39.
8. Rothenburg and Mateluf.
9. Simon, see note 1.
10. Milgram, see note 6.
11. A. O. Ross, "The Case of the Innocent Model," *The Clinical Psychologist*, 1971, 24:2–3, 6.
12. A. Broskowski, "Clinical Psychology: A Research and Development Model," *Professional Psychology*, 1971, 2:235–42.
13. For an informative analysis of fundamental differences between practitioners and basic scientists in the man-environment field, see I. A. Altman, "Some Perspectives on the Study of Man-Environment Phenomena," *Representative Research in Social Psychology*, 1973, 4:1. The issues he highlights have relevance also for clinical psychology.
14. Stein et al., see note 7.